ANTI-BIAS BUILDING BLOCKS:
AN ELEMENTARY CURRICULUM

Anti-Defamation League

Marvin Nathan, *National Chair*

Jonathan Greenblatt, *CEO* and *National Director*

Kenneth Jacobson, *Deputy National Director*

Miriam Weisman, *Chair, Education Committee*

David S. Waren, *Director, Education Division*

Lorraine Tiven, *Associate Director of Education/Director of Education Programs*

Jinnie Spiegler, *Director of Curriculum*

© 2016 Anti-Defamation League
All rights reserved

Printed in the United States of America

No part of this book may be reproduced or utilized in any form or by any means, electronic or mechanical, including photocopying and recording, or by an information storage and retrieval system for any purposes other than intended and described in this publication without permission in writing from the publisher.

Anti-Defamation League
605 Third Avenue
New York, NY 10158-3560
(212) 885-7700/885-7800
(212) 867-0779/490-0187 (Fax)
www.adl.org

TABLE OF CONTENTS

INTRODUCTION 9
About the Anti-Defamation League 9
About the A WORLD OF DIFFERENCE® Institute 9
Goals of A CLASSROOM OF DIFFERENCE™ 10
The Rationale for Anti-Bias Education 11
What Is Anti-Bias Education? 12

ABOUT THIS CURRICULUM 13
Overview of Units 13
Overview of Lesson Structure 14
Instructional Methods and Strategies 15
Additional Resources 16

BACKGROUND INFORMATION FOR EDUCATORS 17
Creating an Anti-Bias Learning Environment 17
Social and Emotional Development 18
Creating a Gender Inclusive Classroom Environment 19
Responding to Name Calling and Bullying in the Classroom 20
Importance of Multicultural and Anti-Bias Children's Literature 20
How Children Develop Racial and Cultural Identity and Attitudes 21
Teacher and Classroom Self-Assessment 24

UNIT I. CREATING A SAFE AND COMFORTABLE CLASSROOM ENVIRONMENT 27
Goals for Kindergarten Through Fifth Grade 27

Grades K–2
Lesson 1. Ground Rules 29
Lesson 2. Communicating Well 31
Lesson 3. Listening 35

Lesson 4. My Feelings 39
Lesson 5. Cooperation 45
Who, What, Why and How Worksheet *(Student Handout)* 48

Grades 3-5
Lesson 1. Developing Classroom Guidelines... 49
Ground Rules for Respect Worksheet *(Student Handout)* 52
Lesson 2. Nonverbal Communication and Miscommunication 53
Lesson 3. Active Listening 57
Paraphrase Worksheet *(Student Handout)* 61
Lesson 4. Understanding, Managing and Expressing Feelings.. 63
Lesson 5. Collaboration and Teamwork 71

UNIT II. UNDERSTANDING MY STRENGTHS, SKILLS AND IDENTITY 75
Goals for Kindergarten Through Fifth Grade 75

Grades K-2
Lesson 6. Self-Portraits 77
Lesson 7. Likes and Dislikes 81
Lesson 8. Things I'm Good At 85
Things We Can Do *(Student Handout)* 88
Lesson 9. My Family 89
Lesson 10. My Neighborhood 93

Grades 3-5
Lesson 6. Identifying Unique Physical Characteristics.. 97
Describe Myself *(Student Handout)* 101
Lesson 7. Respecting Opinions 103
Persuasive Essay Graphic Organizer *(Version 1 Student Handout)*............................. 106
Persuasive Essay Graphic Organizer *(Version 2 Student Handout)*............................. 107
Lesson 8. Skills and Abilities 109
Find Someone Who... (Opposites) *(Student Handout)* 112
My Skills, Talents, Interests and Hopes *(Student Handout)* 113
Lesson 9. Many Kinds of families 115
My Family Suitcase Worksheet *(Student Handout)* 119
My Heritage *(Student Handout)* 120
Lesson 10. What is Community? 123
My Neighborhood Map *(Student Handout)* 127

UNIT III. UNDERSTANDING AND APPRECIATING DIFFERENCES...129
Goals for Kindergarten Through Fifth Grade 129

Grades K-2
Lesson 11. I Belong to Many Groups 131
Groups I Belong To *(Student Handout)* 134
Lesson 12. My Cultural Flag 135
Lesson 13. Similarities and Differences 139
Who is Similar, Who is Different? *(Student Handout)* 141

Grades 3-5
Lesson 11. What is Culture? 143
Aspects of Culture *(Student Handout)* 146
Autobiography Worksheet *(Student Handout)* 147
Lesson 12. Learning About Different Cultures 149
World Map *(Student Handout)* 153
Lesson 13. Feelings About Differences 155

UNIT IV. UNDERSTANDING BIAS AND DISCRIMINATION 159
Goals for Kindergarten Through Fifth Grade 159

Grades K-2
Lesson 14. What are Stereotypes? 161
Lesson 15. Dislike vs. Prejudice 165
Lesson 16. Unfairness and Discrimination 169
Lesson 17. Equality and Inequality 173
Lesson 18. Teasing, Name-Calling and Bullying 177
Lesson 19. Cycle of Inequality 181

Grades 3-5
Lesson 14. Perspective and Stereotypes 185
Photos #1-3 *(Student Handout)* 189
Stereotypes *(Student Handout)* 192
Media Stereotypes Log *(Student Handout)* 193
Lesson 15. Forms of Prejudice 195
Definitions: Forms of Prejudice and Discrimination *(Student Handout)* 198
Prejudice Scenarios *(Student Handout)* 199
Lesson 16. Discrimination 201
Prejudice and Discrimination: Definitions *(Student Handout)* 204
Prejudice, Stereotype or Discrimination? *(Student Handout)* 205
Lesson 17. Inequality Past and Present 207

Equality for People with Disabilities *(Student Handout)* 210

Lesson 18. Bullying and Identity-Based Bullying 211

Lesson 19. Three Is of Injustice 215

The Three Is of Injustice and Their Connection *(Student Handout)* 219

The Three Is of Injustice Worksheet *(Student Handout)* 220

UNIT V. CONFRONTING/CHALLENGING BIAS AND BULLYING.....221

Goals for Kindergarten Through Fifth Grade 221

Grades K-2

Lesson 20. Responding to Bullying and Teasing 223

Roles in Bullying and Prejudice *(Student Handout)* 226

Lesson 21. Being Brave and Standing Up 227

Be an Ally Scenarios #1–4 *(Student Handout)* 230

Lesson 22. One, Some, Many, All—Standing Up to Prejudice 235

Lesson 23. Together We Can Make a Difference 239

Pros and Cons of Working with Others *(Student Handout)* 242

Boy Allowed to Bring 'My Little Pony' Backpack Back to School *(Student Handout)* 243

Lesson 24. Standing Up to Inequality 245

Sylvia Mendez and Segregated Schools in California *(Student Handout)* 248

Sylvia Mendez Photos *(Student Handout)* 249

Lesson 25. Making a Difference in My School 253

Grades 3-5

Lesson 20. Roles We Play in Bullying and Bias 257

The New Girl *(Student Handout)* 261

The Roles We Play *(Student Handout)* 262

Lesson 21. Being an Ally 263

Be an Ally Self-Reflection *(Student Handout)* 267

Lesson 22. Challenging Prejudice and Discrimination 269

Strategies to Challenge Prejudice and Discriminatio *(Student Handout)* 272

Addressing Different Levels of Prejudice and Discrimination *(Student Handout)* 273

Lesson 23. Strength in Numbers 275

Advertisement: The Fire of Hate Consumes Us All *(Student Handout)* 278

Letters to the Burned Churches *(Student Handout)* 279

Lesson 24. Exploring Social Change Movements 281

Segregation Photos *(Student Handout)* 285

Activism During the Civil Rights Movement *(Student Handout)* 291

Steps in Writing and Presenting a Research Project *(Student Handout)* 292
Lesson 25. Social Action Projects 295
A Case Study in Community Activism *(Student Handout)* 299
Group Action Plan *(Student Handout)* 303

APPENDIX. CORRELATION OF LESSONS TO THE COMMON CORE LEARNING STANDARDS 305

Unit I. Creating a Safe and Comfortable Classroom Environment 305
Unit II. Understanding My Strengths, Skills and Identity 307
Unit III. Understanding and Appreciating Differences 309
Unit IV. Understanding Bias and Discrimination 311
Unit V. Confronting/Challenging Bias and Bullying 313

Bibliography 317
Glossary 321

INTRODUCTION

Anti-Bias Building Blocks: An Elementary Curriculum is a K-5 teaching guide designed for elementary educators who want to promote anti-bias concepts in order to create safe, inclusive and respectful classroom and school environments. The materials have been designed to assist educators and students in exploring ways to ensure that the principles of respect for diversity, freedom and equality become realities. The curriculum provides teachers with lessons that encourage students to reflect on their identity, understand and appreciate differences, explore societal issues arising from bias and discrimination, understand how historically people have combated prejudice and injustice and take leadership roles in promoting justice and equity in their schools, communities and society at large. By teaching this curriculum, you will be making an important contribution by helping children explore valuable principles that they will bring into their social and peer interactions throughout their lives.

ABOUT THE ANTI-DEFAMATION LEAGUE

The Anti-Defamation League (ADL) was founded in 1913 "to stop the defamation of the Jewish people and to secure justice and fair treatment to all." Now the nation's premier civil rights/human relations agency fighting anti-Semitism and all forms of bigotry, ADL defends democratic ideals and protects civil rights for all.

ABOUT THE A WORLD OF DIFFERENCE® INSTITUTE

The Anti-Defamation League's A WORLD OF DIFFERENCE® Institute is a market leader in the development and delivery of anti-bias training and resources. Human relations and education professionals design training modules and produce curricula that provide the necessary skills, knowledge and awareness to promote and sustain inclusive and respectful school, work and home environments. Customized to meet the changing needs of a wide range of audiences, programs are available to schools, universities and community-based organizations throughout the United States and abroad.

The origins of the A WORLD OF DIFFERENCE Institute date back to 1985, when ADL and WCVB-TV in Boston initiated the A WORLD OF DIFFERENCE campaign, a year-long series of education and media-driven programs designed to combat prejudice and create effective tools to address these issues in the classroom and community. The campaign's immense success led to ongoing programs in Boston and 28 U.S. cities and several national awards including a Peabody, Gabriel and Scripps-Howard.

In 1992, in an effort to meet the increasing demand for its services and to formalize and coordinate its anti-bias research, programming and training efforts, ADL created and officially launched the A WORLD OF DIFFERENCE Institute.

A WORLD OF DIFFERENCE Institute collaborates with universities, colleges and national funding sources to study and enhance the efficacy of its programs. These collaborations have included formal evaluation studies with prominent institutions including Yale University, Columbia University Teachers College, Claremont Graduate School and the University of Pennsylvania.

Through the development and delivery of its programs and resources, the Institute seeks to help participants recognize bias and the harm it inflicts on individuals and society; explore the value of diversity; improve intergroup relations and combat racism, homophobia, anti-Semitism and all forms of prejudice and bigotry.

A CLASSROOM OF DIFFERENCE™ is at the heart of the Institute, developed to address diversity in the pre-kindergarten through 12th grade school communities. Programs include workshops for teachers, classified staff, administrators, students and family members.

GOALS OF A CLASSROOM OF DIFFERENCE™

The following are the overall goals of A CLASSROOM OF DIFFERENCE for all audiences:

- To promote respectful, inclusive and safe learning environments and communities,
- To build understanding of the value and benefits of diversity,
- To improve intergroup relations,
- To eradicate anti-Semitism, racism, homophobia and all forms of bigotry, and
- To encourage personal responsibility in the promotion of justice and equity.

THE RATIONALE FOR ANTI-BIAS EDUCATION

Schools in the United States have long played a vital role in supporting the nation's democratic ideals. Providing all students with a quality education—one in which academic and social development are inseparable goals—is essential to creating equal access to opportunity and fostering responsible citizenship. The challenges of fulfilling this obligation are heightened in an educational climate whose primary focus is accountability for student achievement as measured by standardized test scores. Recognizing the need to prepare students to live and work successfully in a pluralistic national and a global community, educators can engage in a collaborative process to achieve the ideals of justice and equality upon with the nation was founded.

The inequities and social tensions that exist in U.S. society are also present in the hallways of our nation's schools. Because schools are both educating and socializing institutions, the potential exists for them to establish frameworks that challenge intolerance and promote safety, fairness and respect. Students' successful pursuit of academic excellence depends on their ability to learn in a safe and inclusive environment.

The rapidly increasing diversity of our nation presents both a windfall of benefits and new challenges. When diversity—differences in race, religion, sexual orientation, language, culture, learning style, socioeconomic class, body type and ability—is not understood, valued or respected, the resulting fear and misunderstanding can fuel intergroup tension. The potential for conflict, bullying, discrimination and scapegoating is high when bias and stereotypes go unchallenged or are ignored. Left unexamined, biased attitudes can lead to biased behaviors, which have the potential to escalate into violent acts of hate. Youth violence, hate crimes, bullying and harassment occur today at alarming rates, have a powerful impact on the entire educational community and underline the imperative for schools to address prejudice and discrimination directly.

Biased behavior can be subtle or overt. In schools, name calling and acts of social exclusion are the common examples of discriminatory behavior and prejudicial thinking. Although children are not born prejudiced, from as early as six months of age, infants can distinguish differences in physical appearances and by ages 3–5, children may also begin to develop negative attitudes toward differences. In an attempt to minimize the development of prejudice, well-meaning adults often teach children to ignore differences and focus only on similarities—also known as being "color blind"—and do not teach children about bias and discrimination. Just as common experiences are part of the "glue" that holds communities together, understanding and respecting differences are essential for successful multicultural societies.

References

Henze, Rosemary, A. Katz, E. Norte, S.E. Sather and E. Walker. 2002. *Leading for diversity: How school leaders promote positive interethnic relations.* Thousand Oaks: Corwin Press.

Stern-LaRosa Caryl, and E.H. Bettmann. 2000. *Hate hurts: How children learn and unlearn prejudice.* New York: Scholastic.

WHAT IS ANTI-BIAS EDUCATION?

Anti-bias education is a comprehensive approach to learning designed to actively challenge stereotyping, prejudice and all forms of discrimination. Anti-bias education incorporates curricular content that reflects diverse experiences and perspectives; it includes instructional methods that advance the learning of all students and tools to establish and sustain a safe, inclusive and respectful learning environment and school community. Ultimately, anti-bias education engages students in the exploration of social problems and empowers them to take active steps to create a more just and peaceful world, where all groups share equal access to opportunity and every person can flourish.

With comprehensive anti-bias education, the mastery skills that participants acquire include the following (specific activities and curricula are tailored for each age group):

- Children understand the various dimensions of identity and apply this understanding to their thinking and behavior.
- Children develop an understanding of basic terms and concepts relating to prejudice and discrimination and apply this understanding to their interactions with others.
- Children increase their understanding of the impact of culture on communication and apply this understanding to their interactions with others.
- Children develop the capacity to recognize and acknowledge bullying, prejudice and discrimination in themselves, in others and within institutions.
- Children develop and put into practice skills to challenge bullying, bias and discrimination in themselves and others.

ABOUT THIS CURRICULUM

Anti-Bias Building Blocks: An Elementary Curriculum is divided into five instructional units. Each unit has lessons grouped for Grades K-2 and for Grades 3–5. Although there might be instances when using a lesson or lessons from a particular unit out of sequence may be useful, we recommend that whenever possible, the units be used sequentially. By progressing through the units in this manner, students build a strong foundation for analyzing and confronting bias.

During the elementary school years, the social and emotional development of students is a core part of their school experience. We suggest making *Anti-Bias Building Blocks* a regular part of your weekly lesson plans. With twenty-five lessons for each grade level, it is ideal to do one lesson per week. Each lesson has children's literature suggestions as well as writing activities and fits within English Language Arts (ELA) curriculum. The curriculum also connects with social studies as well as other subject areas. An integrated approach to anti-bias education is significantly more powerful than tying it to one subject area.

OVERVIEW OF UNITS

Below is an overview of the curriculum, including the goals for each section as well as the specific lessons for each grade level.

Unit I: Creating a Safe and Comfortable Classroom Environment provides lessons to build a solid foundation for the students' social and emotional skill development. The lessons help students feel safe in their classrooms, develop the skills to communicate effectively, gain a vocabulary for the different feelings that may emerge and learn how to work collaboratively in small and large groups.

Unit II: Understanding My Strengths, Skills and Identity provides lessons to build a strong sense of self in children, exploring the concepts of identity and differences. The lessons help students understand factors that shape their identity, acknowledge their likes and dislikes and reflect on the differences between themselves and their classmates.

Unit III: Understanding and Appreciating Differences provides lessons to explore students' cultural and other identities and differences so that they can learn to play and work together effectively. The lessons help students reflect on their own cultural identities, learn about the culture of others and understand when differences arise.

Unit IV: Understanding Bias and Discrimination provides lessons to create a viable and inclusive school and classroom climate by helping students understand bias and discrimination. The lessons help students explore bullying, stereotypes, prejudice and discrimination (and the differences between those) and reflect on the cycle of inequality.

Unit V: Confronting/Challenging Bias and Bullying provides lessons to empower students to do something about the bias, discrimination and bullying they encounter. The lessons help students learn how to be an ally on an individual level and by working with others, explore social change movements over history and work on a social action project that improves their school and community.

OVERVIEW OF LESSON STRUCTURE

Each unit consists of 3–6 lessons. All of the lessons build upon the previous lessons/units and are highly interactive, modeling a participatory process that encourages students to actively engage with issues that affect their classroom, school and community. As students work together and share diverse perspectives and backgrounds, solving problems, brainstorming and discussing the material, they learn to communicate respectfully, cooperate and improve their critical thinking skills. Research indicates that all of these abilities are associated with decreased discriminatory behavior.

Lesson Structure

Rationale: a statement that identifies the purpose of the lesson and the topic(s) to be explored.

Objectives: the anticipated student outcomes that will occur as a result of the lesson.

Grade Level: the approximate grades for which the lesson is appropriate (all lessons are either K–2 or 3–5 and in some cases, the K–2 lessons are designed for just grades 1 and 2, where indicated).

Strategies and Skills: a list of instructional techniques (e.g. role play) and skills (e.g. writing skills) practiced or reinforced in the lesson.

Key Words and Phrases: a list of vocabulary, organized alphabetically, which students will need to know in order to effectively participate in the lesson.

Time: the suggested block of time that teachers will need to schedule for the lesson. Most K–2 lessons are 35 minutes and most Grades 3–5 lessons are 45 minutes.

Procedures: step-by-step teacher instructions to implement the lesson. Also included throughout this section are special considerations and cautions to the teacher, highlighted as NOTE as well as alternative methods for a procedure, highlighted as ✍.

Flipped Classroom Idea: suggestions for "flipping" your classroom which include videos you can make and have students watch prior to the lesson (included only for Grades 3–5 lessons). These ideas are designated by the symbol 📹.

Extension Activities: a list of additional activities to continue and extend the learning of the lesson's objectives and concepts.

Children's Books: a list of three or more children's books that have a similar theme and learning objective to the lesson. These recommended books are located either at the beginning or the end of the lesson and are identified by the image:

Handouts/Support Documents: additional materials that are needed to implement lessons can be found at the end of the lesson they accompany.

Other Materials: additional items needed to implement the lesson that can likely be found in most elementary classrooms (e.g. paper, art supplies) or a website that will need to be used.

Academic Standards: a list of common core learning standards that are met by teaching the lesson. (See the Appendix for a comprehensive list of the standards.)

INSTRUCTIONAL METHODS AND STRATEGIES

A variety of instructional methods are used to implement the lessons in this curriculum. The strategies provide opportunities for students to talk with each other in order to connect and learn. They also provide opportunities for students to tie historical and contemporary information to their own understanding of bias and discrimination. Other methods invite students to examine information critically and personally clarify their own opinions on a variety of topics. The following five methods are used most often through the curriculum although other techniques are also used.

1. **Directed Discussions:** The lessons include discussion questions that are intended to help facilitate student discussions for partner, small group and whole class dialogue. Some of the questions assess student comprehensions of the concepts presented and others ask students to formulate feelings, opinions, draw conclusions or connect material to parallel situation.

    The material in Unit I, "Creating a Safe and Comfortable Classroom Environment," provides a helpful framework for having these discussions. The material in this section should be reviewed and reinforced regularly and especially when sensitive topics are under discussion.

2. **Small Group Work:** Numerous opportunities for students to work collaboratively are provided throughout. Teachers may want to enlist a variety of grouping methods, including randomly assigned groups, self-selected groups and teacher-selected groups. Providing opportunities for students to interact with as many of their classmates as possible will increase the likelihood that students will be exposed to a greater number of perspectives and communication styles. The instructional technique also gives students the opportunity to learn the behaviors that foster and undermine effective group process. To maximize student participation in small group work, teachers should make sure that all students clearly understand what is being asked of them and circulate around the room during small group work.

3. **Brainstorming:** Brainstorming sessions are often used a springboard for discussing new concepts. Because the process of coming up with ideas is distinct from the process of judgment, brainstorming provides an opportunity to generate ideas that have no right or wrong answers and often creative ideas are generated from this process because students build on each other's thoughts. It is important to remind students throughout brainstorming sessions not to criticize any of the ideas that are shared, to work quickly, not to censor their own ideas, and whenever possible, to expand on the ideas of others.

4. **Role Playing:** One of the most effective ways to get students involved in the learning process is through role play. By experimenting with various roles and considering the implications of each, students begin to understand the complexity of social issues and to develop empathy. Stress to students that the purpose of role playing is to practice new responses, to consider alternative points of view and to experience some of the feelings that occur in real-life situations. Whenever students are asked to develop or act out role plays (either with puppets or students themselves), it is important that they not use real names of other students or teachers or details about a situation that would reveal something that should be private.

5. **Defining Terms:** It is critical that students gain an understanding of the language of diversity, bias and social justice as well as the distinction between words. Often in the lessons, there is a discussion about terminology that is related to the concepts being taught, that includes words and phrases for which many students may be unfamiliar. In most cases, we suggest providing an opportunity for students to reflect on and share what they may have heard or already know about the term and then provide the definition for the students as well as an example to help them better understand the word. Provided in the Appendix is a glossary of all the words defined throughout the curriculum.

ADDITIONAL RESOURCES

In addition to the resources used to conduct the exercises in the lessons, you may also find many of ADL's online educational resources useful at www.adl.org/education-outreach, including:

Anti-Bias Education, www.adl.org/education-outreach/anti-bias-education
Provides information on anti-bias trainings, programs, webinars and other resources offered for schools and campuses.

Curriculum Resources, www.adl.org/curriculum-resources
A collection of free original lesson plans and resources that help K-12 educators integrate multicultural, anti-bias and social justice themes into their curricula.

BACKGROUND INFORMATION FOR EDUCATORS

CREATING AN ANTI-BIAS LEARNING ENVIRONMENT

Educational environments that reflect the rich diversity of the community, nation and world assist in opening students' minds and actively engaging them in their own learning. Research has shown that prejudice is countered when schools and classrooms foster critical thinking, empathy development and positive self-esteem in students.

It is important for teachers to consider how they can most effectively raise complex issues of identity, hate, bias, bullying and exclusion with their students. Educators should keep in mind that conversations about understanding and respect should not be limited to commemorative events or special programs and holidays but should be a part of everyday classroom life. Creating inclusive, respectful classrooms where students feel comfortable talking about difficult but important issues is an ongoing effort and working for social justice is a life-long endeavor.

To prepare for successful learning of anti-bias concepts in the classroom, teachers should consider making the following practices an integral part of their everyday practice.

1. **Self-exploration:** Examine your own cultural biases and assumptions. Explore your perceptions and understanding of situations by developing an awareness of your cultural "filters."
2. **Comprehensive Integration:** Integrate culturally diverse information and perspectives in all aspects of your teaching. Relegating equity issues to special of "multicultural" time sends a message to students that such lessons are unimportant relative to other aspects of the curriculum.
3. **Time and Maturation:** Allow time for the process to develop. Introduce less complex topics first and create time to establish trust. Develop ground rules for discussion which allow for honest conversation within a respectful context.
4. **Accepting Environment:** Establish an environment that allows for mistakes. Since most of us have been unconsciously acculturated into prejudicial and stereotypical thinking, we may not be aware that certain attitudes are harmful to ourselves and others. Model how to respond in a non-defensive manner when told something you said or did was offensive. Assume good will and make that assumption a common practice in the classroom.
5. **Intervention:** Be prepared to respond to purposefully directed acts of bias. Students will carefully observe how you intervene when someone is the target of discriminatory or bias-motivated behavior. Silence in the face of injustice conveys the impression that the behavior is condoned or not worthy of attention. Make it clear to students and their families that you will not allow name calling in the classroom.
6. **Lifelong Learning:** Keep abreast of current issues and discuss them with students. Clip articles from newspapers and magazines and post them in the classroom. Use our *Current Events Classroom* lessons (www.adl.org/current-events-classroom) to discuss those topics with your students. Let

students know that you consider yourself a learner in these issues as well and see yourself as part of the learning process.

7. **Discovery Learning:** Avoid "preaching" to students about how they should speak or behave. Research indicates that exhortation is the least effective methodology for changing prejudiced attitudes; in fact, it often produces a result opposite from the desired effect. Provide opportunities for students to resolve conflicts, solve problems, work in diverse teams and think critically about the information they learn.

8. **Life Experiences:** Provide opportunities for students to share life experiences and choose literature that will help students develop empathy. Make your classroom a place where students' experiences are embraced and appreciated, as opposed to marginalized or invalidated. Prejudice and discrimination have a unique impact on each individual, and it is not fruitful to engage in a debate over who has suffered the most.

9. **Resources' Review:** Review materials so that classroom displays and bulletin boards are inclusive of all people. Insure that supplemental books and videos do not reinforce existing stereotypes. When you see such examples in literature, textbooks and the media, point them out to students and encourage them to think critically about and challenge them.

10. **Home-School-Community Connections:** Involve parents, caregivers, family members and the community in the learning process. Find opportunities to invite family and community members into the classroom as teachers and learners. We cannot view the school and the home or school and the community as isolated from one another; we must examine how they interconnect and provide opportunities to share these connections with students.

11. **Examine the Classroom Environment:** What is present and absent in the classroom sends a message to children about whom and what is important. Make every effort to create a setting that is rich in possibilities for exploring cultural diversity. Such an environment assists children in developing their ideas about themselves and others, creates the conditions to initiate conversations about differences and provides teachers with a setting for introducing activities about diversity.

SOCIAL AND EMOTIONAL DEVELOPMENT

During the elementary school years, the social and emotional development of children is a high priority for teachers. Social and emotional learning (SEL) is the process through which children and adults acquire and effectively apply the knowledge, attitudes and skills necessary to understand and manage emotions, set and achieve positive goals, feel and show empathy for others, establish and maintain positive relationships, and make responsible decisions. Before students can understand and address bullying, bias, discrimination and injustice, they first need skills in communicating effectively, empathizing with others, understanding and managing their feelings and the feelings of others and working collaboratively. As such, we have provided social and emotional skill development as part of the first unit's lessons and we encourage the review of these and other lessons when topics arise in the classroom.

CREATING A GENDER INCLUSIVE CLASSROOM ENVIRONMENT

By the time children arrive to elementary schools at the age of four or five, they already have well developed notions and stereotypes about gender identity and expression. Students tend to have very clear ideas about what girls and boys are "supposed" to wear, like, do, and how they should behave based on their gender identity. There is often little flexibility within these concepts and any children who act in ways that challenge those gender norms—often referred to as "gender non-conforming"—are often the target of teasing, isolation, name-calling and/or bullying. Gender stereotypes are pervasive in elementary school and should not only be challenged when they arise but teachers should pro-actively work to minimize them.

Beginning with the youngest students and continuing through high school, one of the best ways to create safe and welcoming classrooms is to diminish the focus on the gender binary and instead, create "gender inclusive schools and classrooms."

Gender Spectrum (2015) states the following:

> "As one of the most fundamental aspects of self, gender impacts everybody. All of us can point to a time in our lives when we were burdened by unfair limitations or expectations because of others' beliefs about our gender. Regardless of a student's age, gender impacts a child's experience at school across the grades. There is abundant research about the relationship between students' sense of safety and their ability to succeed in school, and gender is one of the factors that greatly impacts perceptions of safety. As a primary socializing agent, schools have a tremendous opportunity and responsibility to be inclusive of all students, regardless of their Gender identity or expression. In this role, educational institutions and the professionals associated with them can significantly impact the degree to which gender diversity in children and teens is viewed—either positively or negatively.
>
> Beyond supporting our young people as individuals, we cannot afford to have any of our students cut off from interests, talents, or intellectual pursuits that may ultimately contribute to our society. School is the place where our children should be exploring ideas and discovering new skills. It is inexcusable that any child might be prevented from pursuing their passions simply based on others' perceptions of their gender. By sending a message that certain pursuits are off limits simply because of a person's gender, we lose access to an incredible source of human potential. How many great discoveries, new inventions, cures for disease, or works of art have we lost simply because people believed they couldn't, or shouldn't, do something because of their gender?"

Examples of the practical application in the classroom include:
- Do not have students line up as boys and girls or separate them by gender for activities.
- Display visual images that reinforce gender inclusion such as pictures of people who don't fit gender norms.
- Challenge gender stereotypes by looking for and talking with students about examples in the media that reinforce these stereotypes.
- Share personal anecdotes from your own life which reflect gender inclusiveness.

_____

Reference

Gender Spectrum. 2015. *Gender Inclusive Schools – An Introduction.* www.genderspectrum.org/explore-topics/education/#more-239.

RESPONDING TO NAME CALLING AND BULLYING IN THE CLASSROOM

Below are strategies for preventing teasing, name calling and bullying in the classroom and for addressing it when it does arise. In addition, there are several lessons in the *Anti-Bias Building Blocks* curriculum that address name calling and bullying directly.

- Provide students with opportunities to develop cooperative learning and conflict resolution skills, both as independent opportunities and as part of routine instructional methods.
- Provide students who engage in bullying behaviors with opportunities to discuss these behaviors with counseling staff and to develop more effective strategies for managing peer relationships.
- Avoid focusing efforts to eliminate bullying on a few students who are the aggressors. Understanding and communicating the expectations for all members of the school community are needed to create positive change. Those people not directly involved in bullying are often bystanders who can become active allies by supporting those targeted by bullying.
- Implement strategies to increase student reporting of bullying. Have "share boxes" available where students can leave anonymous notes for administrative staff about incidents or problems that occur in the school.
- Offer "ally-building" activities for students to strengthen their skills, teach techniques to prevent or respond to future incidents and build self-esteem.
- Engage students in a campaign to develop a school motto that communicates a commitment to address bullying, e.g., "All students should feel safe in all areas of the school at all times."
- Organize a group or club for students to take action against name-calling and bullying and to develop skills to be allies to targeted students, e.g., "friendship groups."
- Help students develop informal ways to build peer support.
- Develop a system to reinforce pro-social behavior, e.g., "Caught you caring" or "good deed stars," which are especially effective for younger students.

IMPORTANCE OF MULTICULTURAL AND ANTI-BIAS CHILDREN'S LITERATURE

Books have the potential to create lasting impressions. When books contain experiences and characters for which children can relate, they set the stage for fostering children's positive self-concept and respect for diversity.

Unfortunately, although children of color in the United States make up about 40% of the population, recent statistics compiled by the Cooperative Children's Book Center (CCBC) show a lack of racial diversity in children's books. Despite how critical it is to surround children with books that speak to all

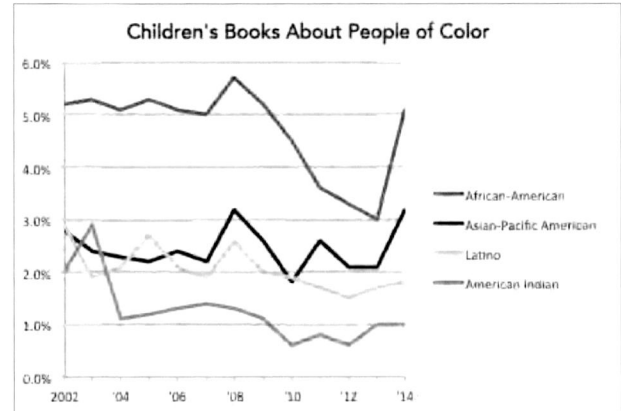

Source: Children's Books By and About People of Color and First/Native Nations Published in the U.S., 2002-2014, Multicultural Cooperative Children's Book Center, University of Wisconsin-Madison, https://ccbc.education.wisc.edu/

children, CCBC found that out of 3,500 children's book titles published in 2014, only 5.1% of the books were about African-Americans, 3.2% were about Asian-Pacific Americans, 1.8% were about Latinos and a mere 1% were about American Indians (Cooperative Children's Book Center, 2014). In addition, there is also a lack of other types of diversity including ability, gender, socioeconomic status, types of families, etc.

Since the books we choose to read with children send messages to them about whom and what is important, book collections should reflect all the children, staff and families in the school and community in which they live. When book collections serve as "mirrors," they contain reflections of the children, their culture, their family type, their abilities, etc. Helping children learn to feel positively about themselves and others also fosters the development of their comfort with human differences.

Helping children gain comfort with differences during their elementary school years has lasting effects, thus underscoring the importance of also including "window books" in children's book collections. When books serve as "windows," they provide a glimpse into the diversity of the world in which children live and help them develop a comfort with and respect for people, places and cultures for which they may be unfamiliar. Books can also illustrate the concept that people from diverse groups can play and work, solve problems and overcome obstacles together.

In addition, books can and should promote social action to combat injustice. Children benefit from hearing stories about people who have been successful in challenging inequality and understanding that they are not powerless in the face of prejudice and discrimination. Books can inspire children by showing them the power of pro-social actions against injustice. They can provide models to help children see themselves as people who can help to enact change.

Because reading is a fundamental part of the elementary curriculum, for each lesson we have provided children's literature suggestions that extend the learning of the lesson or as a way to introduce the concept. You can also check our Books Matter website (www.adl.org/books-matter) for a directory of over 500 books that represents the best anti-bias and multicultural literature for educators and parents of children ages 0–12.

HOW CHILDREN DEVELOP RACIAL AND CULTURAL IDENTITY AND ATTITUDES

Researchers have discovered important information about how young children develop racial and cultural identity and attitudes. Some of the key points are listed below. This information can be used as a framework for observing children and for selecting and creating appropriate lessons and activities.

Two-Year-Olds become increasingly aware of the physical aspects of identity. The awareness of gender is usually noticed first, followed by a curiosity about skin color, hair color and texture, eye shape and color as well as other physical characteristics. Awareness of disabilities tends to come later than the awareness of gender and "race;" however, some two-year-olds may begin noticing more obvious physical disabilities, such as a person using a wheelchair.

Children between the ages of two and three may begin to be aware of the cultural aspects of gender, noticing that girls play more frequently with dolls while boys play more often with trucks. Children at this age may also be aware of ethnic identity, noticing such things as children eating different cultural foods, celebrating different holidays or not celebrating or recognizing holidays or birthdays that they view as important.

Children may show signs of pre-prejudice (the ideas and feelings in very young children that may later develop into "real" prejudices when reinforced by biases that exist in society). Pre-prejudice is often manifested by discomfort, fear or rejection of differences.

Children at this age may take their first steps toward the appreciation of people who are physically and culturally different from themselves if positive interactive experiences are part of the regular home, school and after-school program environments and activities.

Three- and Four-Year-Olds begin to expand their observations of differences and seek greater explanation of those differences. They are aware of their own and others' physical characteristics. Constructing their identity is a primary task. They want to know how they got their skin, hair and eye color and may question why "racial" group "color" names are different from the actual colors.

Preschoolers are curious about variations within their extended family and the reason why two people with different skin colors may be considered part of the same group. They begin to wonder if skin, hair and eye color will remain constant, as they begin to recognize that getting older brings physical changes. Children at this age may ask questions like, "Will my skin color change when I grow up?" Or, "Will you always be white?"

Five-Year-Olds begin to build a group ethnic identity, as well as an individual identity. They can more fully explore the range of differences within and between "racial" and ethnic groups as well as the range of similarities between groups.

Children at this age begin to understand scientific explanations for differences in skin color, hair texture and eye shape. They are also beginning to understand the concept of family traditions and family history.

Six- to Eight-Year-Olds continue to recognize other group members and begin to realize that their ethnicity is not changeable. They are beginning to become aware of history, local actions and attitudes for and against cultural groups. Such new knowledge, influenced in part by the media, may foster personal prejudices that may become an integral part of a child's attitudes and behaviors.

Children at this age are highly influenced by the way they see people interact and resolve conflicts. Many children in this age group learn about culture and "race" with greater cognitive depth and emotional connection than they did at earlier stages. They may begin to take pride in their own cultural identities and understand the experiences of others.

Nine- to Twelve-Year-Olds are gaining a greater understanding of the geographic and historical aspects of culture. Although many 9-12-year-olds may still be concrete thinkers primarily focused on their own experiences, many may be moving into more abstract thinking. They may become aware of the attitudes and behaviors of persons in positions of authority within institutional settings, such as schools, places of worship and youth agencies. They may also begin to gain an awareness and understanding of the various perspectives that have surrounded historical events.

Children at this age may understand personal and family struggles against bias and are often willing to discuss culture, "race" and differences. A more complex understanding of personal, family and community identity based on cultural values may emerge. Children at this age are becoming increasingly aware of the valuing and de-valuing of culture and "race" by their peers, the media and the larger community. The advantages and disadvantages of some groups politically, educationally and economically are becoming evident and children may informally begin to discuss what they see as unfairness.

Most nine- to twelve-year-olds can understand "racial" and cultural stereotypes; can speak from dominant and non-dominant perspectives; can practice stating the strengths and positive aspects of various cultures; and can discuss how internalizing a negative view about self may affect someone's confidence.

References

Bernal, M., and G. Knight, eds. 1993. *Ethnic Identity: Formation and Transmission among Hispanics and Other Minorities.* New York, NY: SUNY Series/State University of New York Press.

Derman-Sparks, L. 1989. *Anti-Bias Curriculum: Tools for Empowering Young Children.* Washington, DC: National Association for the Education of Young Children.

Holmes, R. M. 1995. *How Young Children Perceive Race.* Newbury Park, CA: Sage Publications.

McCarthy, C., and W. Crichlow, eds. 1993. *Race Identity and Representation in Education.* New York, NY: Routledge Publishing.

Phinney, J., and M. Rotheram, eds. 1987. *Children's Ethnic Socialization: Pluralism and Development.* Newbury Park, CA: Sage Publications.

Schultz, F., ed. 1995. *Multicultural Education.* 6th ed. Guilford, CT: The Dushkin Publishing Group/Brown and Benchmark Publishers.

Van Dijk, T. 1987. *Communicating Racism.* Newbury Park, CA: Sage Publications.

TEACHER AND CLASSROOM SELF-ASSESSMENT

The following self-assessment checklist assists educators in reflecting on and gaining insight into their personal, professional and institutional beliefs and attitudes about diversity and anti-bias education. These questions can be used as part of a larger conversation about anti-bias education or by individual teachers to assess their own practice.

Part I. Assessing Yourself

How effective are you in promoting a bias-free educational environment?	I haven't thought about this.	I need to do this better.	I do this well.
1. Have you recently read any books or articles, or watched any documentaries to increase your understanding of the particular hopes, needs and concerns of students and families from the different cultures that make up your school community and beyond?	[ ]	[ ]	[ ]
2. Have you participated in professional development opportunities to enhance your understanding of the complex characteristics of racial, ethnic and cultural groups in the U.S.?	[ ]	[ ]	[ ]
3. Do you try to listen with an open mind to all students and colleagues, even when you don't understand their perspectives or agree with what they're saying?	[ ]	[ ]	[ ]
4. Have you taken specific actions to dispel misconceptions, stereotypes or prejudices that members of one group have about members of another group at your school?	[ ]	[ ]	[ ]
5. Do you strive to avoid actions that might be offensive to members of other groups?	[ ]	[ ]	[ ]
6. Do you discourage patterns of informal discrimination, segregation or exclusion of members of particular groups from school clubs, committees and other school activities?	[ ]	[ ]	[ ]
7. Do the curricular content and wall displays in your classroom reflect the experiences and perspectives of the cultural groups that make up the school and its surrounding community?	[ ]	[ ]	[ ]
8. Have you evaluated classroom materials and textbooks to ensure they do not reinforce stereotypes and that they provide fair and appropriate treatment of all groups?	[ ]	[ ]	[ ]
9. Do you use classroom methods, such as cooperative learning, role-playing and small group discussions to meet the needs of students' different learning styles?	[ ]	[ ]	[ ]
10. Do students have opportunities to engage in problem-solving groups that address real issues with immediate relevance to their lives?	[ ]	[ ]	[ ]
11. Do you use a range of strategies, in addition to traditional testing methods, to assess student learning?	[ ]	[ ]	[ ]

Part II. Assessing Your School

How effective is your school in promoting a bias-free educational environment?	We haven't thought about this.	We need to do this better.	We do this well.
1. Does the school's mission statement communicate values of respect, equity and inclusion?	[ ]	[ ]	[ ]
2. Do students typically interact with one another in positive, respectful ways?	[ ]	[ ]	[ ]
3. Do the school's symbols, signs, mascots and insignias reflect respect for diversity?	[ ]	[ ]	[ ]
4. Do celebrations, festivals and special events reflect a variety of cultural groups and holidays?	[ ]	[ ]	[ ]
5. Is the school staff (administrative, instructional, counseling and supportive) representative of the racial, ethnic and cultural groups that comprise the surrounding community?	[ ]	[ ]	[ ]
6. Are staff or volunteers available who are fluent in the languages of families in the school community?	[ ]	[ ]	[ ]
7. Do students, families and staff share in the decision-making process for the school?	[ ]	[ ]	[ ]
8. Has the school community collaboratively developed written policies and procedures to address harassment and bullying?	[ ]	[ ]	[ ]
9. Are consequences associated with harassment and bullying policy violations enforced equitably and consistently?	[ ]	[ ]	[ ]
10. Do the instructional materials used in the classroom and available in the school library, including text books, supplementary books and multimedia resources, reflect the experiences and perspectives of people of diverse backgrounds?	[ ]	[ ]	[ ]
11. Are equitable opportunities for participation in extra- and co-curricular activities made available to students of all gender, ability, and socioeconomic groups?	[ ]	[ ]	[ ]
12. Do faculty and staff have opportunities for systematic, comprehensive and continuing professional development designed to increase cultural understanding and promote student safety?	[ ]	[ ]	[ ]
13. Does the school conduct ongoing evaluations of the goals, methods and instructional materials used in teaching to ensure they reflect the histories, contributions and perspectives of diverse groups?	[ ]	[ ]	[ ]

UNIT I. CREATING A SAFE AND COMFORTABLE CLASSROOM ENVIRONMENT

As we introduce young children to issues of bias, diversity and social justice, it is critical that we begin by building a solid foundation for their social and emotional skill development. We want to ensure that students feel comfortable in their classrooms; have the skills they need to communicate effectively; have a vocabulary for the different feelings that may emerge and a useful and positive way to deal with those feelings; and have an understanding of how to work collaboratively in small and large groups. Social and emotional skill development is the foundation for any positive and pro-social elementary school classroom, especially in classrooms that aspire to grapple with issues of identity, bias, bullying and diversity. The best learning and insight emerges when children feel supported, safe and skilled.

GOALS FOR KINDERGARTEN THROUGH 2ND GRADE

In Unit I, children in kindergarten through 2nd grade will help to set the ground rules for their classroom so that everyone feels safe and ready to participate. They will reflect on communicating well and understand the difference between good and poor listening, a foundation for effective communication. Children will expand their feelings vocabulary, gaining insight into the connection between actions and feelings. They will explore cooperation and learn techniques for working well with others.

GOALS FOR THIRD THROUGH FIFTH GRADE

For third to fifth graders, children will develop classroom guidelines to maximize their ability to interact with one another and their learning. They will reflect on nonverbal communication and miscommunication and will learn about and practice active listening. Children will deepen and expand their feelings vocabulary and at the same time, will learn how to express and manage their feelings more effectively. Finally, learning to work collaboratively and as part of a team will enhance their learning throughout the course of this curriculum and beyond.

GROUND RULES

Lesson 1

RATIONALE

The purpose of this lesson is for students to consider why rules are important when people are playing, working or learning together. The lesson provides an opportunity for students to develop rules for their classroom. Creating a safe classroom environment which allows for sharing and different ways of being sets a positive tone for discussion and allows for maximum learning and sharing.

OBJECTIVES

- Students will reflect on the importance of rules.
- Students will identify rules that will make them feel safe and able to participate.
- Students will, as a group, come to agreement about their class rules.

WHAT'S NEEDED

Chart paper, markers, construction paper and crayons

PROCEDURES

1. Introduce the lesson by asking students if they have ever played a game. Have them share aloud some of the games they have played. Ask them if they want to play a game of "Duck, Duck, Goose" or another game that they are all likely to know (hot potato, follow the leader). After the class has decided on a game, ask one student to explain how to play the game to the rest of the group. Play the game for several minutes.

2. Stop the game and ask the students how they knew what to do when playing the game. Draw out from students that they knew what to do because the game has rules and someone taught them the rules. To engage them in a class discussion, ask students the following questions:
   - Why do people have rules?
   - Do you think rules are a good thing? (Have students put

GRADE LEVEL
K–2

TIME
35 minutes

COMMON CORE STANDARDS
Reading, Speaking & Listening

STRATEGIES AND SKILLS
Engage in large group discussion, draw, support ideas with examples, come to agreement

KEY WORDS AND PHRASES
Participate
Rules
Safe

 **CHILDREN'S BOOKS**

The Berenstain Bears No Girls Allowed by Stan and Jan Berenstain

Do Unto Otters by Laurie Keller

Never Spit on Your Shoes by Denys Cazet

■ *Anti-Bias Building Blocks: An Elementary Curriculum*   Unit I.29

thumbs up for yes, thumbs down for no and thumbs to the side for not sure.)

- Do we have rules in this classroom? Name a rule you know.
- What are some other places where we have and follow rules?
- Have you ever experienced when a rule was not followed? What happened?
- Do you think we should have rules for when we talk and play together (thumbs up, thumbs down, thumbs to the side)?

3. Ask students to think of rules that they would like to see in the classroom. They should think about what rules would help them to take care of themselves, each other and the classroom. Rules should help them feel safe, able to fully participate and be themselves. If needed, provide an example such as "be a good listener" or "do not make fun of anyone."

4. Distribute construction paper and drawing materials and have students write out a rule they would like to see followed in the classroom. Depending on writing ability, kindergarteners can do a combination of writing a word and/or drawing and other children will write out more of the rule. Have all students illustrate the rule by drawing a picture that symbolizes the rule or important parts of the rule (e.g., an ear for "be a good listener"). Distribute masking tape and have students hang their pictures on the wall. After all the pictures are on the wall, in groups of 4–5, have students come up and look at the pictures. When everyone has a chance to look at the pictures, ask students to share specific rules. As students suggest rules, ask them to explain why this might be a good rule.

5. Write all of the rules on the board and come up with a list of 5–8 rules that the class agrees to, either by working to build consensus or having students vote. Once the class has agreed on these rules, explain that you are going to write the rules on chart paper. Write "Our Rules" in large letters on a piece of chart paper. Write the students' rules in simple language.

6. Review each rule with the class. When finished, ask the students if they agree that these are good rules for everyone in the class to follow. Have the children raise their hands in agreement or say "yes" all together loudly. Remind students that you will be reviewing these rules with them before beginning new activities or at other times when it might be necessary. Explain that sometimes rules need to be changed or depending on the activity, it may be necessary to add a new rule.

EXTENSION ACTIVITIES

- Divide students into small groups based on the number of rules you have for the classroom. Each group will create a mini-skit about the rule not being followed and what the consequences of not following the rule might be. They will then hear suggestions from their classmates about what to do to follow the rule and will act that out as well. An alternative idea is to have students write a story about a situation in which a rule was not followed and what happened as a result.

- Using photos, magazine pictures and Internet art and photos, have students create a collage of words and pictures that illustrate "Rules In Our Lives." This can include sports, games, home, school, etc. Alternately, you can have students collect the words and pictures and create a class bulletin board or mural for "Rules in Our Lives."

- Read aloud and discuss one or more of the children's books from the list provided in this lesson.

COMMUNICATING WELL

Lesson 2

RATIONALE

The purpose of this lesson is for students to understand the different aspects of communication and why it is important to communicate well. Communicating well decreases conflict and helps students discuss issues more effectively. This lesson provides an opportunity for students to understand what communication is, reflect on different ways we can communicate and participate in group interviews to practice speaking and listening.

OBJECTIVES

- Students will communicate something about themselves non-verbally.
- Students will define communication and identify the many ways people communicate.
- Students will practice speaking and listening by conducting group interviews.

REQUIREMENTS

Paper and pencil for each student

PROCEDURES

1. Begin the lesson by having students form a circle. Explain to students that they will tell everyone in the class something about themselves (e.g., one activity they like) but they cannot use words to express themselves. Ask students, "How can we communicate without speaking?" Explain that they will need to use their body or parts of their bodies to share. For example, if you like swimming, you can use your arms or legs to show swimming movements.

2. As students take turns acting out their facial expressions or movements, have the other children guess what the person has shared about themselves.

3. After completing this activity, have everyone go back to their seats. Write the word "communication" on the board, read it

GRADE LEVEL
K–2

TIME
35 minutes

COMMON CORE STANDARDS
Reading, Speaking & Listening, Language

STRATEGIES AND SKILLS
Act out activities, ask and answer questions (interview), engage in large group discussion, take notes

KEY WORDS AND PHRASES
Communication
Interrupt
Interview
Listening
Non-verbal
Speaking

■ *Anti-Bias Building Blocks: An Elementary Curriculum*

aloud and ask if anyone knows what it means. Come to a definition of **communication** as sharing thoughts, feelings or information with another person or group. Ask students, "What are some ways that people can communicate their thoughts, feelings or information?" Brainstorm a list that may include: talk, listen, write, email, use emoticons, symbols, text, sign language, etc. This instruction may be challenging for kindergarteners

4. Explain to students that sometimes communication is non-verbal (i.e. not verbal, not talking) which means people can use other body parts to share feelings, thoughts or information. Ask for an example and refer back to the activity in the beginning of the lesson where everyone shared a favorite activity or feeling without talking.

5. Engage students in a large group discussion by asking the following questions:
   - Do animals communicate (with us and other animals)? If so, how?
   - How do we use our bodies to communicate?
   - Can you think of examples of how people who cannot hear (or hear fully) or speak communicate?

6. Have students brainstorm a list of good communication strategies by asking them what are some ways people can communicate well. Bear in mind that people view communication differently and some of this is based on people's cultural backgrounds and norms. Therefore, remain open to different responses to how we communicate. The list may include the following:
   - Speak so others understand.
   - Say what you mean.
   - Focus on the person.
   - Listen to what the person said.
   - Act interested.
   - Check for understanding.

7. Explain to students that they are going to do interviews with each other to demonstrate communication. With the class, brainstorm a list of questions that students would like to ask about each other. Questions can include:
   - Where do you live?
   - Do you have any pets?
   - What is your favorite game to play?
   - Who is in your family?
   - What languages do you speak?
   - What's your favorite food?

8. One at a time, have each student come to the front of the room and have the rest of the class "interview" that student. You may choose to have all students interviewed or only those who volunteer and want to be the "interviewee." Conduct the group interviews by having students ask questions of the person in the front of the room. Remind students (if it is not part of your class rules) that they have the right to pass if they do not feel comfortable answering a particular question, but encourage as much participation as possible. Have each student answer 3–5 questions and then move to the next person.

9. As students are interviewed, instruct all of the other children to write down one thing about each person that they found out during the interview or for students who are not writing, they may draw a picture instead. Have students share some of those when the interviews are completed.

10. After the interviews are finished, ask students why is communication important? Make the connection between good communication and class rules you determined previously. Point out which rules relate to communication such as listening and not interrupting.

EXTENSION ACTIVITIES

- Play the game of charades, acting out different things (books, characters, activities, etc.) and having the other children guess.

- Have students draw four different facial expressions using a different emotion for each. The four drawings can be four different people or the same person with four different emotions expressed through their facial expressions. If you have time, have them use the facial expressions to create a comic strip or storyboard that has a story plot that goes along with the facial expressions.

- Read aloud and discuss one or more of the children's books from the list provided in this lesson.

CHILDREN'S BOOKS

My Mouth is a Volcano by Julia Cook

Let's Hear it For Almigal by Wendy Kupfer

The Quiet Book by Deborah Underwood

Willow's Whispers by Lana Button

LISTENING

Lesson 3

RATIONALE

The purpose of this lesson is for students to understand the difference between good and poor listening and to practice effective listening strategies. Listening is a critical aspect of good communication. In this lesson, students will have the opportunity to reflect on poor listening practices, identify and examine effective strategies in listening well and practice good listening.

OBJECTIVES

- Students will reflect on and be able to articulate the difference between good and poor listening.
- Students will identify effective listening practices.
- Students will practice good listening and discuss how they feel when listened to.

WHAT'S NEEDED

Board/Smart board or chart paper with the word LISTENING at the top, magic markers

PROCEDURES

1. Begin the lesson by playing the telephone game. Have students sit in a circle if possible. Explain to students that you will be playing a game to learn more about listening. You will whisper a sentence to the first person in the circle and they will pass along the message to the next person. The sentence should go around the entire circle, the goal being that the last person in the circle receives the sentence as it was originally sent. After sending the message around the circle, have the last person in the circle state what they heard.

2. If the sentence is incorrect—which is likely—play the game again but this time allow the students to, if need be, restate back to the person whispering to them what they think they heard and that person can correct them. Note that this can only be done once and then the message has to be passed on. Remind the students

GRADE LEVEL
K–2

TIME
35 minutes

COMMON CORE STANDARDS
Reading, Speaking & Listening

STRATEGIES AND SKILLS
Engage in large group discussion, observe for good and poor listening, practice good listening

KEY WORDS AND PHRASES
Interrupt
Listening
Rephrase

■ *Anti-Bias Building Blocks: An Elementary Curriculum*

to be sure to whisper quietly and if they think they got the sentence right the first time, they do not have to restate it; they can simply move on to the next person. Again, have the message go around the circle and have the last person in the circle state aloud the sentence.

3. After completing the game, engage students in a discussion by asking the following questions:
   - What happened in the first round?
   - What happened in the second round?
   - Why do you think there was a different outcome the second time?
   - What was helpful in getting the right message around the circle?

4. Explain to students that today's lesson will focus on good and poor listening. To demonstrate ineffective listening, either do a role play with another student or use two puppets to demonstrate. If you are acting this out with a student, ask for a volunteer. Ask the student to talk about a topic that you determine before the activity (e.g., my favorite book or movie). As the student speaks (or if you are using puppets and playing both parts), exhibit ineffective listening by looking around the room, interrupting, fidgeting, not paying attention, etc.

5. Engage students in a discussion by asking the following questions:
   - What did you see?
   - Do you think I was listening? Why or why not?
   - How do you think (person being listened to) felt?
   - What should I do differently to listen better?

   As students respond to the last question, "What should I do differently to listen better," record their responses on board/smart board or chart paper with the heading LISTENING. Again, make sure to focus on the larger categories of listening and not the specifics. For example, for some students, keeping one's body still shows good listening. For others, standing up or moving their hands means they are listening. Therefore, if a student responds, "keep your body still," ask students if this works for everyone.

6. Have students pair off with another person. Explain that they are going to take turns listening to each other and that they should consider the LISTENING guidelines. Explain that students will get one minute to talk per person and then they will switch. They should decide who is person A and who is person B. They may also tell each other in advance what they need from the other person to feel like they are listening. Person A will go first and answer the following question: "What is your favorite thing to do on Saturday morning?" Then when you call "time," they will switch and Person B will speak and Person A will listen.

7. After completing their speaking and listening, engage the students in a discussion by asking the following questions:
   - When you were the listener, was it easy or difficult?
   - When you were the speaker, how did you feel while your partner was listening?
   - What were some ways that the person listened well?
   - What were some ways that they didn't listen so well?

8. End the lesson by having students say one word to describe how they felt when their partner listened.

EXTENSION ACTIVITIES

- Play a modified version of "I'm going on a picnic." Have students form a circle and tell them that the class is going on an imaginary picnic. Each person gets to bring one item. The first person will share one item they would like to bring and then the next person has to re-state the first person's item and then say what they want to bring. For example, the first person will say, "I'm going on a picnic and I'm bringing a baseball." Then the next person will say, "I'm going on a picnic and I'm bringing a baseball (from the first person) and some watermelon." And so on. You can start off by having students remember the five people's items before them and then start over and then build up to them remembering everyone in the class.

- Have students write a story about a time in school when either they didn't listen to someone or someone didn't listen to them. Remind them to not use anyone's name in the class nor details that would give away the people who were involved. This could be a realistic fiction story or a made up story. They should include what happened, how the person felt when not listened to, and any consequences that resulted.

- Read aloud and discuss one or more of the children's books from the list provided in this lesson.

CHILDREN'S BOOKS

The Listening Walk by Paul Showers

Oink, Oink Benny by Barbro Lindgren

I Have a Little Problem, Said the Bear by Heinz Janisch

MY FEELINGS

RATIONALE

The purpose of this lesson is to help students understand a wide range of feelings and be able to express those emotions. Understanding and being able to express feelings is an important part of helping children navigate their world and relate to others. Students will have the opportunity to brainstorm feelings' words that they know, connect those feelings to how they feel in different situations and during different activities and use nonverbal communication to act out different feelings.

OBJECTIVES

- Students will be able to make a list of different feelings.
- Students will be able to connect feelings with activities and situations.
- Students will be able to act out and guess expressed feelings nonverbally.

WHAT'S NEEDED

Handouts and Resources: Feelings Cards (optional: purchase a set of feelings flashcards)

Other Material: Scissors, heavier weight paper, hat

Advance Preparation: Reproduce the *Feelings Cards* onto heavier paper. Cut each section into individual card pieces. Place the cards in a hat.

PROCEDURES

1. Begin the lesson by brainstorming and creating a semantic web with feelings words. Ask students, "What are some words that describe feelings or emotions?" While they are sharing feelings, record their responses on the web, connecting words on the web as they make the connections. Read aloud the words as you write

Lesson 4

GRADE LEVEL
K–2

TIME
35 minutes

COMMON CORE STANDARDS
Reading, Speaking & Listening

STRATEGIES AND SKILLS
Engage in large group discussion, act out feelings, brainstorm, turn and talk

KEY WORDS AND PHRASES
Angry
Annoyed
Bored
Brave
Delighted
Disappointed
Emotions
Excited
Feelings
Frightened
Happy
Nervous
Overjoyed
Proud
Sad
Scared
Serious
Shy
Silly
Worried

■ *Anti-Bias Building Blocks: An Elementary Curriculum*

them down. The web might look like this:

```
        Frustrated    Happy —— Glad
              Silly    Proud
         Excite              Shy
    Bold                        Worried
   Brave         ┌─────────┐   Nervous
                 │ Feelings │
     Sad         └─────────┘   Surprised
                                Calm
   Angry —— Mad   Scared
              Confused   Terrified
```

2. After the semantic web is complete, have students get in pairs. For each of the words on the list, have one person in the pair complete a sentence about it ("I feel happy when _____"). Using "happy" as an example, model how to do the activity by saying: I feel happy when it is my birthday. Explain to students that you will call out the word and then each of them will fill in the blank. Use as many words from the semantic web as possible.

3. After the students have shared with their partners, engage them in a discussion by asking the following questions:
   - Was it easy or difficult to connect a feeling with an activity or situation?
   - Were there some feeling words you did not know?
   - If so, how did you figure out the meaning?
   - Are there some feelings' words that have similar meanings? Can you give an example?
   - Did you have different feelings from your partner?
   - What do you notice about the feeling words?

4. Have students form a circle in the center of the room. Using the *Feelings Cards*, explain to students that you are going to have them pick a feeling word/picture and act it out. You will start the activity by giving the students an activity such as brushing teeth or dribbling a basketball. Then they will pick one of the feelings cards out of the hat and will act out the activity (brushing teeth) with the feeling that they chose. Help them read the card after they pick it out.

5. Remind students about nonverbal communication by asking what parts of our bodies can we use to show our feelings if we cannot use words (e.g., facial expression, body language, hand movements, etc.)? As students act out the activity using the feeling, have students raise their hands if they can guess the feeling being expressed.

6. After completing the activity, engage students in a discussion by asking:
   - Was it easy or difficult to guess the feeling that each person acted out?
   - How did you know what the feeling was?
   - Did you learn any new words for feelings?

7. End the lesson by having students say one new feeling they learned today.

> ### Additional Tips To Help Children Understand and Express Feelings
>
> 1. In the morning, regularly have a "feelings' check-in" where you ask the students how they are feeling or they paste a feeling word (or emoji) next to their name in the morning.
>
> 2. Whenever you read a children's book, ask how they feel about different parts of the book and specifically ask how different characters are feeling at different times.
>
> 3. When things happen during the school day, especially when there are conflicts or strong feelings, be sure to ask how the students are feeling, either individually or as part of a group discussion.

EXTENSION ACTIVITIES

- Using pictures and photos students find in magazines, newspapers and on the Internet, have students create Feelings' Collages by cutting out different pictures and photos, gluing them on a piece of paper and marking each of the pictures with feelings words (with you writing for the children who are not writing yet). Alternately, you can create a class mural or larger collage with different feelings and add to it throughout the course of the year as their feelings vocabulary develops.

- Have students make their own feelings cards. Give each of them a feeling that is either part of the list or a new one that would be useful for students to learn. Have students create the card by writing the feeling word in magic marker and/or creating an emoticon (emoji) that expresses that feeling.

- Read aloud and discuss one or more of the children's books from the list provided in this lesson.

CHILDREN'S BOOKS

The Feelings Book by Todd Parr

Sometimes I'm Bombaloo by Rachel Vail

When Sophie Gets Angry— Really, Really Angry... by Molly Bang

Wemberly Worried by Kevin Henckes

Feelings by Aliki

The Way I Feel by Janan Cain

FEELINGS CARDS

Happy	Sad
Excited	Shy
Brave	Angry

Images reprinted with permission from Todd Parr, *Feelings Flashcards* (San Francisco: Chronicle Books, 2010).

FEELINGS CARDS

Delighted	Proud
Serious	Bored
Disappointed	Scared

Images reprinted with permission from Todd Parr, *Feelings Flashcards* (San Francisco: Chronicle Books, 2010).

■ *Anti-Bias Building Blocks: An Elementary Curriculum* | Unit I.43

FEELINGS CARDS

Nervous	Annoyed
Overjoyed	Worried
Frightened	Silly

Images reprinted with permission from Todd Parr, *Feelings Flashcards* (San Francisco: Chronicle Books, 2010).

COOPERATION

Lesson 5

RATIONALE

The purpose of this lesson is for students to learn about cooperation and what is involved in working together on a project, activity or goal. Working as a team member is an important social skill and students will be expected to work cooperatively in groups throughout this curriculum. In this lesson, students will have the opportunity to define cooperation, discuss and explore their experiences with cooperation and teamwork and work on something together as a small group and reflect on that experience.

OBJECTIVES

- Students will be able to define cooperation and provide examples from their own lives.
- Students will work cooperatively with others to create something.
- Students will explore and reflect on real life experiences with cooperation.

WHAT'S NEEDED

Handouts and Resources: Who, What, Why and How Worksheet (one for each student)

Other Material: 26 index cards (or small pieces of paper) with the letters A-Z, one on each card; bag

PROCEDURES

1. Begin the lesson by playing an observation game where students have to work together. Explain to students that they will pair off with someone sitting near them and then decide who will be Person A and Person B. Explain that Person A will change three things in their appearance and it is Person B's job to guess the changes. Person B will take about 30 seconds to closely observe Person A—their dress and appearance. You will call "time" and then students will stand with their backs to one another while Person A changes three things about their appearance (e.g.,

GRADE LEVEL
K–2

TIME
35 minutes

COMMON CORE STANDARDS
Reading, Writing, Speaking & Listening

STRATEGIES AND SKILLS
Define terms, engage in small group cooperative work, engage in large group discussion

KEY WORDS AND PHRASES
Cooperation
Decision
Planning
Team

removing glasses, rolling up a sleeve, untying a shoe, etc.). After changing those three things, they will turn around and Person B has to guess what they changed. After one round, Person A will observe and Person B will change their appearance. If interest remains high, you can conduct another round by changing partners.

2. Model this activity to the group.

3. After completing the game, ask students the following questions:
   - Was it difficult or easy to guess what your partner changed?
   - What made it easier?
   - How did you work together or not work together?

4. Ask students, "What are some examples of people working together?" Brainstorm a list of ideas which could include the following:
   - Playing on a sports team
   - Playing a game with teams
   - Working on a group project for school
   - Cooking something with my family
   - Taking care of a pet with my sister
   - Building something with my friends

5. Tell students that all of those activities require cooperation. Write the word COOPERATION on the board and ask does anyone know what cooperation means? Come to a definition of **cooperation** as people working together to do something. Using the examples students shared in #4, ask "How did people cooperate and what was the outcome? Can you think of other examples of cooperation?"

6. Divide students into groups of 3–4. Explain to students that they are going to work together cooperatively to make the shape of a letter of the alphabet while they are laying on the floor. Assign each group a letter by having them pick the letters out of a bag that you have prepared in advance. Give students 7–10 minutes to talk together to plan out how they are going to form the letter with their bodies, practice and then do it. Taking turns, have each group display their letter one at a time and have the rest of the students guess what letter they have displayed.

7. Engage students in a discussion by asking the following questions:
   - How did your group work together?
   - What worked well?
   - What didn't work so well?
   - How did you decide how to create the letter?
   - Was everyone included in planning and making the decision?
   - How did you feel about your work together?

8. Have students think about a real-life example of working together with other people on something. It can be something they shared at the beginning of the lesson or another project or activity. Using the *Who, What, Why and How Worksheet,* have students write the details of a story outline by including more details about the situation. Students should write just one or a few words after each of these questions and/or they can illustrate it if time permits.

9. After working on the story beginnings, have students share them with the class either individually or hang them up and have students do a gallery walk. You may choose to have students elaborate on these and create a full story (see Extension Activities).

EXTENSION ACTIVITIES

- Challenge your students to convert a game that involves individual competition to a game that requires teamwork and cooperation. Model the activity by playing "team tag" instead of individual tag, so that students work as teams to tag other teams. Start by having them brainstorm a list of games they enjoy. Then they can work in groups to change one of the games into a cooperative game and write out the rules and any necessary illustrations.

- Have students go home and talk with their parents, caregivers, family members and other adults about what they do in the course of their day that takes cooperation. They can also ask about what happens when people do not cooperate but should. Then have students come back to class and report back what they found out and either write or draw about the activities described.

- Read aloud and discuss one or more of the children's books from the list provided in this lesson.

CHILDREN'S BOOKS

Swimmy by Leo Lionni

Anansi the Spider by Harcourt School Publishers

The Crayon Box that Talked by Shane Derolf

WHO, WHAT, WHY AND HOW WORKSHEET

[Student Handout]

Instructions: Think about a real-life example of working together with other people on something. Write the details of a story outline by including more details about the situation. Write just one or a few words after each of the following questions and/or illustrate it if time permits.

WHO was involved? _____

_____
_____
_____
_____

WHAT was the activity? _____

_____
_____
_____
_____

WHY did you work together? _____

_____
_____
_____
_____

HOW did it turn out? _____

_____
_____
_____
_____

Unit I.48 | Creating a Safe and Comfortable Classroom Environment

DEVELOPING CLASSROOM GUIDELINES

Lesson 1

RATIONALE

The purpose of this lesson is for students to consider why rules are important when people are working, playing or learning together. Creating a safe classroom environment sets a positive tone for discussion and allows for maximum learning and sharing. The lesson provides an opportunity for students to develop rules for their classroom.

OBJECTIVES

- Students will reflect on the purpose and advantages of having rules.
- Students will identify guidelines for the class.
- Students will understand the importance of being flexible about classroom guidelines and that sometimes rules need to be added or changed.

WHAT'S NEEDED

Handouts and Resources: Ground Rules for Respect Worksheet (one for each student)

Other Material: A few decks of cards (at least one per four students)

PROCEDURES

1. Begin the lesson by asking students to name their favorite games, which can include sports, board games, computer games or apps. Brainstorm a list of games and record them on the board.

2. Divide students into small groups of 3–4 students each and have them decide together on a card game that at least some of those in the group know. For about five minutes, have the students play the card games in their small groups.

3. Ask students, "For those in the groups who did not know the card game, how did you know how to play?" Explain that for those who did not know the game, someone had to explain the rules. Ask them to picture the game being played without any rules.

GRADE LEVEL
3–5

TIME
45 minutes

COMMON CORE STANDARDS
Reading, Writing, Speaking & Listening, Language

STRATEGIES AND SKILLS
Engage in large group discussion and small group cooperation, create a game

KEY WORDS AND PHRASES
Abide
Confidential
Conflict
Environment
Participate
Respect

■ *Anti-Bias Building Blocks: An Elementary Curriculum*   Unit I.49

Encourage students to consider what would happen if the rules that had been established for their game (or other game) were not followed. Have students share examples and experiences that they have had with rules not being followed. Ask students the following questions:

- What happened when the rules were not followed? How did people feel?
- Why are rules established in the first place?
- What is the advantage of having rules?
- Why do rules sometimes have to be changed or new rules added?
- What games have you played where the rules had to change?
- What is the purpose and advantages for having rules?

Discuss the purpose and advantages for having rules, helping students understand that rules serve as a guide for learning, discussion and playing games. Rules in the classroom help everyone feel safe and able to fully participate.

4. Write the term "Ground Rules" at the top of a piece of chart paper. Write the letters R-E-S-P-E-C-T along the left-hand side of the paper. Define and discuss the meaning of respect. Ask students for examples of how they show respect to others as well as the ways in which they feel they are shown respect.

5. Explain to students that their task is to develop ground rules for the class. These rules will help create an environment in the class where everyone feels safe and able to participate in discussions honestly and respectfully. Tell them that the seven letters in "respect" will help guide them in the development of the ground rules.

6. Distribute the *Ground Rules for Respect Worksheet* to each student. Instruct students to think about words that begin with each of the seven letters of "respect" and then write their suggestions after each corresponding letter (e.g., confidential for the letter "c"). They should come up with at least one word per letter but ideally more than one for each letter.

    Example:

    R   Respect everyone's opinions
    E   Enjoy listening to others
    S   Steer clear of put-downs
    P   Participate
    E   Energy
    C   Confidential
    T   Trust

7. Begin with R and ask the first student to share their word choice for R. The next person should share their choice for E and so on. Explain to students that if the same word or general concept they have is already up there, to share something new. Go through the word RESPECT at least twice getting as much input as possible. After you have gotten suggestions from as many people as possible, come up with a word or concept for each letter that students can agree to.

8. If there are any important rules that are missing (listen, speak from own experience, participate, confidentiality, no put-downs, respect others' points of view), add those in and make sure students agree.

9. Ask students if they agree to abide by the ground rules developed by the class. If students cannot

agree to the rules, ask what they need added or changed in order to agree. Continue the discussion until everyone is satisfied with the ground rules. Have students verbally agree to the rules by saying "yes!," raising their hands in agreement to the rules or signing the piece of chart paper.

10. Post the ground rules in a location where all students can see them. Remind students that you will review the rules with them often. Ask students, "Did you ever play a game and you had to change the rules at the beginning or midway through the game?" Explain to students that depending on the activity and what is happening in the classroom, sometimes rules need to be changed or new rules need to be added depending on the situation.

EXTENSION ACTIVITIES

- Have students choose one of the rules they came up with and write a persuasive essay about the rule. In the essay, they will need to provide evidence to persuade the reader as to the importance of the rule. They should include what the rule is, why they think it is important and what happens if the rule is not followed and provide an example. They can illustrate their essay and/or create a storyboard/comic book about it.

- Have students design a bulletin board entitled "Rules In Our Lives." Encourage them to use signs and symbols that most people know (e.g., stop sign) as well as signs with which some people might be unfamiliar (e.g., parking spaces for people with disabilities). Also ask them to think about rules as they relate to sports and other activities, clubs, etc. in which they participate. They can use original drawings, pictures from magazines or photos. Review all of the signs and symbols with the students and discuss how rules can help people.

- Read aloud and discuss one or more of the children's books from the list provided in this lesson.

FLIPPED CLASSROOM IDEA

Make a video of yourself reading one of the books in the recommended Children's Books section. As you would with any read aloud, ask a few prediction questions at the beginning, a few questions while you are reading and a few questions for students to think about at the end of the story.

CHILDREN'S BOOKS

Miss Nelson is Missing by Harry Allard

If Everybody Did by Jo Ann Stover

Officer Buckle and Gloria by Peggy Rathmann

GROUND RULES FOR RESPECT WORKSHEET

[Student Handout]

Instructions: Think about words that begin with each of the seven letters of "respect" and then write your suggestions after each letter. For example, the word confidential for the letter "c". Come up with at least one word per letter but ideally more than one for each letter.

R _____   _____   _____

E _____   _____   _____

S _____   _____   _____

P _____   _____   _____

E _____   _____   _____

C _____   _____   _____

T _____   _____   _____

Unit I.52 | Creating a Safe and Comfortable Classroom Environment

NONVERBAL COMMUNICATION AND MISCOMMUNICATION

Lesson 2

RATIONALE

The purpose of this lesson is for students to understand and analyze the causes of miscommunication and the role of nonverbal communication in giving and receiving information. Students will define communication, miscommunication and nonverbal communication, provide examples of and act out nonverbal communication and learn how to recognize miscommunication and nonverbal communication.

OBJECTIVES

- Students will analyze how missing information leads to miscommunication.
- Students will define communication, miscommunication and nonverbal communication.
- Students will understand aspects of nonverbal communication and act out examples of nonverbal communication.

WHAT'S NEEDED

Chart paper and markers

Advance Preparation: Write the definitions of communication, miscommunication and nonverbal communication on board/smart board or chart paper (see #2, 3 & 4)

PROCEDURES

1. Begin the lesson by modeling a role play on miscommunication. You will describe an object without conveying all of the necessary details to identify the object, in order to demonstrate the importance of sharing all of the relevant information. Explain to students that you are going to describe something simple. For example, you might describe a cherry and say it is small, red and round but leave out that it has a pit and that it is a fruit. Your job is to describe the object but leave something out and see if they can guess what the object is. Ask students if they can guess. If they do not get it, you can explain that you left some key information

GRADE LEVEL
3–5

TIME
45 minutes

COMMON CORE STANDARDS
Reading, Writing, Speaking & Listening, Language

STRATEGIES AND SKILLS
Give and receive instructions, role play nonverbal communication, brainstorm, engage in large group discussion

KEY WORDS AND PHRASES
Culture
Facial expression
Gestures
Listening
Miscommunication
Nonverbal communication
Posture
Thorough
Tone of voice
Volume

■ *Anti-Bias Building Blocks: An Elementary Curriculum*

out and try again including that information the next time. If time permits, allow a few students to be the ones to do the describing of an object. Explain the importance of giving as much information as possible and being clear.

2. Ask students to define communication. Come to the definition of **communication** as sharing thoughts, feelings or information with another person or group. Ask students what are the different ways we communicate? The list will look something like this:

   - Talk
   - Listen
   - Text
   - Send email
   - Use hand signals
   - Use emoticons
   - Send messages in video games
   - Use sign language

3. Engage students in a discussion by asking the following questions:

   - Do people communicate differently?
   - Where do you first learn how to communicate?
   - Do you think people communicate differently based on who they are, their family background, their culture, etc.?

   Then ask students, "What is miscommunication?" Define **miscommunication** as failure to communicate clearly.

4. Ask students for some reasons why people miscommunicate. Have students talk with a person sitting next to them for a minute and talk about why people miscommunicate. Then reconvene the whole group and create a list, which may include the following:

   - Lying about something
   - Not giving all the information (as in the example above)
   - Having a different point of view
   - Previous conflict with the person
   - Language barriers
   - Different understanding of word meanings or interpretation
   - Not listening well
   - Making assumptions
   - Nonverbal communication

   If students do not add nonverbal communication, add that as the last item. Explain that sometimes someone says one thing but

FLIPPED CLASSROOM IDEA

Make a video of yourself having a conversation with another person and make sure to use lots of nonverbal communication like body language, tone of voice, facial expression, posture etc. After the conversation is over, ask what type of nonverbal communication the students noticed and list a few examples of what you did nonverbally that conveyed a message.

their nonverbal communication conveys a different message, and that can lead to miscommunication. Define **nonverbal communication** as aspects of communication, such as gestures and facial expressions, which do not involve speaking but can also include nonverbal aspects of speech (tone and volume of voice, etc.).

5. On a board/smart board, make a semantic web with the words "Nonverbal Communication" written inside the circle. Ask students, "What words, phrases and feelings come to mind when you hear nonverbal communication?" Have students brainstorm different aspects of nonverbal communication and feelings associated with it. The web may look like the following:

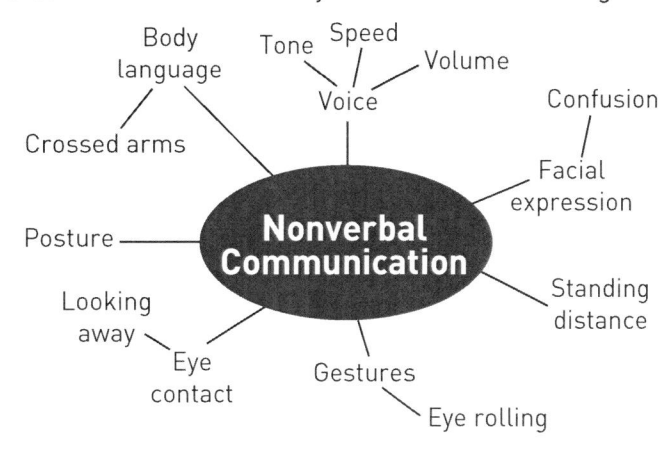

6. After brainstorming, engage students in a discussion by asking the following questions:
    - What do you notice about the web?
    - Which examples of nonverbal communication were new to you?
    - Choose something on the web (like gestures) and show me an example.
    - What types of nonverbal communication do you use?

7. Remind students the different ways people communicate nonverbally. Explain that they will be doing an activity to learn more about nonverbal communication. Instruct students to form into a circle in the center of the room. (If space does not allow, have half the students form a circle and have the other students observe and they can switch places halfway through the activity.) Tell students you are going to give them a sentence to say and that they will take turns changing their tone of voice to convey a specific feeling or emotion (you can brainstorm emotions or just list them: anger, boredom, frustration, sadness, happiness, interested, disinterested, silliness). Examples of sentences to use are: "Vanilla is my favorite flavor ice cream," "I can't wait to go to camp this summer" or "I have so much homework." Model the activity, using an angry tone of voice to say "I can't wait to go to camp this summer." As students say the sentence and use a tone of voice, ask students to guess the emotion they are conveying.

8. After doing this for a few minutes, add facial expression. Students will then need to use both tone of voice and facial expression to convey the feeling they wish to convey. If time and interest permits, add gestures so that they will be using tone of voice, facial expressions and gestures while the other students guess.

9. After conducting the activity for about 10 minutes, have everyone go back to their seats and engage them in a class discussion by asking the following questions:
    - What happened?

- How did you know what someone was feeling?
- Did the nonverbal communication match the verbal communication?
- How did you feel when the verbal and nonverbal communication did not match up?
- Has something like this ever happened to you?
- How can we avoid miscommunication?

10. Make the point that being aware of the nonverbal messages you send and receive is an important aspect of understanding what someone is trying to express to you. In our communication, it is important to be thorough, complete and clear (reminding them of the instruction activity at the beginning of the lesson), and to try to match our words with our nonverbal communication.

EXTENSION ACTIVITIES

- Have students cut out pictures from magazines and the Internet that are examples of nonverbal communication. Have them create a collage that shows different forms of nonverbal communication and label each picture.

- Have students write a story about a miscommunication. The story should not involve any members of the class or details that would give away a real-life situation. They can illustrate the story with pictures, create a storyboard or comic strip or act it out with other students.

- Read aloud and discuss one or more of the children's books from the list provided in this lesson.

CHILDREN'S BOOKS

No Talking by Andrew Clements

The Quiet Book by Deborah Underwood

ACTIVE LISTENING

Lesson 3

RATIONALE

The purpose of this lesson is for students to understand effective listening strategies and learn specific skills in active listening. Listening is a key component of effective communication. Students will have the opportunity to identify elements of effective listening, define and delineate active listening techniques, learn how to paraphrase and practice active listening with several partners.

OBJECTIVES

- Students will identify elements of effective listening.
- Students will be able to define active listening.
- Students will practice and improve their active listening strategies.

WHAT'S NEEDED

Handouts and Resources: Paraphrase Worksheet (one for each student)

Other Material: Active Listening Strategies, board/smart board or chart paper, markers

Advance Preparation: Write the "Active Listening Strategies" listed at the end of this lesson on board/smart board or chart paper

PROCEDURES

1. Begin the lesson by asking students, "How do you know when someone is really listening to you?" Allow several students to share their thoughts and keep the discussion going for several minutes. Affirm their responses and add your own.

2. Explain to students that you are going to demonstrate listening and you want them to pay close attention and let you know how you did. Ask for a volunteer to come to the front of the classroom and talk about something (you can come up with the topic in advance). As the student talks, demonstrate poor listening. You should interrupt the person, look away, be distracted, etc.

GRADE LEVEL
3–5

TIME
45 minutes

COMMON CORE STANDARDS
Reading, Writing, Speaking & Listening, Language

STRATEGIES AND SKILLS
Engage in large group discussion, observe for effective listening, define terms, engage in listening and speaking practice

KEY WORDS AND PHRASES
Active listening
Feedback
Paraphrase
Respond
Restate

■ *Anti-Bias Building Blocks: An Elementary Curriculum* Unit I.57

FLIPPED CLASSROOM IDEA

Make a short video of two conversations. The first one will be a model of you listening to someone but it will be clear in the video that you are not listening effectively. Then you can ask your viewers "Was I listening? How could you tell?" The second conversation will be one in which it is clear you are paying attention, responding appropriately, focusing on the speaker. Ask again, "Was I listening? How could you tell?"

3. Ask students, "Did I listen well to _____? Why or why not?" Create a T-Chart (see sample below) on the board with "Good Listening" and "Poor Listening" in the two columns. Record their responses as they discuss what they observed. If students say that you did not listen well, ask, "What can I do differently to listen better?" As you engage students in the discussion, record what they share about good listening and what you did well under "Good Listening" and record their comments about what you did not do well under "Poor Listening." Remind students about the nonverbal communication discussed in the previous lesson.

Good Listening	Poor Listening

Re-do the role play and this time, demonstrate good listening based on their suggestions. After the role play, ask again whether you listened well.

4. Explain to students that we are going to talk about "active listening" and ask if anyone knows what the term means. Come to a definition of **active listening** as listening clearly to understand the feelings and views of the speaker by being very attentive to what they say.

5. Demonstrate active listening. Display board/smart board or chart paper of "Active Listening Strategies" (prepared in advance) and review with the students asking for examples of each. Bear in mind that people view communication differently and some of this is based on people's cultural backgrounds and norms. Therefore, remain open to different responses as to how we best communicate and listen effectively. For example, students may give differing responses to how they pay attention but validate that paying attention can look differently depending on who you are.

   Highlight the "Provide Feedback" section by discussing paraphrasing in more depth.

6. Ask students, "Does anyone know what paraphrase means?" Come to a definition of **paraphrase** as a statement that says something another person has said or written in a different way. Paraphrasing is part of active listening because we are checking out whether we understood what the speaker said.

7. Distribute the *Paraphrase Worksheet* to each student and have them pair up. Explain to students that they will be practicing paraphrasing and they are to work with their partners to come up

with four paraphrased statements based on the sentences on the worksheet. After completing, they will share aloud a few of their paraphrased statements.

8. Tell students that now we are going to practice active listening. Instruct students to count off by twos—1,2,1,2, etc. Have students who are #1's form a line on one side of the room. After the line is formed, have all of the #2's form a second line facing the #1s so that each student has a partner facing them.

9. Explain to students that they will practice active listening by talking with the person standing opposite them. You will read a question and they will respond to the question and talk with the other person for one minute. Explain that when the minute is up, you will signal "change" at which time the speaker will become the listener, the listener will become the speaker and a new question will be read. Remind students that they should practice active listening skills. Before they begin, give a minute for each student to tell their partner what they need to feel listened to. For some students, this may be no interrupting at all and for others, they may like/need some intermittent short verbal words (i.e. "yes," "I see," "uh huh.")

Possible questions:

- Share with your partner something about your first, middle or last name.
- What is your favorite thing to do on the weekend and what do you like about it?
- What is your favorite holiday and how do you celebrate it?
- Who do you admire (look up to) and why?
- Tell me about a pet you have or one that you want?

10. After completing the activity, instruct all students to go back to their seats and engage them in a class discussion by asking the following questions:

- How did it feel to be the speaker?
- How did it feel to be the listener?
- Was it easy or difficult to be an active listener?
- When you were the speaker, did you feel that the listener was actively listening? How did you know?
- What, if anything, did you learn from this activity?

ACTIVE LISTENING STRATEGIES

Pay Attention
(Examples include: look at speaker and explain that for some cultural groups, eye contact can be a sign of disrespect; don't prepare response while other person is speaking; don't be distracted; pay attention to speaker's body language/nonverbal communication)

Show that You are Listening
(Examples include: nod; facial expression; smile/look concerned where appropriate; attentive posture; without interrupting, use short verbal words such as "yes," "uh huh," "hmmm," go on, etc.")

Provide Feedback
(Examples include: paraphrase—say back what you heard to make sure you got it right; remember to paraphrase both ideas and feelings; ask clarifying questions)

Respond
(Examples include: ask questions to continue the conversation; say what you think if asked, etc.)

EXTENSION ACTIVITIES

- Have students create a group story. You can start off the story by creating a first sentence (e.g., "It was a cold and snowy night in October...."). Then the next person should say the next sentence and so on. Remind the last few students that it is their job to conclude the story. You may want to have someone write down the story so you can edit and publish it.

- Play the birthday line-up game. Explain to students that they are going to line up according to their birthdays in order, starting with January and ending with December. You will show them where the start of the line is. Their challenge is to do this nonverbally. When they are finished lining up, start at the beginning and ask each student to state their birthday as a way to check if they got it right.

- Read aloud and discuss one or more of the children's books from the list provided in this lesson.

CHILDREN'S BOOKS

The Other Way to Listen by Byrd Baylor

Listen and Learn by Cheri Meiners

PARAPHRASE WORKSHEET

[Student Handout]

Instructions: Below are four sentences that could be said during a conversation. Read each sentence and come up with a paraphrase of that sentence. **Paraphrasing** is a statement that restates something another person has said or written as a way to check whether you understood the speaker.

1. I'm really excited to go to the movies this weekend because I'm seeing a movie of a book I recently read. I liked the book a lot and I don't know if I will like the movie as much.

   Paraphrase: _____

   _____

   _____

   _____

2. I wish we didn't have so much homework this weekend. My grandparents are coming to visit but I have Math, ELA and social studies homework. I hope I can get it all done and still do fun things with my grandparents.

   Paraphrase: _____

   _____

   _____

   _____

3. Playing soccer is awesome. I love running around the field and passing the ball with my foot and I especially like to play goalie. I get nervous when the ball comes close to me but then I can bend down and pick it up.

   Paraphrase: _____

   _____

   _____

   _____

■ Anti-Bias Building Blocks: An Elementary Curriculum | Unit I.61

4. Social Studies is my favorite subject. I like it because there are facts but things aren't right or wrong the way they are with Math. I have a hard time with Math; it gives me a headache.

Paraphrase: _____

_____

_____

_____

UNDERSTANDING, MANAGING AND EXPRESSING FEELINGS

Lesson 4

RATIONALE

The purpose of this lesson is to expand student's vocabulary of feelings' words and to help them understand, manage and express their feelings. Students will have the opportunity to act out feelings, identify feelings' words they know and learn new ones, reflect on particularly strong feelings they have and explore actions that help or worsen the situation.

OBJECTIVES

- Students will be able to use nonverbal communication to express feelings.
- Students will identify feelings' words and expand their feelings' words vocabulary.
- Students will reflect on strong feelings they have and both helpful and not helpful responses to those feelings.

WHAT'S NEEDED

Handouts and Resources: Feelings Cards and *Feelings Words ABCs*

Other Material: Board/Smart board, chart paper (at least 12 pieces), markers

Advance Preparation:
- Reproduce the *Feelings Cards* onto heavier paper. Cut each section into individual card pieces and set aside.
- Write the ABCs on 12 pieces of chart paper using the *Feelings Words ABCs* as a guide and post around the room or, make enough copies of the handout for each participant (see procedure #4).

PROCEDURES

1. Start the lesson by playing a quick game of feelings charades. Explain to students that they will be choosing a feeling word to act out that feeling without using words or sounds. Remind them about the role nonverbal communication (facial expression, posture,

GRADE LEVEL
3–5

TIME
45 minutes

COMMON CORE STANDARDS
Reading, Writing, Speaking & Listening, Language

STRATEGIES AND SKILLS
Act out feelings, engage in large and small group discussion, brainstorm

KEY WORDS AND PHRASES
Emotions
Feelings
Feelings words
I-messages
Respond

hand movement, body language) plays in conveying feelings.

2. Model the activity for the group.

3. Conduct a few rounds of this exercise and ask students, "How did you know what feeling was being expressed?"

4. Explain to students that we are going to make a long list of feelings' words. Ask students, "What are some feelings' words?" To elicit ideas, ask the following questions:

    - How do you feel when someone says something about you that is untrue?
    - How do you feel on your birthday?
    - How do you feel when you get a lot of homework?
    - How do you feel when your favorite sports team loses?
    - How do you feel when you receive a gift you did not expect?
    - How do you feel when someone has something you want but do not have?

    Continue to brainstorm and record the feelings' words on the board/smart board until they come up with ten or so. Explain to students that they are going to expand their "feelings vocabulary" by brainstorming and talking about many different feelings' words. Explain to students that when you say "go," they will have about 10 minutes to walk around the classroom and write feelings' words beginning with the letters on the chart paper posted around the room ( ). For example, on the A-B piece of chart paper, they might write anger and bashful. To model, write those words on the paper.

ALTERNATIVE
Instead of walking around the classroom, distribute the *Feelings Words ABCs* handout to each student and have them complete it alone or in pairs at their seats.

5. After recording all the words they can think of, have students do a quick walk around the room and write a check mark next to the words they do not know on the chart paper or each student's handout, depending on which method you used. Make a note of the words without many check marks. Identify those words which may not actually be feelings' words and explain why.

6. Have students come back to their seats and engage them in a group discussion by asking the following questions:

    - Was it difficult or easy to come up with feelings' words for each letter?
    - What new feelings' words did you learn?
    - Are there some feelings' words that have the same or similar meanings? If so, can you give an example?
    - Can you describe feelings you have for which you do not know the word that describes that feeling?
    - Based on the check marks, what words on the lists do most

people not know? (Ask for feedback on those words or provide definitions for them.)

7. 📷 In order to expand their feelings vocabulary, come up with five additional feelings' words for which your students may be unfamiliar (e.g., jealousy, irritating, grumpy, concerned, joyful). State the word and ask if anyone knows what it means or a similar feeling word. If they do not know, define the feeling and give an example and add the feeling word to the list.

8. Ask students, "From all the words we came up, what are some examples of very strong feelings? Examples may include: angry, terrifying, frustrated, excited.

9. Ask students, "When you have a strong feeling like anger or frustration, what do you do?" Write their responses on the board, which may include some of the following:

- Cry
- Yell
- Talk to someone
- Take a walk
- Be by myself
- Punch something
- Play sports
- Tell the person how I feel
- Blame other people
- Run

10. For each of the above responses, ask students, "Does this make the feeling and situation worse or does it help?" Put a "W" (worse) or "H" (help) next to the action based on their responses. Explain to students that having strong feelings is a normal part of life and everyone has strong feelings. The important thing is how we deal with our feelings.

11. Divide students into small groups of four students each. Explain that you are going to ask three questions about strong feelings and they are to talk in small groups about these feelings that they may have had and how they respond to those feelings. This is a timed activity and each student will get one minute to respond to each question without interrupting or cross-talk. When you call time, they should move to the next person in the group. After each of the four students has spoken to a question, you will move to the next question. Remind students about active listening that they learned in the previous lesson.

- Describe a time you felt excited.

FLIPPED CLASSROOM IDEA

Make a short video about 5–7 feelings words your students are unlikely to know. Possibilities include: jealousy, irritating, grumpy, concerned, joyful. State each of the words, spell them, define them, use them in a sentence and finally make a facial expression that conveys the feeling.

- Describe a time you felt angry.
- Describe a time you felt disappointed.

12. After each of the four students has discussed each of these questions, engage students in a group discussion by asking the following questions:
    - How did it feel to do that activity?
    - Was it difficult to just listen and not talk when others were sharing?
    - What did you learn about how people respond to strong feelings?
    - Did most of your responses to the strong feelings make it worse or help?
    - Thinking about it now, was there anything you could have done differently? If so, what was it?

13. Wrap the lesson up by having each student say one thing they learned as a result of the lesson.

EXTENSION ACTIVITIES

- Have an in depth lesson and discussion on "I-messages" or "I statements," giving students time to learn more about the use and purpose of I-messages. Use role plays and/or puppets to demonstrate and practice giving and receiving I-messages.

- Have students write acrostic poems using feelings' words. Acrostic poems use the first letter of each line to spell out a word or phrase. In this case, the word will be a feeling word and each of the lines in the poem should relate to the overall topic. Acrostic poems do not have to rhyme and each line can be as short or long as you like. For example, using the word Calm, you can create an acrostic poem like this:

    > Chillin'
    > Always feels relaxing
    > Like the mood
    > Makes me feel like I'm dreaming.

- Read aloud and discuss one or more of the children's books from the list provided in this lesson.

CHILDREN'S BOOKS

Alexander and the Terrible, Horrible, No Good, Very Bad Day by Judith Viorst

The Invisible Boy by Trudy Ludwig

Yesterday I Had The Blues by Heron Ashford Frame

Mouse Was Mad by Linda Urban

Grappling with the Grumpies by Deborah Fannie Miller

FEELINGS CARDS

Happy	Sad
Excited	Shy
Brave	Angry

Images reprinted with permission from Todd Parr, *Feelings Flashcards* (San Francisco: Chronicle Books, 2010).

FEELINGS CARDS

Delighted	Proud
Serious	Bored
Disappointed	Scared

Images reprinted with permission from Todd Parr, *Feelings Flashcards* (San Francisco: Chronicle Books, 2010).

FEELINGS CARDS

Nervous	Annoyed
Overjoyed	Worried
Frightened	Silly

Images reprinted with permission from Todd Parr, *Feelings Flashcards* (San Francisco: Chronicle Books, 2010).

FEELINGS WORDS ABCs

[Student Handout]

A-B	C-D	E-F	G-H
I-J	K-L	M-N	O-P
Q-R	S-T	U-V	WXYZ

COLLABORATION AND TEAMWORK

Lesson 5

RATIONALE

The purpose of this activity is to help students explore collaboration, an important social skill that will be used throughout the curriculum. This lesson provides an opportunity for students to define collaboration, discuss its pros and cons, practice collaborating through a variety of activities and analyze how to make it more effective.

OBJECTIVES

- Students will be able to define collaboration.
- Students will practice their collaboration/teamwork skills through a variety of activities.
- Students will identify the pros and cons of collaboration.

WHAT'S NEEDED

Small *Post-it Notes*® (two different colors), pens or pencils

PROCEDURES

1. Begin the lesson by playing a game called Count to 5. The goal of the game is to have students in the class call out numbers from 1–5 without having two or more people talk at once. The rules are:

    a. Anyone can call out a number starting with one;

    b. Only one person can call out a number at a time;

    c. The numbers have to be in order;

    d. Students cannot talk to each other or use body signals to "plan" who calls out a number.

    Make sure everyone understands the rules. If students need a challenge, do Count to 10.

2. Ask students, "What made this easy or difficult? How did you work together?"

3. Ask students if they know what collaborate means. Come to a definition of **collaborate** as to work with another person or group in order to achieve or do something. Ask for suggestions of

GRADE LEVEL
3–5

TIME
45 minutes

COMMON CORE STANDARDS
Reading, Writing, Speaking & Listening, Language

STRATEGIES AND SKILLS
Define terms, turn and talk, explore pros and cons, engage in small group collaborative work and large group discussion

KEY WORDS AND PHRASES
Charades
Collaboration
Negative
Positive
Teamwork

FLIPPED CLASSROOM IDEA

Have students watch the 3.5-minute YouTube video *Student Groups Divide Work* at https://www.youtube.com/watch?v=EtqS5CHndyo, which shows small groups of children working together on a project. Before showing the video, explain to students that they should pay attention to how the students work or do not work together. Ask students,"Does everyone have a role? Is there a leader? What role do you think you might play if you were in the group?"

synonyms for collaborate (such as cooperate, teamwork).

4. Ask students for examples of times when they collaborated or worked as a team on something recently. Using the turn and talk strategy, have students talk with the person sitting next to them and talk about a time they collaborated on something. Explain to students they are to share with their partners:

   - What happened.
   - Whether the collaboration was positive or negative.
   - How they felt in the end.

5. Discuss the positive and negative aspects of collaboration by having students think about one positive and one negative aspect of working/collaborating with others. Distribute two *Post-it Notes®* to students (ideally, two different colors). Have students write a positive aspect on one post-it and a negative aspect on the other and have them come up and paste them on different sides of the board or room. Read some of the responses aloud and record them on a chart like the following:

What's Positive about Collaboration	What's Negative about Collaboration

6. Engage students in a group discussion by asking the following questions:

   - What do you notice about the pros of collaboration?
   - What do you notice about the cons of collaboration?
   - Do you notice any patterns or similarities?

7. Explain to students that they are going to work in collaborative small groups to accomplish a task. Ask them if they are familiar with the game "Charades." Explain that this activity is a variation of Charades. Divide students into groups of 4–6 per group. Assign each group a machine (i.e. dishwasher, cell phone, television, lawnmower, supermarket cash register, popcorn popper, etc.). Instruct students to work together in their small groups to develop a "charade" that demonstrates the qualities and functions of their assigned machine. Explain that they cannot use sounds or speaking and that all members of the small group must have a role in the group's charade. Allow about ten minutes for small groups to prepare their presentations.

8. Reconvene the whole class and have each group present their machine charade to the class. After each group presentation, allow students to guess the machine.

9. After all small groups have presented, lead a whole group discussion by asking the following questions:
   - What worked well?
   - What was difficult about the activity?
   - What were some of the benefits of having a team to work together to accomplish the assigned task?
   - What was your role in your group? Was the role "assigned" or did you volunteer to take it on?
   - What were some of the challenges you faced in involving all members of your team? How did you address these challenges?
   - How could the collaboration have been more effective?
   - What did you learn from this activity?

10. As a way of ending the lesson, have each student complete this sentence for themselves: "I used to think _____ about collaboration, but now I think _____.

EXTENSION ACTIVITIES

- Have students develop a research project where they learn about successful collaborations in history. Be creative with the collaborations; they could be a social change/justice movement, a musical group, a sports team or a political movement. Have students either work on these projects individually or they can model collaboration by working on it as a group, assigning different roles or parts of the research to different members of the group.

- Do a reading activity using a "jigsaw" strategy, which enables students to be introduced to new material and to teach others what they learned. You can either divide a larger reading assignment into four parts, or have four shorter pieces of reading material. Divide students into four or five groups. Within each group, you will give each individual student a part of a larger document or they will each have a different shorter article. The goal is for each of the individual students in the group to read their portion and then share it back with the rest of the group. In this way, the group is learning more by dividing up the reading material. You can find age appropriate non-fiction reading material at THE TIME for Kids website, www.timeforkids.com.

- Read aloud and discuss one or more of the children's books from the list provided in this lesson.

CHILDREN'S BOOKS

999 Tadpoles by Ken Kimura

The Biggest Snowman Ever by Steven Kroll

UNIT II. UNDERSTANDING MY STRENGTHS, SKILLS AND IDENTITY

Before young children can understand bias and how to address it, they need to have a sense of who they are and of differences between people. Self-esteem is strengthened by a sense of self and appreciating diversity is critical to a child's development. The concepts of identity and differences will be explored in this section. Students will reflect on a variety of identity factors such as appearance, family, likes and dislikes, opinions, community and strengths and abilities. Through these explorations, they will understand factors that shape their identity, learn that there are differences between them and their classmates and understand that those differences are positive, and in fact, make life interesting.

GOALS FOR KINDERGARTEN THROUGH 2ND GRADE

In Unit II, children in kindergarten through 2nd grade will study their own physical characteristics and create self-portraits. They will reflect on their likes and dislikes and gain insight into their classmates' preferences. Children will understand what their skills are and be able to teach each other something new. They will explore their family characteristics and notice the similarities and differences of other families. Finally, students will look at their communities and think about what all communities need.

GOALS FOR THIRD THROUGH FIFTH GRADE

For third to fifth graders, children will identify their unique physical characteristics. They will understand the difference between fact and opinion, what opinions they hold and the importance of respecting differing opinions. Children will reflect on their own abilities, skills, talents and interests and those of their classmates. They will investigate the concept of family and expand their understanding of many different kinds of families. Finally, they will explore the people, services and places that are part of any community, and will consider what improvements can be made in their own communities.

SELF-PORTRAITS

RATIONALE

The purpose of this activity is for students to consider the physical characteristics of themselves and others. Understanding similarities and differences is an important part of being able to appreciate diversity and understand bias. This lesson provides an opportunity for students to describe themselves and other people, create self-portraits and identify and understand the similarities and differences of their classmates.

OBJECTIVES

- Students will be able to describe themselves and other people using adjectives and descriptive language.
- Students will draw or paint self-portraits, noting their unique characteristics.
- Students will identify the similarities and differences they notice amongst their classmates.

WHAT'S NEEDED

Large drawing paper, markers, crayons, colored pencils and paint (make sure to have markers, crayons and paint that reflect the colors, shades and complexions of children in your classroom); several mirrors for students to use; paper and pencil for each student

PROCEDURES

1. Begin the lesson by reading the following excerpt from the book, *I'm Your Peanut Butter Big Brother* by Selina Alko (Alfred E. Knopf, 2009). First explain a little bit about the book by telling students that the book is about a boy whose mother is pregnant. The boy's father is black with brown skin and his mother is white with pink skin and the boy wonders what his baby brother or sister will look like.

    > *Baby brother or sister, will you look like me?*
    > *I blend from semisweet dark Daddy chocolate bar and strawberry cream Mama's milk.*

Lesson 6

GRADE LEVEL
K–2

TIME
35 minutes

COMMON CORE STANDARDS
Reading, Writing, Speaking & Listening

STRATEGIES AND SKILLS
Large group discussion, describe people, draw/paint creating self-portraits, gallery walk

KEY WORDS AND PHRASES
Adjective
Appearance
Color
Complexion
Describe
Prejudice
Self-portrait
Shape
Size
Texture

My hair is soft, crunchy billows of cotton candy.
I'm your peanut butter big-brother-to-be.

2. Ask students the following questions:
   - How did the the boy in this poem describe himself?
   - What parts of his appearance did he describe?
   - What kind of words did he use?

3. Write the following categories/descriptions below on the board/smart board and explain what each means, asking students first to define them. Then, using these categories, ask children to describe what you look like. Tell students not to describe clothing, glasses, etc. and anything else that is not part of your body or face. Stand where all the children can see you up close and ask them to describe your face, including the following descriptors:
   - Hair: color, texture, style
   - Skin color and complexion
   - Eyes: shape, color
   - Shape of face
   - Other characteristics like birth marks, freckles, etc.

   If they do not include certain features, ask questions about hair color and texture, skin color and complexion, eye color as outlined above. Remind them about what adjectives are (words used to describe a person, place or thing) and to use as many different adjectives and be as specific and descriptive as possible. They can compare colors and shapes to other things ("her light brown skin was the color of caramel") as the narrator did in the book excerpt read aloud earlier.

4. Instruct students to work in pairs with someone sitting near them to describe each other. Have them take turns looking at each other closely and verbally describe their partner as much as possible. Be sure to remind them to use only kind descriptions. When finished, the person described should take a few minutes to write down the words and adjectives they heard. Then switch and reverse the roles, if they are able. Next have students individually look in mirrors. If they notice anything else about their appearance, have them add that to the description.

5. Explain to students that now they are going to draw self-portraits of themselves. Ask students, "What is a self-portrait?" If they do not know what a self-portrait is, ask if they know what a portrait is and then have them guess what a self-portrait is. Tell them that a **self-portrait** is a painting or drawing of yourself that is done by yourself. Distribute large drawing paper and painting supplies and explain that they should make self-portraits of just their faces and include details about their faces that were described

Self-Portrait

Give me a mirror and I'll show you what I see. Spiky hair, kind eyes behind glasses, and a great smile. That's me!

by their partners and themselves. If you have more time, you can use paint and have the students make sketches first. If you have less time, use markers and crayons. When the self-portraits are completed, hang them around the room and do a "gallery walk" where the students get to look at all of the self-portraits.

6. After the gallery walk, engage students in a discussion by asking the following questions:

    • What do you notice about the self-portraits?

    • What are some of the similarities you see?

    • What are some of the differences?

    • Why do we all look different?

    • What different skin colors, hair, etc. do we see in our classroom and school?

    • Can you think of any examples or times when someone teased, bullied or showed prejudice against someone else because of their physical appearance?

EXTENSION ACTIVITIES

- Provide students with wooden clothespins and assorted art supplies (yarn, scraps of fabric, cotton balls, buttons, markers, etc.) and have them create clothespin dolls that reflect their physical characteristics. Allow time for students to work on their dolls with family members. Display dolls in the classroom or in a showcase. Take photos and create a photo exhibit either in the school or online.

- Have students write an acrostic poem that describes what they look like. Acrostic poems use the first letter of each line to spell out a word or phrase. In this case, the word can be their name and each line in the poem should relate to the overall topic, which is their physical appearance. Acrostic poems do not have to rhyme and each line can be as short or long as you like. For example, using the name Jaden, you can create an acrostic poem like this:

    Jaden's hair is short and black
    Almond shaped,
    Dark
    Eyes
    Neck and rest of my skin is tan

- Read aloud and discuss one or more of the children's books from the list provided in this lesson.

CHILDREN'S BOOKS

The Colors of Us by Karen Katz

Shades of People by Shelley Rotner

I'm Your Peanut Butter Big Brother by Selina Alko

Nina Bonita by Ana Maria Machado

LIKES AND DISLIKES

Lesson 7

RATIONALE

The purpose of this activity is for students to share some of the things that they like and dislike and to consider what has influenced those choices. Understanding the concept of opinions (likes and dislikes) is an important part of forming one's sense of self and is the foundation for learning about dislike versus prejudice. This lesson provides an opportunity for students to explore their likes and dislikes, the reasons why people like and dislike certain things and the concept of opinions.

OBJECTIVES

- Students will identify things they like and dislike.
- Students will examine possible reasons why people like and dislike certain things.
- Students will explain their unique likes and dislikes.

WHAT'S NEEDED

Brown paper lunch bags (two per student), markers or crayons, assorted art supplies, magazines/newspapers with relevant pictures, drawing paper

PROCEDURES

1. Begin the lesson by having students participate in a stand-up (or hand-raising) exercise. Ask them to stand as you call out the name of an item or activity they like. Encourage students to look around the room to see how many other people like or do not like the same things they do. Remind students to sit down before calling out a new item.

    Sample items to call out:

    Ice cream, listening to music, playing video games, vegetables, playing in snow, going to the beach, playing on an app, cooking, doing homework, reading, pizza, swimming, riding a bicycle, shopping, animals, drawing, playing basketball, tacos, visiting relatives, beading, skateboarding, churros, going to the beach, ice

GRADE LEVEL
K–2

TIME
35 minutes

COMMON CORE STANDARDS
Reading, Speaking & Listening

STRATEGIES AND SKILLS
Large group discussion, draw, grouping information, oral presentation, listening, explaining an opinion

KEY WORDS AND PHRASES
Dislike
Like
Opinion
Prefer
Unique

skating, snow cones, making jewelry, scootering, writing, donuts, playing card games, playing an instrument, playing dress up

2. Engage students in a discussion by asking them the following questions:

    - Did everyone in the class like the same things?
    - Were there some things that many people liked? If so, what were they?
    - Were there some things that few people liked? If so, what are they?
    - Are there things that you do not like or dislike? (For example, maybe you do not dislike ice skating but you do not particularly like it either. Maybe you prefer ice skating over roller skating. Explain the difference and the meaning of preference.)
    - Were you ever standing or raising your hand with a large group? How did that feel?
    - What are some reasons people like the things they do?
    - What are some reasons people do not like certain things?

3. Distribute to each student two paper lunch bags and a marker or crayon. Have students make a large smiley face (☺) on one bag and a frowning face (☹) on the other bag. Have students write their names on the back of their bags. Explain to students that they will identify five things they like for the smiley face bag and five things they do not like for the frowning face bag. These should be items, activities, food, etc. but not people. They can draw pictures of the items, cut out pictures from magazines/newspaper, find pictures online or bring photographs from home. Tell students that they will be explaining their choices later to the class.

4. When students have completed their bags, have them sit in a large circle in the center of the classroom. The faces on the bags should be pointed toward the middle of the circle. Give each student the opportunity to share one or two things from each of their bags, explain why they like and dislike the selected items. After all the students have presented their items, engage them in a discussion by asking the following questions:

    - How was it to share with others about the things you like and dislike? Why?
    - Are there certain kinds of things you noticed that most people in our class like?
    - What kinds of things do most people dislike?
    - Did anyone have the same likes and dislikes as you? Do you think it would be unlikely for that to happen? (Reinforce the concept of uniqueness).

My Likes and Dislikes

In my smiley face bag I drop gummy bears, patty cake, my purple blanket, kite flying and my teddy bear foo foo too.

But my frowning face bag, I throw in coloring in the lines, hide and go seek, bugs, spinach and beets—eek!

5. Ask students, "Does anyone know what an opinion is?" Point out that students in the class like and dislike different things and these are called "opinions." Opinions are what people think and feel about certain things and it is natural to have different opinions from other people—even from friends and family members.

6. End the lesson by playing two different songs or reading two different stories or poems and asking students to decide which one of the two they liked better and explain their choice using as many details as possible. They should begin their explanation with the phrase, "In my opinion...."

EXTENSION ACTIVITIES

- Create a class bulletin board, mural or PowerPoint called "We All Like Different Things" in which students contribute pictures, photographs or drawings to the display that depict things they like, things they enjoy doing, foods they like, places they like to go.

- Have students work in small groups to create an opinion poll with their class members and others in their family and school. They can create opinion questions based on favorite (1) meal, (2) color, (3) sport, (4) day of week and (5) activity or any other categories they develop. Have each student poll 5–10 classmates, friends and family members, bring back the results and work together to develop graphs or other visual illustrations of the results.

- Read aloud and discuss one or more of the children's books from the list provided in this lesson.

CHILDREN'S BOOKS

I Am the Dog I Am the Cat by Donald Hall

Sunny Sunday Drive by Janine Scott

Red is Best by Karen Stinson

I Will Never Eat a Tomato by Lauren Child

THINGS I'M GOOD AT

Lesson 8

RATIONALE

The purpose of this activity is for students to reflect on their skills and abilities and understand the skills and abilities of others. Recognizing skill-sets is part of their identity development as well as understanding and accepting differences. This lesson provides an opportunity for students to teach another student something they know how to do, reflect on what they do well, categorize those skills and identify something new they want to learn.

OBJECTIVES

- Students will teach another student something they know how to do.
- Students will be aware of some activities they can do well, skills that are needed to do it and the category of skill it fits into.
- Students will identify something new they would like to learn.

WHAT'S NEEDED

Handouts and Resources: Things We Can Do (one for each student)

Other Material: Chart paper or boards/smart boards, markers

Advance Preparation: On chart paper or a board/smart board, write at the top the heading WE CAN DO MANY THINGS; on another piece of chart paper or board/smart board create three columns labeled THINGS WE CAN DO, SKILLS NEEDED and TYPE OF SKILL (see #4).

PROCEDURES

1. Begin the lesson by having students form a circle in the center of the classroom and ask them, "What are some things that you do well?" List students' responses on the previously prepared board/smart board or chart paper with the heading WE CAN DO MANY THINGS. Examples could include: draw, play soccer, write my name, jump rope. Make sure that all students who want to contribute to the list are able to do so. When completed, ask,

GRADE LEVEL
K–2

TIME
35 minutes

COMMON CORE STANDARDS
Reading, Speaking & Listening

STRATEGIES AND SKILLS
Teach another student, large group discussion, categorize

KEY WORDS AND PHRASES
Academic
Artistic
Physical
Skills
Social

■ *Anti-Bias Building Blocks: An Elementary Curriculum*

"What do you notice about the list? Are any of the items on the list surprising?"

2. Remaining in the circle, have the students pair off with a person standing next to them. Explain that each of two students in the pair will take a few minutes to teach the other person something they know how to do. It can be a dance movement, a sports activity, words or a sentence in another language, a food you know how to cook, how to draw something, a hand game you know, how to make something.

   Explain what a skill is (the ability to do something well). Explain to students that some skills are physical like running, balancing, throwing a ball, etc. Some skills are artistic like acting, drawing, making a bracelet. Other skills are social like listening, getting along with others, expressing your feelings (refer to those lessons in the first unit) and others are academic skills like reading, writing, doing math problems and doing science experiments.

   They can either demonstrate the skill or explain to the other person how to do it. They need to explain it well enough so that the person listening can demonstrate it to others. Give them 5–7 minutes total to practice both skills.

3. Come back to the circle and each pair will demonstrate the two new things or skills they just learned. After completing the demonstrations, engage students in a discussion by asking:

   - How did it feel to teach something you can do well to another person?
   - Did you learn something new from your partner?
   - Was it easy or difficult?

4. Have students sit down in their seats and display the board/smart board or chart paper divided into three columns (see sample below) prepared in advance. List the skills and things that students taught, shared in the brainstorm or their demonstration on this chart. After listing what they already discussed, have students add other things they can do to the list.

   After getting all of items in the "Things We Can Do" column, ask them questions to get them to fill in the "Skills Needed" and "Type of Skill" sections of the chart. Use a larger version of the chart (Things We Can Do worksheet) to have the students write along with you.

THINGS WE CAN DO	SKILLS NEEDED	TYPE OF SKILL
Write our names	Hold a pencil, form letters	Academic

5. Reflecting on the experience of teaching another student something and discussing and charting "Things We Can Do," engage students in a discussion by asking:

   - Is there a pattern to what kinds of things people in our class can do (e.g., more physical activities and less artistic)?
   - What kinds of skills do people need for certain activities?
   - Did you hear about something that you would like to learn how to do?

6. Reinforce the concept that all people have unique talents, abilities and skills by pointing out the "We Can Do Many Things" list and by summarizing the variety of things students taught each other. Explain that people learn how to do things all the time and with practice they can become talented in skills in multiple areas.

7. As a way to close the lesson, ask students to think about and each state aloud something new they would like to learn how to do or something they want to do better.

EXTENSION ACTIVITIES

- Take turns having students teach the whole class something they know how to do. Create a calendar in advance and make sure that everyone's name is on it. Give them advance notice and tell them they can bring in materials, props etc. for their instruction. Alternately, they can make a video of themselves doing something like cooking something at home that they narrate with instructions of how to do it.

- Following up on what students said about something new they want to learn, have them develop an action plan for developing that skill and write a plan for learning or improving that skill. Have students consider the following:
  - What do I want to learn how to do, or do better?
  - Why do I want to learn this?
  - What skills would I need to practice?
  - What materials would I need?
  - Who can help me?

- Have students share their action plans with a partner or in groups of three. Devote time at a future date for students to demonstrate or share their new abilities and the extent to which they followed their action plans.

- Read aloud and discuss one or more of the children's books from the list provided in this lesson.

CHILDREN'S BOOKS

Penguin's Hidden Talent by Alex Latimer

My Family Plays Music by Judy Cox

THINGS WE CAN DO

[Student Handout]

THINGS WE CAN DO	SKILLS NEEDED	TYPE OF SKILL

MY FAMILY

RATIONALE

The purpose of this lesson is for students to reflect on the concept of family—their own and others—and to expand their notions of family. Understanding what is similar and different about families is key to children's identity development and their ability to observe and appreciate diversity. This lesson provides an opportunity for students to explore the word "family," reflect on the characteristics of their own family by drawing a picture and expand their concept of different kinds of family structures and sizes.

OBJECTIVES

- Students will explore and understand the meaning of "family."
- Students will reflect on family characteristics and draw a picture of their family.
- Students will identify the similarities and differences among different types of family structures and sizes.

WHAT'S NEEDED

Drawing paper, markers, crayons, colored pencils or paint (make sure these reflect the colors, shades and complexions of children in your classroom)

PROCEDURES

1. Begin the lesson by having students think about the word "family." Using a semantic web, chart student responses to the following question: What words, phrases and feelings come to mind when you hear the word family?

2. After brainstorming, engage students in a discussion by asking the following questions:
   - What do you notice about the words and phrases on the web?
   - Are there things that all families have in common? What are they?
   - How are families different?

Lesson 9

GRADE LEVEL
K–2

TIME
35 minutes

COMMON CORE STANDARDS
Reading, Speaking & Listening

STRATEGIES AND SKILLS
Brainstorm, semantic web, draw, large group discussion, gallery walk

KEY WORDS AND PHRASES
Family
Size
Members
Structure

■ *Anti-Bias Building Blocks: An Elementary Curriculum*

- What are the different types of family structures, sizes and people who are in the family (members)?

Explain to students that just as their names, physical characteristics, likes/dislikes and abilities are unique, so are their families and no two families are exactly the same. Explain that in the next part of the lesson, they will have a chance to delve deeper into their family and think about other types of families.

3. Distribute drawing materials and instruct students to create a picture representing their family. The picture should (1) include all the members of the family, including pets, (2) show them in their home and (3) show their family doing an activity they like to do together (e.g., eating, celebrating a holiday, playing a game). They may also write the names of people in their families, dialogue words for things certain family members say, or other words or pictures of things that are important to their family. Circulate around the room asking questions to get the students to show more detail in their drawings. If time permits, students can take their pictures home and work on them more for homework.

4. When students have completed their drawings, hang them up in an area of the classroom and allow them to take a "gallery walk" in order to see all of the pictures. If time permits, have each student come to the front of the classroom and present their picture. After students have had a chance to look at all the pictures, engage them in a discussion by asking the following questions:

   - Were any two pictures in the gallery exactly alike?
   - Did you notice any similarities in the family structures? If so, what were they?
   - Did you notice any differences in the sizes of the families? If so, what were they?
   - What were some of the different family structures you saw in the pictures?
   - Are there any family structures that are not represented in these pictures (in our classroom)? What are they?

5. Depending on the family structures portrayed in the pictures, ask students about family structures not portrayed and for each, ask, "Is this a family?" Examples include:

   - A family with two Moms
   - A family with a Mom and a Dad
   - A family with two Dads
   - A family with one parent
   - A family with a grandparent, aunt or other relative living with them or head of household
   - A parent and a step-parent

6. Explain that all of these examples are families because they all have some of the key ingredients: they live together in a home, they take care of and love each other and they share money and home responsibilities.

7. End the lesson by asking each student to say the first word they can think of when they hear the word "family."

EXTENSION ACTIVITIES

- Using clippings from magazines/newspapers, photographs, original drawings and pictures from the Internet, have students create a collage about different aspects of their family. This can include their family structure/configuration, activities their family likes to do, places their family has visited, etc. As an alternative, create a class bulletin board or mural that includes everyone's pictures.

- Invite family members to come in for a "gallery opening." Have students act as tour guides, explaining the purpose of "The Family Gallery" exhibit. Have books about families available in the classroom for family members to review. Take photos of students with their family members and in small groups, have students interview the different family members.

- Read aloud and discuss one or more of the children's books from the list provided in this lesson.

CHILDREN'S BOOKS

Who's in a Family? by Robert Skutch

The Family Book by Todd Parr

Daddy, Papa and Me by Leslea Newman

I Love You Like Crazy Cakes by Rose A. Lewis

All Families Are Special by Norma Simon

Stella Brings the Family by Miriam Schiffer

MY NEIGHBORHOOD

Lesson 10

RATIONALE

The purpose of this activity is to explore the concept of community and how it fits into student's identity. Understanding your own community and how it might differ from other communities is a part of understanding differences and culture. This lesson provides an opportunity for students to identify different elements in communities, consider important aspects of their community and as a class create a story quilt about their community.

OBJECTIVES

- Students will identify elements of their community, including people and places.
- Students will draw representations of important aspects of their community.
- Students will reflect on their community as a whole.

WHAT'S NEEDED

Board/Smart board; picture of a quilt (see #4); colored drawing paper cut into 4" x 4" squares (at least four per student); crayons, markers and other art supplies; computer/LCD projector and Internet access (optional)

PROCEDURES

1. Begin the lesson by reviewing some of the concepts covered so far in this unit which focuses on all aspects of who students are: physical characteristics, likes and dislikes, skills and talents and families. Explain to students that another key aspect of their identity is where they live, their neighborhood or community.

2. Have students turn and talk with the person sitting next to them and respond to the question, "What is something you like about where you live?"

3. Have students come back to the large group and ask them, "What are some of the places and people who are in your

GRADE LEVEL
K-2

TIME
40 minutes

COMMON CORE STANDARDS
Reading, Writing, Speaking & Listening

STRATEGIES AND SKILLS
Large group discussion, turn and talk, small group discussion, brainstorm, create quilt

KEY WORDS AND PHRASES
Community
Identity
Neighborhood
Quilt

community?" Explain that these can be people doing certain jobs in the community like "community helpers" in our classroom or neighborhood, people who live here, places in the community where people work or services that the community provides. Give an example such as hospital, park or librarian. Make a list on the board/smart board. It could look something like this:

- teacher
- park
- movie theater
- babies
- schools
- daycare centers
- subway
- hardware store
- grocery store
- firefighter
- mail carrier
- playground
- toy store owner
- temple
- teachers

Ask students, "Do you think all communities have the items on this list? Do you think all communities need everything on the list?"

4. Show students a picture of a quilt and explain that quilts often tell stories. Ask students if they have ever seen a quilt, and if so, ask them to explain where they saw it and what it looked like. Explain that as a class, we are going to make a quilt that tells the story of our community. Explain to students that each of them will design four quilt squares that will represent how they see their community and what in their community is most important to them. Once all the squares are completed, they will be joined together to make a quilt for the class called "Our Community."

5. Provide each student with four different colored squares (4" x 4") of colored paper and various art supplies. If you think four is too many for them, give them two or three instead. You may choose to prescribe a theme for each of the four squares (as outlined below) or make it more open ended and allow students to choose the theme for each square. Instruct students to write their initials on the back of each of their squares. Possible themes include:

- Square that represents people in the community who are important to you
- Square that represents places in the community that are important to you
- Square that represents what you most like about your community
- Square that represent things you and/or your family do in the community

6. After all the squares are complete, collect them and mix them all together. With student helpers, lay the squares out face down on a large, flat surface and carefully tape the seams vertically and horizontally until all the squares are attached. Carefully lift

NOTE 4

PBS America Quilts (www.pbs.org/americaquilts/century/stories/) has some examples that can be projected to share with the students.

the quilt and secure it to a wall in the classroom. Have students sit in a large circle and observe its many colors and designs. Ask students to consider what story this quilt tells about the community in which the students live. You may want to invite other classes and family members into the classroom to see the quilt.

7. Engage the students in a discussion by asking the following questions:

    - If you did not know anything about your community and saw this quilt, what would you say about the community?

    - Is there anything that you would like to share about one of your quilt panels?

    - Did you enjoy making the quilt? Why or why not?

    - What did you learn about community while participating in the project?

EXTENSION ACTIVITIES

- As a class brainstorming activity, identify the things about your community that you do not like, things that are missing or improvements that are needed. Narrow down the ideas to four or five and for each of them, identify something you can do about it, either individually or as a class. It can be a project or service that already exists (e.g., if there is a homeless population in your community, there may already be a shelter or soup kitchen) or you can develop a community service project for something that is needed in your community.

- Have students interview someone in their community and learn more about their background, history, role in the community and what they like and dislike about the community. This could be a public official, a public service worker (firefighter, police officer, mail carrier, etc.) or someone who works in a business in the community. Brainstorm the questions in advance, have students record the interviews and when they have all finished, put them together into a book, calendar or an online blog called "People In Our Community."

- Read aloud and discuss one or more of the children's books from the list provided in this lesson.

CHILDREN'S BOOKS

Old Henry by Joan W. Blos

Welcome to My Neighborhood by Quaira Alegria Hudes

A Chair for My Mother by Vera Williams

IDENTIFYING UNIQUE PHYSICAL CHARACTERISTICS

Lesson 6

RATIONALE

The purpose of this activity is to explore the physical attributes each student has and to gain insight into similarities and differences and what makes each of them unique. In order to appreciate diversity and understand bias and prejudice, it is important that students explore theirs and others' physical characteristics. This lesson provides an opportunity for students to learn how to describe themselves and other people, use metaphor and simile to write a poem about their physical appearance and reflect on how biases and attitudes about physical appearances are sometimes used to foster prejudice and bully other children.

OBJECTIVES

- Students will be able to describe objects, themselves and other people with specificity and descriptive language.
- Students will understand metaphors and similes and use them in poems about their physical appearance.
- Students will reflect on the similarities and differences of their physical traits and make connections between using those differences as an excuse for prejudice and bullying.

WHAT'S NEEDED

Handouts and Resources: Describe Myself (one for each student)

Other Material: Pencil and paper; (optional) definitions of *simile* and *metaphor* written on board/smart board or chart paper (see #7 for definitions)

PROCEDURES

1. Begin the lesson by asking students to describe the physical characteristic of several items in the classroom. Start with a simple item like a desk. Ask students, "How would you describe this desk?" Think about as many aspects of the desk as possible including shape, size, texture, color and size (length, height and weight)

GRADE LEVEL
3–5

TIME
45 minutes

COMMON CORE STANDARDS
Reading, Writing, Speaking & Listening, Language

STRATEGIES AND SKILLS
Describe self and other's physical appearance, small group work, write poetry using metaphor and simile, large group discussion

KEY WORDS AND PHRASES
Identity
Metaphor
Prejudice
Race
Simile
Tease
To Bully

After describing the desk, move to more complex items like a pencil sharpener. You can do this part by dividing students into groups of 4–5 and providing each group with a different item. Have students list on a piece of paper as many physical characteristics of the items as they can. If possible, do not allow the groups to see each other's objects being described. When all the groups are finished, have students read their descriptions and let students who were in other groups guess what the item is.

2. Point out how some of the descriptive words used by students could possibly have a wide range of interpretation. For example, if something is described as "big," it is unclear how big it is and in comparison to what. An elephant could be described as big and a desk can too, but they are very different sizes. Further, explain that if students use colors to describe something or someone, they can get more specific by comparing it to a food or something in nature (e.g., green like a lime or medium brown like a chocolate bar).

3. Explain to students they are now going to describe their own physical characteristics. Tell them to pretend they are going to meet someone on the playground that they have not met before and consider how they would describe themselves to ensure that the person finds them. First ask, "What are all the different things about yourself you should describe?" Create a list like this and add any of the following that the students do not mention:

   - Hair color
   - Hair texture
   - Hair style and length
   - Skin color and complexion
   - Height
   - Ear shape (almond shape, round, small, large)
   - Eye color
   - Eye shape
   - Eyebrows (thick, thin, light, dark)
   - Eyelashes (long or short, curly or straight)
   - Nose shape (short, long, broad/wide, narrow)
   - Mouth (wide, small, thin or narrow lips)
   - Body shape
   - Other distinguishing characteristics (e.g., birthmark, freckles)

4. Distribute the *Describe Myself* handout to each student. Using the list above, have students describe as many of their physical characteristics as possible and record them on the handout.

Describing Myself

Do I look like me, the me I described myself to be?

Unit II.98 | Understanding My Strengths, Skills and Identity

Encourage students to use adjectives in their descriptions and be as specific as possible. Remind students not to describe their clothing.

📷 Model the process by describing yourself and be sure to explain the different categories above, giving examples for each.

5. To add to their description of themselves, have students get into groups of four and take turns pairing off within their group. Each pair will have 30 seconds total to share one description of their partner facing them and then they will switch. Remind students about the Classroom Guidelines and that there should be no put-downs or judgments, just descriptions. Instruct students to add any descriptors to their *Describe Myself* handout that they did not have before.

6. Have students return to their seats and ask for students to share the descriptions they and their partners came up with. After a few have shared, engage students in a discussion by asking the following questions:

    - In what ways are some of the descriptions different?
    - Did some of the physical characteristics fall into the same general category but still show differences (e.g., several shades of "brown" skin, light, medium or dark complexion)?
    - How do people get their physical characteristics?
    - What does it mean to be unique?
    - How have you changed since you were a baby, a toddler and now?
    - How does one's race or ethnicity connect with physical appearance?
    - Are physical characteristics ever used to tease, bully or be prejudiced? If so, how?

7. Explain to students that they are going to write poems about their appearance, using metaphors and similes. Explain that both similes and metaphors are good to use in poems because they compare something to another thing that is usually unrelated. If you have already taught metaphors and similes, remind students of their meanings. If not, ask, "Does anyone know what a metaphor is? Does anyone know what a simile is?" Give definitions and examples as follows (and write definitions on board or chart paper):

Metaphor: A word or phrase that is used to make a comparison between two people, things, animals or places. (Examples: The snow is a white blanket. Life is a roller coaster. It is raining cats and dogs.)

FLIPPED CLASSROOM IDEA

Make a short video of yourself describing your own physical appearance using the identifying characteristics listed in #3. As you describe different features, point to them. Define adjective, simile and metaphor and use those as you describe yourself, citing examples of each.

■ *Anti-Bias Building Blocks: An Elementary Curriculum*

Simile: A figure of speech that compares two things or persons which are not similar. The simile is usually in a phrase that begins with "as" or "like." (Examples: "as boring as watching paint dry," "as sweet as pie," and "brown like a chocolate kiss.")

8. Have students write poems, using their *Describe Myself* handout and other descriptive words used by their classmates. You may want to model this exercise. An example is provided below.

    My hair is ripples across the ocean

    My skin is light brown like a cinnamon bun

    My eyes are blades of grass

9. After completing their poems, have students read them aloud. Consider publishing them in a book, conducting a reading for the rest of the school and invite parents in for the event or use social media (blog or Tumblr page) to share the poems with others. You can also combine several lines from each of the student's poems into a group poem called "Who We Are."

EXTENSION ACTIVITIES

- Divide students into small groups and give each group a website, television show or children's book to analyze in terms of its accurate portrayal of diversity of physical characteristics among humans. Students should ask and answer the following questions about what they analyzed:

    – Do the characters represent many possible human body types?

    – Do the characters represent the many shades of skin color and races of people in the world?

    – Do the characters represent different hair textures and colors?

    – Do the characters represent people who wear glasses or hearing aids or use wheelchairs, braces or crutches?

- Using magazines, newspapers, photos and Internet pictures/photos, have children cut out pictures of people representing the many possible shades of skin color, hair, body types and other characteristics and have them design individual collages or a group bulletin board entitled "People Come in Many Sizes, Colors and Shapes."

- Read aloud and discuss one or more of the children's books from the list provided in this lesson.

CHILDREN'S BOOKS

All the Colors of the Earth by Sheila Hamanaka

All the Colors We Are by Katie Kissenger

Black is Brown is Tan by Arnold Adoff

DESCRIBE MYSELF

[Student Handout]

Instructions: Using the list below, describe yourself by writing as many of your physical characteristics as possible.

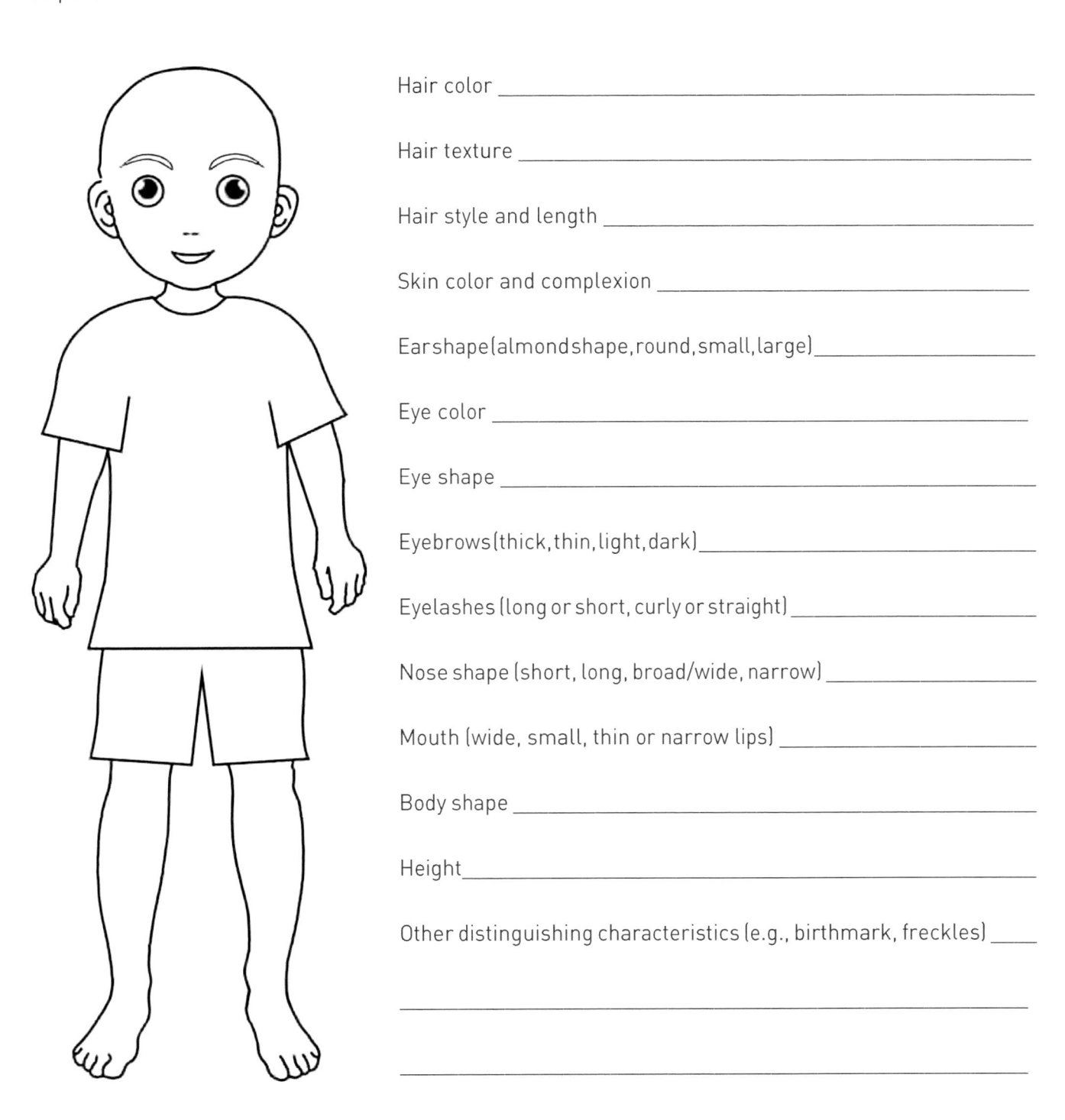

Hair color _____

Hair texture _____

Hair style and length _____

Skin color and complexion _____

Ear shape (almond shape, round, small, large) _____

Eye color _____

Eye shape _____

Eyebrows (thick, thin, light, dark) _____

Eyelashes (long or short, curly or straight) _____

Nose shape (short, long, broad/wide, narrow) _____

Mouth (wide, small, thin or narrow lips) _____

Body shape _____

Height _____

Other distinguishing characteristics (e.g., birthmark, freckles) ____

_____

_____

■ *Anti-Bias Building Blocks: An Elementary Curriculum* | Unit II.101

RESPECTING OPINIONS

Lesson 7

RATIONALE

The purpose of this activity is for students to understand the difference between facts and opinions and to explore their own opinions about things. Understanding and accepting that people have different opinions are important concepts that help students grapple with other topics in the curriculum, as well as develop a sense of self. This lesson provides an opportunity for students to understand the difference between facts and opinions, explore and reflect on their own opinions and write a persuasive essay.

OBJECTIVES

- Students will understand the difference between facts and opinions.
- Students will explore and reflect on their own and their classmates' opinions about certain topics.
- Students will write persuasive essays to provide justification for their opinions.

WHAT'S NEEDED

Handouts and Resources: Persuasive Essay Graphic Organizer (Version 1 or 2), one for each student

Other Material: Post-it Notes® (four per student in two different colors), chart paper, markers, pens or pencils

Advance Preparation: Create five signs individually labeled STRONGLY AGREE, STRONGLY DISAGREE, AGREE, IN BETWEEN/NOT SURE, and DISAGREE

PROCEDURES

1. Begin the lesson by asking, "What is the difference between a fact and an opinion?" Explain that **facts** are absolutely true statements (something that truly exists or happens) and **opinions** are what people feel and think about something and that there can be a wide range of opinion or point of view about something. Share an

GRADE LEVEL
3–5

TIME
45 minutes

COMMON CORE STANDARDS
Reading, Writing, Speaking & Listening, Language

STRATEGIES AND SKILLS
In My Opinion, write persuasive essay, large group discussion

KEY WORDS AND PHRASES
Example
Evidence
Fact
Opinion
Persuade
Persuasive essay
Quote
Reason

■ *Anti-Bias Building Blocks: An Elementary Curriculum*

example of a fact about yourself (e.g., I am a teacher) and an opinion you hold (e.g., Teaching is the best profession). As a quick example, ask students to raise their hands if they agree with the following statement: "Dogs are the best pets to have." Point out that some agree and some don't, so they have different opinions.

2. To make sure students understand the difference, make a few statements aloud and have students first raise their hands if they think it is a fact and then raise their hands if they think it is an opinion. If there is disagreement or misunderstanding, have students explain their responses.

   - Snow is white.
   - Cats are the best pets.
   - Sunday comes after Saturday.
   - Chocolate cake tastes really good.

3. Distribute four *Post-it Notes*® to each student, two of one color and two of another color. Instruct them to write two facts about themselves and two opinions they have, using one color for facts and the other color for opinions.

4. Have students stick their post-its on the wall or chart paper, one side marked FACTS and another side marked OPINION. Give students a few minutes to come up and look at all the notes. Ask, "What do you notice about the facts and opinions? Do you see any patterns?"

5. Explain to students that they will be conducting an activity called "In My Opinion," in which they will listen to some statements and decide to what extent they agree or disagree with the statement. They will be indicating their opinion about each topic by positioning themselves along an imaginary line, depending upon how strongly they agree or disagree with a statement.

6. Select a large open space and indicate the position of an imaginary line with the farthest right point representing a STRONGLY AGREE response and the farthest left point a STRONGLY DISAGREE response. In between, place AGREE, IN BETWEEN/NOT SURE and DISAGREE along the continuum. Hang signs, prepared in advance, on the wall as indicated.

7. Read each statement below, requesting students to take a few minutes to decide their opinion on the statement and walk to the place on the continuum that represents that opinion. Instruct them to observe where others choose to stand. After everyone has chosen their spot, have students spend 3–5 minutes talking amongst themselves about why they are standing where they are.

   - Chocolate ice cream is the best.
   - Students should have less homework.
   - Kids our age should be able to have cell phones.
   - Students should get paid for getting good grades.
   - Girls and boys are treated equally at this school.
   - Video games cause children to be violent.

8. Lead a whole group discussion, using the following questions:

   - Was it easy or difficult to decide where to stand? Were some statements easier to decide and some more difficult?
   - How did it feel when most people had the same response as you?
   - If there was a time when you were alone in where you chose to stand, how did it feel?

- Did you ever feel you needed to explain where you chose to stand? If so, why did you feel this way?
- Did you ever decide to change your position when you saw you did not agree with a majority of the group, or after hearing others' points of view?

9. As a final activity, have students choose one of the statements they discussed in "In My Opinion" and write a persuasive essay about their opinion on the subject. If you have not done persuasive essays with them previously, explain that the goal of persuasive writing is for the writer to convince the reader to believe as they do. The writing uses evidence or reasons (facts, examples, quotes) to convince others of their opinions. Distribute the *Persuasive Essay Graphic Organizers* handout to each student to aid them in developing their persuasive essays. This exercise will take a few class periods to bring to completion.

EXTENSION ACTIVITIES

- Have students create an opinion poll using the questions in the "In My Opinion" activity and/or create new ones of their own. They can be either yes or no responses or multiple choice with different possible responses. Have students ask the poll questions of at least ten other students in the school (this would have to be planned and organized in advance with other teachers in the school) and compile all of the information together and make a graph with the results.

- Have students think about some controversial issues they care about—homework, school violence, technology, etc. Instruct students to conduct some background research about the topic and write a persuasive letter to a stakeholder on the topic, using evidence and facts from their research to support their points of view.

- Read aloud and discuss one or more of the children's books from the list provided in this lesson.

CHILDREN'S BOOKS

I Wanna Iguana by Karen Kaufman Orloff

I Wanna New Room by Karen Kaufman Orloff

PERSUASIVE ESSAY GRAPHIC ORGANIZER

[Version 1 Student Handout]

Student Name: _____

Title of Essay:

Opinion Statement:

Reason #1:	Facts, Quotes and Examples:

Reason #2:	Facts, Quotes and Examples:

Reason #3:	Facts, Quotes and Examples:

Summary:

Unit II.106 | Understanding My Strengths, Skills and Identity

PERSUASIVE ESSAY GRAPHIC ORGANIZER

[Version 2 Student Handout]

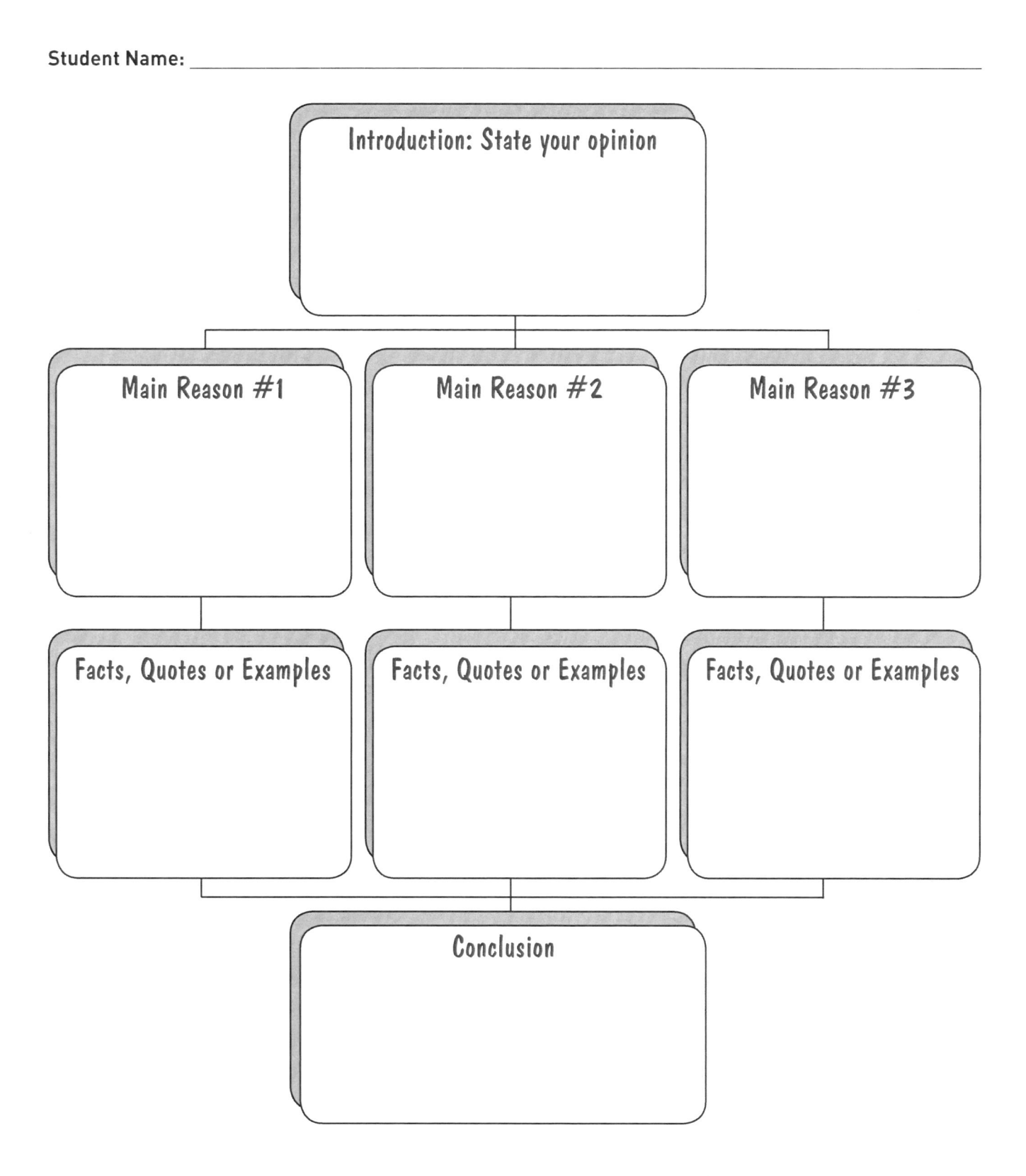

Student Name: _____

- **Introduction: State your opinion**

- **Main Reason #1**
- **Main Reason #2**
- **Main Reason #3**

- **Facts, Quotes or Examples**
- **Facts, Quotes or Examples**
- **Facts, Quotes or Examples**

- **Conclusion**

■ *Anti-Bias Building Blocks: An Elementary Curriculum* | Unit II.107

SKILLS AND ABILITIES

Lesson 8

RATIONALE

The purpose of this activity is for students to identify their own abilities and skills as a way to reflect on their identities and the identities of others, noting both similarities and differences. Gaining insight into their identity is an important aspect of self-esteem and understanding differences forms the basis of diversity appreciation and respect. This lesson provides an opportunity for students to define terms, gain awareness of their abilities and skills and reflect on similarities and differences with others.

OBJECTIVES

- Students will be able to define skill, interest, talent and hope.
- Students will connect with peers who share skills, interests, talents and hopes.
- Students will understand peers whose skills, interests, talents and hopes differ from their own.

WHAT'S NEEDED

Handouts and Resources: Find Someone Who...(Opposites) and *My Skills, Talents, Interests and Hopes* (one of each for each student)

Other Material: Pens or pencils

PROCEDURES

1. Begin the lesson by defining these four words by first eliciting the definition from the students and coming to the definitions as follows. Provide a quick example for each.

   Skill: the ability to do something well

   Talent: a special ability that allows a person to do something well

   Interest: something that a person enjoys learning about or doing

   Hope: something you want to happen

2. Have students stand up and make sure there is room in the classroom for them to move around. Explain that you are going to

GRADE LEVEL
3–5

TIME
45 minutes

COMMON CORE STANDARDS
Reading, Writing, Speaking & Listening, Language

STRATEGIES AND SKILLS
Define terms, attribute linking, small group discussion, assumption

KEY WORDS AND PHRASES
Hope
Interest
Skill
Talent

call out a question related to skills, talents, interests and hopes and they are to walk around the room and try to find others who share the response. For example, you might ask, "What is your favorite color?" Then students will walk around the room to find others who have the same favorite color as them. Instruct students, when they get to their groups, to spend a few minutes talking with each other about it. Then have students call out their groups. For example, in the first grouping below "On Saturday mornings, I like to," point to the sports group and have them call out "SPORTS!" and so on.

Use the questions below or create your own:

a. On Saturday mornings, I like to (1) play sports, (2) watch TV, (3) play video games, (4) visit relatives or (5) something else.

b. I am best at (1) fixing things, (2) making new friends with other people, (3) schoolwork, (4) physical things like sports and dance, (5) art activities, (6) computers and technology or (7) something else.

c. I want to learn (1) how to read or write better, (2) a specific sport, (3) something artistic (4) technology, (5) getting along with others or (7) something else.

d. In the future, I hope to have a job (1) as a teacher, (2) as an artist/dancer/singer, (3) as an athlete, (4) in business, (5) in the health field—doctor, nurse, (6) working with technology or computers or (7) something else.

3. Have everyone go back to their seats and engage students in a discussion by asking the following questions:

- Did you learn something new about others in the class?
- Did you notice any patterns?
- Which of the choices were skills, talents, interests and hopes?
- As a whole, was our class good at and skilled in certain things and not in others?

4. Explain to students that they are now going to do an activity where they will learn about some of the ways they differ from each other. Distribute the handout *Find Someone Who... (Opposites)* to each student and have them look at it briefly. Instruct students to take a few minutes and fill out the handout about themselves and their preferences. Once completed, explain that when you say "begin" they are to move around the classroom to find students in the class who have a different or the opposite characteristic/interest/ability based on what is written in each box—this includes different skills, talents, hopes, interests and identity items. When they receive an answer from someone, have them write their name in the square. When a person signs their worksheet ask that person for specifics. Each person may only sign one square of another student's sheet. Once someone has all of her or his squares filled out or when ten minutes have passed, instruct students to stop and take their seats.

5. Engage students in a discussion by asking the following questions:

- How did it feel to ask people for information?
- Was it easy or difficult to find people who were opposite in some way from you?
- Did you make any assumptions about some of your classmates as you approached them? Were the assumptions correct or incorrect?
- Did you learn anything new or surprising about yourself or others?

6. Distribute the *My Skills, Talents, Interests and Hopes* handout to each student. Based on everything that was discussed in this lesson, have students list a few things in each of the boxes about their skills, talents, interests and hopes for the future. They can illustrate them as well. When completed, have students present their sheets one at a time. Hang them up and have students look at their classmates' work and note new things they learned about classmates including similarities and differences.

EXTENSION ACTIVITIES

- Have a container in the classroom labeled "Let's Learn Something New." Write tasks that will be unfamiliar to many of the students (e.g., say thank you in sign language) on slips of paper and put them in the container. When time permits, have a volunteer choose one of the new skills that they would like to learn from the container and then have the student develop an action plan to learn and practice the skill/task.

- Create learning centers organized by different students where they can teach each other things they know how to do (e.g., a string game center, Spanish center, basketball corner, etc.). Once a week, have 4–5 children set up their own learning centers and take turns teaching the other students in the class. Rotate this. They can also watch and make instructional videos to teach something.

- Read aloud and discuss one or more of the children's books from the list provided in this lesson.

FLIPPED CLASSROOM IDEA

Make a short instructional video of you doing something you are skilled in, like cooking something, fixing something, drawing something or a sporting activity. The video should include you giving instructions to model how you can teach others something you know how to do.

CHILDREN'S BOOKS

Athlete vs. Mathlete by W.C. Mack

Happy Like Soccer by Maribeth Boelts

Willow by Denise Brennan-Nelson

Elena's Serenade by Campbell Geeslin

FIND SOMEONE WHO… (OPPOSITES)

[Student Handout]

Instructions: Fill in your preference for each box beside the word "Me." Then, find someone with the opposite preference of the skill, ability, characteristic or like. For example, if your favorite type of music is rap, write that choice for you, then find someone who prefers another type of music. Have them sign in the box where it says "Other Person" and have them tell you more about their choice. When you have all of your boxes filled in, call "Done!"

Favorite Type of Music	Favorite Art Activity	Wants a Career in the Arts	Family Origin (country, city, state)
Me:	Me:	Me:	Me:
Other Person:	Other Person:	Other Person:	Other Person:
Shy vs. Outgoing	**Favorite Snack**	**Eye Color**	**Family Size**
Me:	Me:	Me:	Me:
Other Person:	Other Person:	Other Person:	Other Person:
Prefers Indoors vs. Outdoors Activities	**Best Sport**	**Favorite Holiday**	**Wants to Work in Business**
Me:	Me:	Me:	Me:
Other Person:	Other Person:	Other Person:	Other Person:
Good at Technology	**Wants to Work in Medicine** (doctor, nurse)	**Handedness**	**Skin Color/Complexion**
Me:	Me:	Me:	Me:
Other Person:	Other Person:	Other Person:	Other Person:

MY SKILLS, TALENTS, INTERESTS AND HOPES

[Student Handout]

My Skills/Abilities: _____
_____
_____
_____
_____

My Talents: _____
_____
_____
_____
_____

My Interests: _____
_____
_____
_____
_____

My Hopes: _____
_____
_____
_____
_____

Anti-Bias Building Blocks: An Elementary Curriculum | Unit II.113

MANY KINDS OF FAMILIES

RATIONALE

The purpose of this activity is to understand that family is a major part of identity and there are many different kinds of families. In order to reflect on themselves and appreciate differences, young people need to analyze elements of family and expand their definitions of family. This lesson provides an opportunity for students to identify different types of families, reflect on their own family structure and traditions and interview family members to gain insight into their family's background and heritage.

OBJECTIVES

- Students will identify different kinds of families based on size, structure, race/ethnicity and heads of household.
- Students will reflect on different important elements of their families and create a family suitcase.
- Students will interview a family member to learn more about their family background and heritage.

WHAT'S NEEDED

Handouts and Resources: Family Suitcase Worksheet and My Heritage (one of each for each student)

Other Material: Colored file folders (one per student), magazines/newspapers for cutting out pictures, drawing paper, markers, crayons, yarn, buttons and scissors, index cards and paper

PROCEDURES

1. Begin the lesson by having students "turn and talk" with a person sitting next to them. They should share something unique about their family or a funny story about their family that they enjoy telling.

   After the pairs have shared, ask if anyone would like to share with the whole class.

Lesson 9

GRADE LEVEL
3–5

TIME
45 minutes

COMMON CORE STANDARDS
Reading, Writing, Speaking & Listening

STRATEGIES AND SKILLS
Turn and talk, large group discussion, family suitcase creation, interviews

KEY WORDS AND PHRASES
Ancestor
Celebration
Extended family
Geography
Heritage
Holiday
Multiracial
Relative
Religion
Tradition
Transracial
Unique

2. Explain to students that there are many different types of families with varying sizes, structures, parents, relatives and races. Brainstorm different kinds of families by asking, "What are all the different kinds of families you know, have read about or can think of?"

   Make sure all of the following are included by infusing them into the conversation or listing them at the end. If listing at the end, as you name each of the families, have students raise their hands (or stand up) if they know anyone with a family like that.

   - **Size:** Families with no children, one child or families with many children
   - **Parents/Configuration:** Families with two Moms, two Dads, one Mom and one Dad, one Mom or one Dad, a parent and step-parent
   - **Relatives (heads of household):** Families with Grandparents, Aunts/Uncles or other relatives who are main caregivers of children
   - **Children:** Families with biological children, foster children, adopted children or a combination
   - **Race/Ethnicity:** Families where all members are of same race, where the family is a mixed race family or where there is transracial adoption (where some/most family members are one race and foster or adopted child is different race)

3. Explain to students that they will be creating a "family suitcase" which will include words, pictures, drawings, etc. that represent different aspects of their family.

4. Distribute the *Family Suitcase Worksheet* to each student and read the worksheet together. Have students spend 8–10 minutes filling out the worksheet. For those who would like to talk with a partner (sometimes working with others helps them to think and come up with ideas), allow them to do that but only when they have worked independently for at least five minutes.

5. Engage students in a large group discussion by asking the following questions:
   - Was it easy or difficult to fill out the sheet?
   - Do you have more information for certain boxes?

6. Explain to students that they will be creating a family suitcase to share with the class. The things in the suitcases will reflect different aspects of their family that they wrote about on the *Family Suitcase Worksheet* and any other ideas they come up with.

FLIPPED CLASSROOM IDEA

Make a video of you talking about your family background, going through each of the four categories on the *Family Suitcase Worksheet*, explaining each category and sharing what you would write on the sheet. Then, give instructions as to how to complete the worksheet.

7. Distribute a file folder to each student. Have students write their names on the tab and explain that the folder will serve as their suitcase. Provide art supplies, magazines/newspapers and pieces of paper to write on.

8. Instruct students to look through the magazines and newspapers and cut out pictures illustrating some or all of the following: members of their family, activities their family likes to do together, something important about their family's race or culture, family stories, etc. Tell students to also create "thought bubbles" for family stories or funny or interesting things said by family members. They are to place their pictures, words, thought bubbles and anything else they created in their folder.

   After students have completed this activity, instruct them to tape the sides of the folder together to make a "suitcase" but one that can be opened so they can share it with others.

9. When the suitcases are complete, have students present their Family Suitcases to the class or create a Family Suitcase Gallery where students circulate around the room and examine each other's work.

10. Engage students in a group discussion by asking the following questions:

    - What were some of the similarities in the suitcases? Did you notice everyone included some similar things?
    - What were some of the differences?
    - Did you discover anything new about your classmates?

11. As a homework assignment, distribute the *My Heritage* handout to each student and instruct them to use it to conduct an interview of their parents/caregivers and other family members in order to learn more about their family history and heritage.

NOTE 8

This may take more than one class period and you can also explain the project in advance so students can bring items in from home to include in their family suitcases. This could also be a family activity that students work on at home.

EXTENSION ACTIVITIES

- Have students watch at least five television shows and five commercials that include families and keep a log of what they observe. After doing their observations and recording them on a log, have them share with the rest of the class. Discuss what families are not included at all or as often and how they feel about that.

- Have students write stories or poems about their family or a family they know. Instruct them to decide in advance what the main plot to the story is (or the theme of the poem) and include the type of details in their story about the family that are included

CHILDREN'S BOOKS

Families are Different by Nina Pelligrini

Over the Moon: An Adoption Tale by Karen Katz

And Tango Makes Three by Justin Richardson

Of Many Colors: Portraits of Multiracial Families by Peggy Gillespie

in the *Family Suitcase Worksheet*.

- Read aloud and discuss one or more of the children's books from the list provided in this lesson.

MY FAMILY SUITCASE WORKSHEET

[Student Handout]

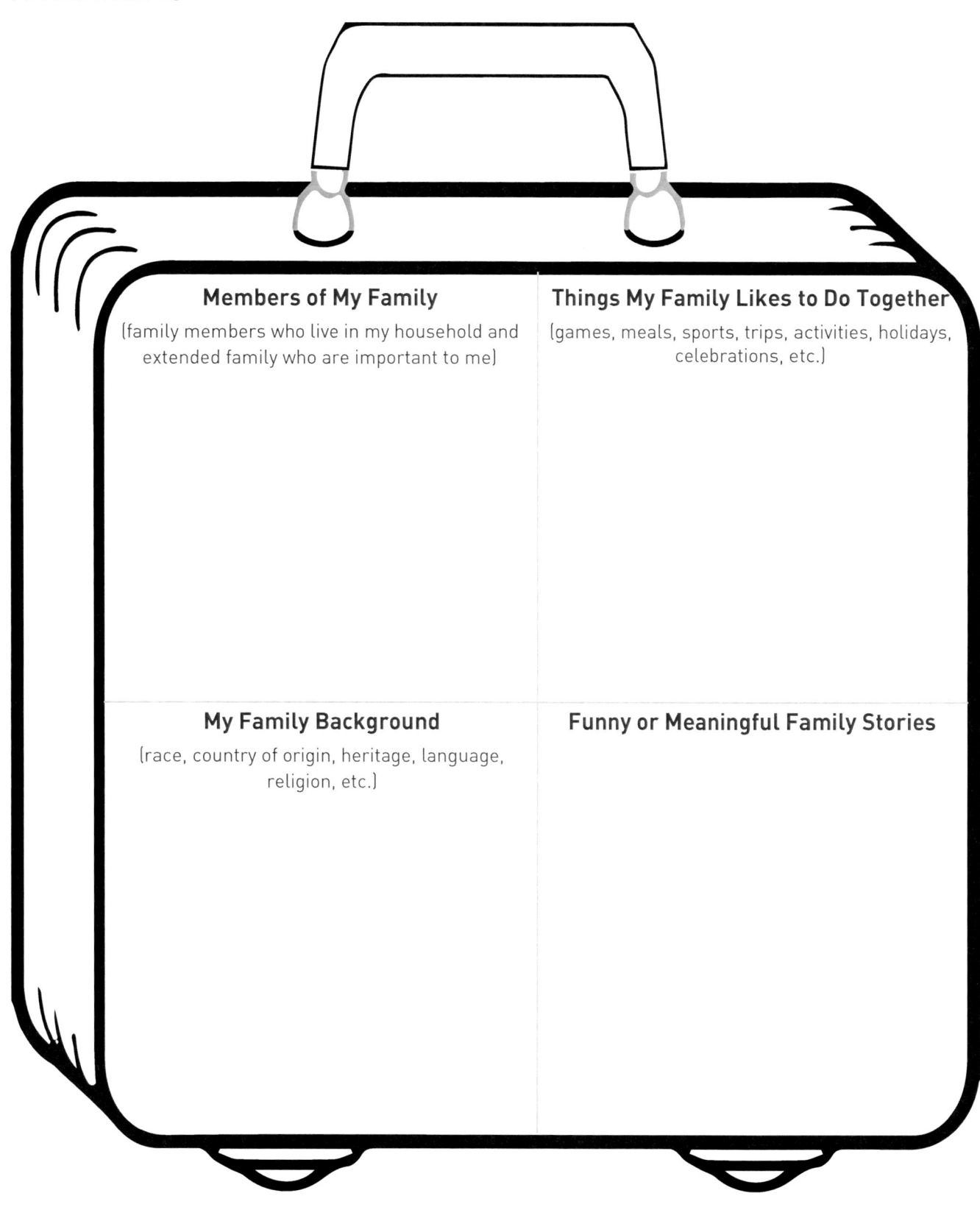

Members of My Family
(family members who live in my household and extended family who are important to me)

Things My Family Likes to Do Together
(games, meals, sports, trips, activities, holidays, celebrations, etc.)

My Family Background
(race, country of origin, heritage, language, religion, etc.)

Funny or Meaningful Family Stories

MY HERITAGE

[Student Handout]

Instructions: Write the name of each family member you are interviewing and indicate their relationship to you (e.g., mother, grandfather, etc.). Conduct interview using the interview questions below to help you learn more about your family history and heritage.

Family Member(s)
Name & Relationship:

Interview Questions
1. How long have you lived in this country?
2. How long has your family lived in this country?
3. In what other parts of the United States have you or other members of your family lived?
4. Do you know where your ancestors/relatives came from? If so, where?
5. What language(s) do you speak?
6. What language(s) did your ancestors speak when they came to the United States?

7. Tell me about a cultural holiday or celebration that you enjoyed as a child.

8. Tell me about some of your favorite cultural foods.

9. Tell me about a favorite story you heard growing up.

10. Are there other aspects of your culture or heritage that you would like to share?

11. In what ways have you tried to teach someone in your family about your family's cultural background?

WHAT IS COMMUNITY?

RATIONALE

The purpose of this activity is for students to understand the concept of community, how their community may differ from others and some of the essential elements of any community. Gaining insight into the strengths and challenges of their community and the differences between one's community and others are helpful tools in empathizing with other people. This lesson provides an opportunity for students to identify the different parts of a community, create their own neighborhood maps and identify improvements for their community.

OBJECTIVES

- Students will identify different people, services and places that are in their community.
- Students will create their neighborhood maps.
- Students will consider what areas of improvement in their community are needed and engage in a community service project to address it.

WHAT'S NEEDED

Handouts and Resources: My Neighborhood Map (one for each student)

Other Material: Paper, pencils, markers, crayons, colored pencils, sharpies

PROCEDURES

1. Begin the lesson by asking, "What is community? When you hear the word community, what words, phrases and feelings come to mind? What things, places and people are in a community?" Create a semantic web using the responses you receive.

   When the web is complete, ask the following questions:
   - What do you notice about the web?
   - Do you have everything written here that is in your community?

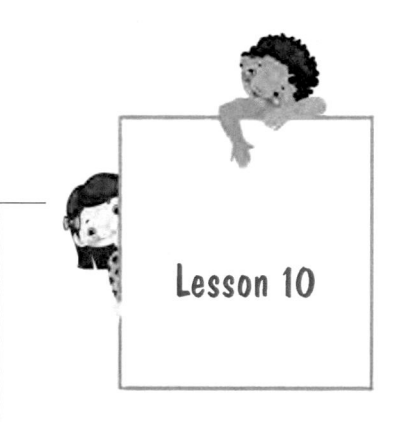

Lesson 10

GRADE LEVEL
3–5

TIME
45 minutes

COMMON CORE STANDARDS
Reading, Writing, Speaking & Listening, Language

STRATEGIES AND SKILLS
Semantic web, define terms, create map, community service

KEY WORDS AND PHRASES
City
Community
Neighborhood
Rural
Service
Small town
Suburb

■ *Anti-Bias Building Blocks: An Elementary Curriculum*

- Are there any parts of your community you do not like or you feel need improvement?
2. Define **community** as a group of people who live in the same area (such as a city, town or neighborhood). Also explain that there are many different kinds of communities and places where people live. In the United States, there are cities, small towns, suburbs and farm or rural areas. For each of these, ask what students know about them and briefly explain the differences.
3. Explain to students that an important part of who they are, their identity, is the community in which they live. Tell them that we will be exploring the idea of community in this lesson. In any community, there are people, services and places. Divide students into three groups. Working together, have each of three groups list (1) people, (2) services and (3) places as follows:

    Group #1: People—Identify people in the community by what they do (e.g., firefighter) and also by who they are (e.g., teenagers)

    Group #2: Services—Identify what services are provided by the people in the community (e.g., garbage pickup, sale of products)

    Group #3: Places—Identify buildings and other places that people go to or gather (e.g., park, movie theater)

4. Give each group 5–7 minutes to come up with as many ideas on their papers as possible and then share with the rest of the class, either noting their ideas on chart paper or board/smart board as students read them aloud. You might put them all on a table as follows:

People	Services	Places
bus driver	garbage pickup	park
teenagers	sale of groceries	post office
usher at movie theater	teach children	supermarket
doctor	foster stray dogs	pizza shop

    If there are significant things missing, prompt the students to get some of those ideas on the list and add your own.

5. Engage students in a discussion by asking the following questions:
    - Are there things on the list you had not thought of before? If so, what?
    - Is there anything on these lists that you do not have in your community? If so, what? What are some reasons it may not be in your community?
    - Would you say that all communities have a lot in common with each other in terms of people, places and services?
    - Thinking about different kinds of communities (cities, suburbs, small towns, farms), do you think certain communities have more of certain services and places and less of others? If so, what do you think those are?
    - What aspects of your community do you like?
    - What aspects of your community do you think need improvement?

6. Explain to students that they are now going to each create a map with some of the people, services and places they just discussed. First ask, "What is a map?" Explain that a **map** is a picture or chart that shows the streets, places, rivers, mountains, etc. in a particular area.

7. 📷◀ Distribute the *My Neighborhood Map* handout to each student. The map will have streets but explain to them that they are going to draw and write different pictures and symbols on the map about their neighborhood. Take a few minutes and have them put a house or apartment that is their home. Next, have them draw in some grass, trees, flowers and other natural things (mountain, river, etc.) based on what they know about the area near their home. Finally, have them identify at least three places and at least three people and draw them in somewhere on the map. For the places, they can use a symbol (e.g., a cross for a church or Star of David for a synagogue) or draw the place itself.

8. After students have completed their maps, have each student tape the map to their desk or table area and have students walk around the room and look at all the maps. When they have finished looking at all the maps, engage students in a discussion by asking the following questions:

    - How was it to create your map?
    - What did you include in your map?
    - Were all of the maps the same?
    - Did you notice any patterns to the maps overall?
    - What interesting things did others include that you didn't?
    - What did you learn?

9. Remind students about the parts of the lesson where they discussed the things they do not like about their community and need to be improved. Ask, "Are there other things about the town that you would like to change?" Brainstorm a list of ideas of what they want to change about their community and have a brief conversation about how to do that. For example, maybe there are too many stray dogs in their neighborhood and they feel sorry for the dogs and they also feel it is unsafe. Or there isn't a grocery store nearby with healthy food options. As a follow-up, decide on what area they want to put their energy and create a social action project based on the problem they identified. Or, they can decide to join a community service project that already exists (e.g., help walk dogs at a local dog rescue center).

EXTENSION ACTIVITIES

- Have students create a photo or video essay about their community. Together you can go on a community or neighborhood walk, allowing the students to take photos of important people and places. They can also interview people along the way about what they do, what they like about the community, what improvements

---

NOTE 7

Be aware and sensitive to the fact that some students in your class may be homeless, transient or may have moved around a lot and therefore, their sense of "community" will be impacted by those experiences.

FLIPPED CLASSROOM IDEA

Make a short video of you talking about your own neighborhood or community. In the video, you can show the blank *My Neighborhood Map* and then talk about all of the important things in your neighborhood. During the video, draw in your home, trees, etc. and a few relevant people and places that are part of your neighborhood.

they think need to be made. To get students to think critically about access to resources, you may also have them take note of how far away different resources are and how this can impact people in a community. You can exhibit the photos in a class gallery or share on social media through Instagram or Pinterest.

- Have students develop and implement a survey about their community. First have students create a list of 5–10 survey questions. Then have them brainstorm different people in the community they can interview for the survey (classmates, family members, other community members). If possible, have students interview people from different generations. After completing the survey, have students create graphs that organize the findings and they may also include video interviews and photographs. They can publish their results online or in a local newspaper with recommendations.

- Read aloud and discuss one or more of the children's books from the list provided in this lesson.

CHILDREN'S BOOKS

A Castle on Viola Street by DyAnne DiSalvo

Dear Primo by Duncan Tonatiuh

Me On the Map by Joan Sweeney

MY NEIGHBORHOOD MAP
[Student Handout]

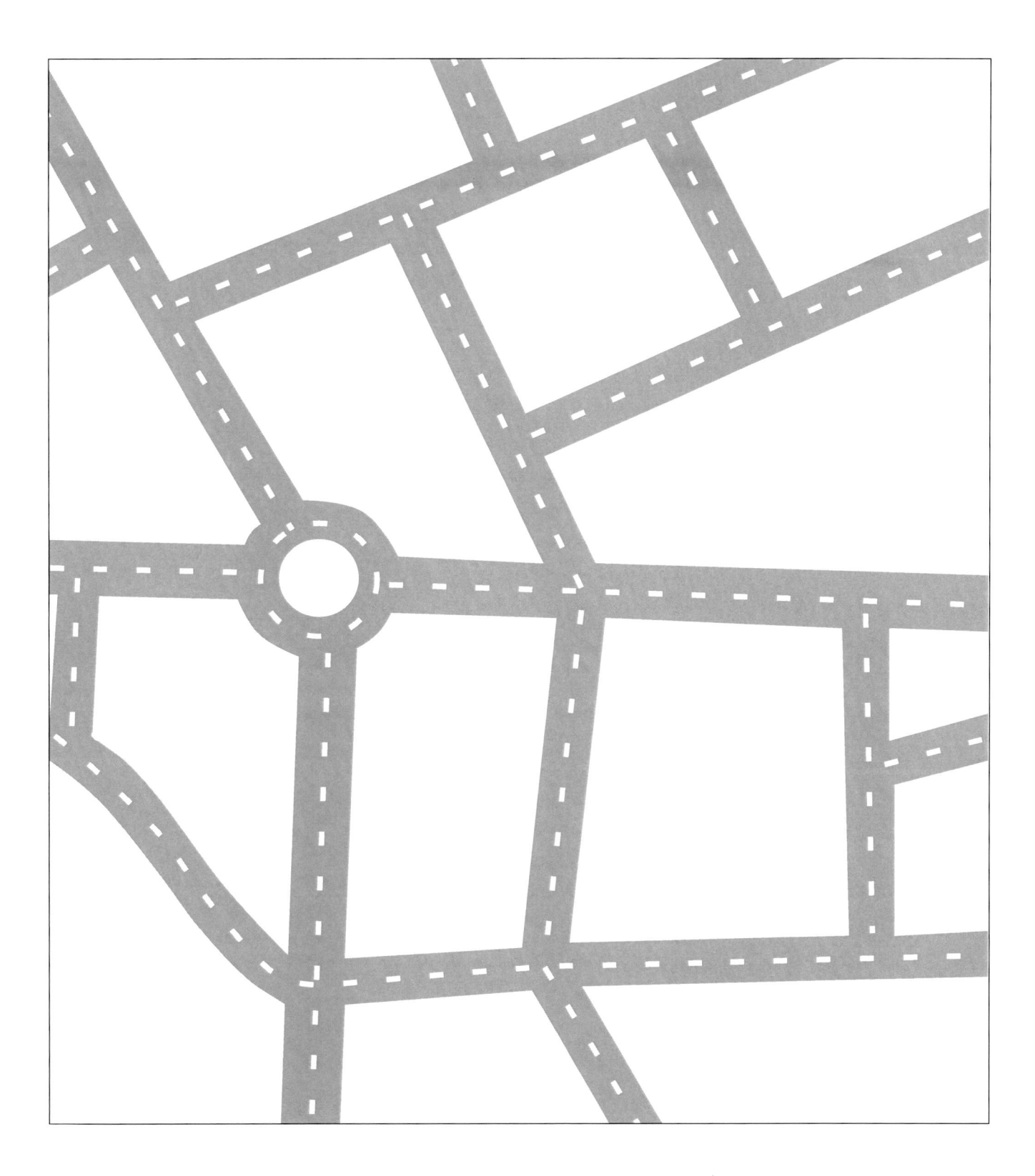

Anti-Bias Building Blocks: An Elementary Curriculum | Unit II.127

UNIT III. UNDERSTANDING AND APPRECIATING DIFFERENCES

Culture is a central part of one's identity. Cultural differences and misunderstandings often lead to conflict, bullying and bias. In Unit III, students will explore their own culture, learn about the cultures of others and be able to express the feelings they have when differences arise. The overall goal is for children to understand cultural and other differences in identity so that they can play and work together effectively. In the process, they will discover that differences are positive and lead to an expanding world view and perspective.

While it is important and relevant for students to learn about and discuss different cultures and identities, it also can lead to stereotyping and generalizations. In your discussions about culture, be careful and mindful not to reinforce stereotypes by portraying cultures in a homogeneous way. We know that, within any culture, there are similarities as well as many differences and a wide variation of people's interests, identities and backgrounds. In addition, we are all multicultural because we are multi-faceted and often have a variety of cultural backgrounds. Culture is complex and ever changing. This nuance can be challenging to convey to young children but it is essential.

GOALS FOR KINDERGARTEN THROUGH 2ND GRADE

In Unit III, children in grades kindergarten through second grade will identify different societal and cultural groups that they belong to and then create pie graphs that illustrate those groups. They will explore what the word "culture" means, identify elements of their culture and create a "culture flag" that represents their cultural identity. Finally, students will articulate the ways in which they are similar to and different from their classmates and explore their feelings around those differences.

GOALS FOR THIRD THROUGH FIFTH GRADE

For third to fifth graders, children will first define culture and then will reflect on what they know about cultures around the world as well as their own. They will explore one country or culture in depth by doing a research project. This unit will culminate in a review of their identity characteristics and an exploration of their feelings around differences.

I BELONG TO MANY GROUPS

Lesson 11

RATIONALE

The purpose of this activity is for students to understand the concept of group affiliation and that they belong to many groups while maintaining their unique identity. This lesson provides an opportunity for students to identify the groups that they belong to, prioritize those that are most important to them and reflect on similarities and differences within their class.

OBJECTIVES

- Students will identify groups to which they belong.
- Students will prioritize the groups that are most important to their identity.
- Students will reflect on the similarities and differences within their class.

WHAT'S NEEDED

Handouts and Resources: Groups I Belong To (one for each student)

Other Material: Markers, crayons or colored pencils

PROCEDURES

1. Begin the lesson by having students think about groups to which they belong. Provide them with several examples of different types of groups—grade/age (first grader), place in family (only child), race/ethnicity (African American), language spoken (Chinese/Mandarin speaker), clubs (Girl Scouts), religion (Muslim), gender, etc. Ask students to add to the list of examples.

   [NOTE: While a child's gender is one group they may consider an important aspect of their identity, this will not be true for all children and may be complex for some. Do not overemphasize gender or the idea of "two genders" (i.e. the gender binary, just boys and girls) in these conversations. There are students who do not identify strongly with gender, especially traditional gender norms. Do not assume that all girls identify strongly as female or that all boys identify stronger as male and avoid promoting stereotypes about gender (e.g., all boys

GRADE LEVEL
K–2

TIME
35 minutes

COMMON CORE STANDARDS
Reading, Writing, Speaking & Listening, Language

STRATEGIES AND SKILLS
Large group discussion, making a pie graph, working with partner, comparing and contrasting

KEY WORDS AND PHRASES
Identity
Groups
Pie graph

cannot sit still and all girls like to read). Visit Gender Spectrum at www.genderspectrum.org for more information on this topic.]

2. Distribute the *Groups I Belong To* handout to each student. Ask students to think about groups to which they belong and how each of those groups is a piece of who they are. Each group is a part of their identity and includes (1) groups they have no choice about as well as (2) groups they choose to belong to.

   Give students some general categories such as family (remind them about previous lesson about different kinds of families), race/ethnic groups, religion, gender, language(s) spoken, school groups (e.g., chorus, basketball team) and community groups (e.g., Boy Scouts). Distribute writing materials and explain to students that they will choose four of the most important groups to them and write those in each of the four pieces on the pie. For younger students who are not writing yet, they can draw a picture.

3. After students have completed their pie graphs, have each pair off with a partner. Have partners compare their pies, looking for similarities and differences. If they have something similar, they should each put an "S" in that part of the pie chart and where there are differences, both pairs should write a "D" in that piece of pie.

4. Have the students come back together and ask for volunteer pairs to share their pies with the rest of the class, explaining the groups they belong to and the groups they have in common and where there are differences. Continue until all pairs have shared their pie graphs.

5. Engage students in a discussion by asking the following questions:
   - As a class, do we have a lot of differences? Do we have many similarities?
   - Which groups, if any, did many in the class have in common?
   - Which groups, if any, did few (or none) of you have in common?
   - What are some groups that people choose to belong to?
   - What are some groups that people have no choice about?

EXTENSION ACTIVITIES

- Continue to provide opportunities for students to share aspects of their identity by creating a "Student of the Week" activity. Designate one student each week to do a variety of things including (1) create a bulletin board about themselves with photographs and other important items, (2) have other students interview the student of

---

FLIPPED CLASSROOM IDEA

Make a short video of yourself talking about the groups to which you belong. You can include more than four (e.g., woman, teacher, Latina, Christian, parent, softball player) and talk briefly about each and how you are a member of that group. Then talk about the four most important and write those in your pie graph.

the week and videotape the interview. After all the children have had a turn to be Student of the Week, put all the videos together to make a class video, (3) invite the student's parents/caregivers in to talk with the rest of the class about their family history and culture.

- Create a list together of famous and important people (both living and dead) from different walks of life that represent different racial, ethnic and religious groups, different families and communities, variety of abilities, age levels, etc. Have students work individually or in small groups to research and identify the many groups to which each of the individuals belongs.

- Read aloud and discuss one or more of the children's books from the list provided in this lesson. In addition to the suggested books, see ADL's Books Matter: The Best Kid Lit on Bias, Diversity and Social Justice at www.adl.org/education-outreach/books-matter/people-identity-culture.html for books about specific cultural groups. Following are tips on selecting books about culture:
    - Look for books that show people from other cultures in contemporary times with contemporary roles.
    - Avoid books that perpetuate stereotypes and those that elevate the status of one cultural group over another.
    - Try to balance books you share with students among many cultures, especially those represented in your classroom, but if you can't find books for all cultures, don't avoid the ones you have.

CHILDREN'S BOOKS

Whoever You Are by Mem Fox

Thank You, World by Alice McGinty

GROUPS I BELONG TO

[Student Handout]

Student Name: _____

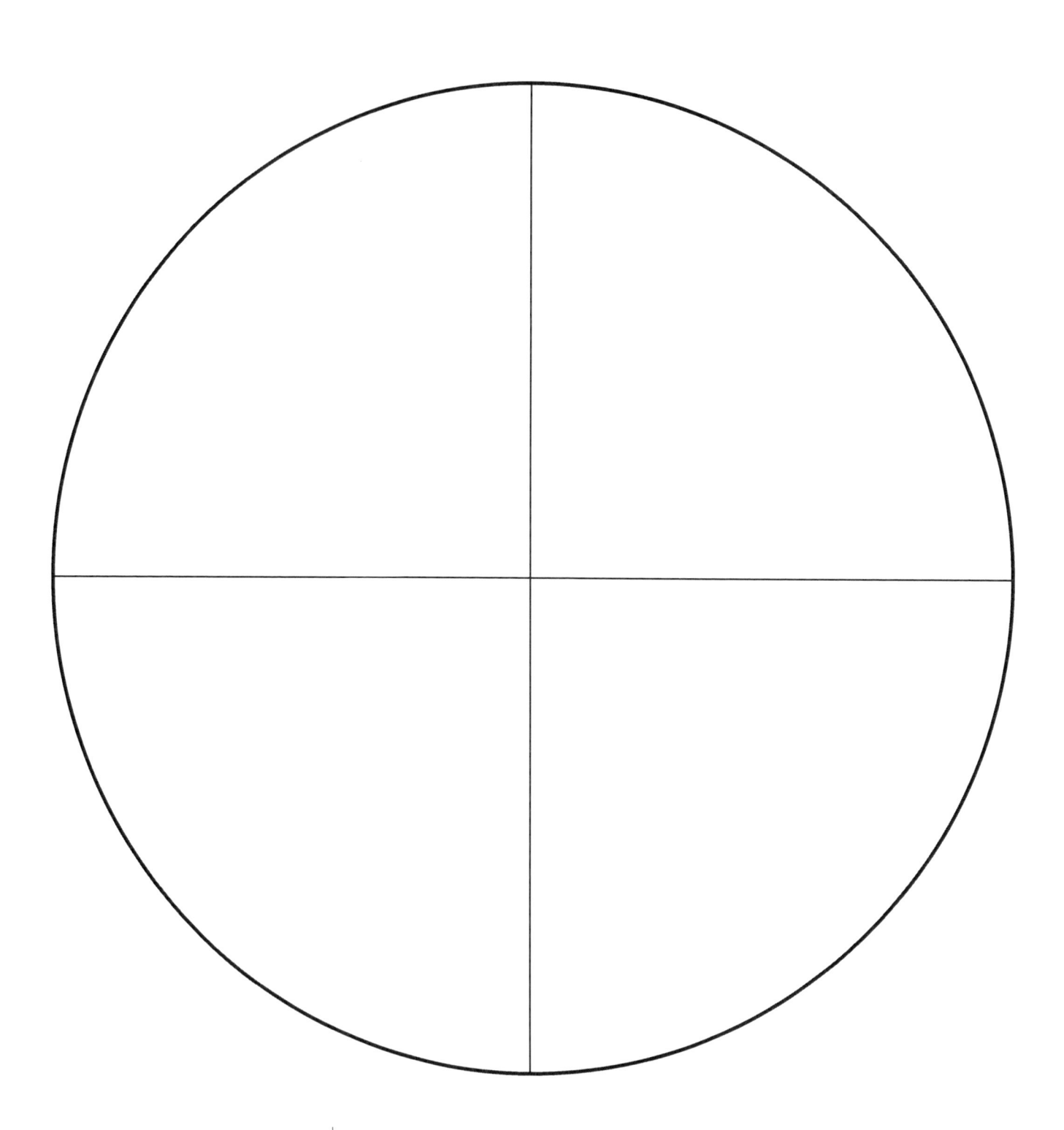

Unit III.134 | Understanding and Appreciating Differences

MY CULTURAL FLAG

Lesson 12

RATIONALE

The purpose of this activity is to explore the idea of culture and to help students articulate aspects of their own culture. Because cultural differences and misunderstandings sometimes lead to bias and bullying, it is important to set a foundation for understanding similarities and differences. This lesson provides an opportunity for students to define and consider examples of culture and create a culture flag which represents aspects of their cultural identity.

[**NOTE:** While it is important and relevant for students to learn about and discuss different cultures and identities, it also can lead to stereotyping and generalizations. In your discussions about culture, be careful and mindful not to reinforce stereotypes by portraying cultures in a homogeneous way. We know that in any culture, there are similarities as well as many differences and a wide variation of people's interests, identities and backgrounds. In addition, we are all multicultural because we are multi-faceted and often have a variety of cultural backgrounds. Culture is complex and ever changing. This nuance can be challenging to convey to young children but it is essential.]

OBJECTIVES

- Students will understand what the term "culture" means.
- Students will identify examples of culture.
- Students will reflect on aspects of their own culture and create a "culture flag" that represents parts of their cultural identity.

WHAT'S NEEDED

World map, "culture flag," construction paper (one piece per student), markers, crayons or colored pencils, popsicle sticks or a wooden dowel, glue

Advance Preparation: Create a sample "culture flag" that includes a variety of things reflective of your culture (e.g., Samosas, Ramadan, games you play with your family, Christmas Eve dinner, Purim, Haitan-Creole, jazz music, kimono, Irish stepdance, favorite expression, etc.).

GRADE LEVEL
K–2

TIME
35 minutes

COMMON CORE STANDARDS
Reading, Writing, Speaking & Listening, Language

STRATEGIES AND SKILLS
Define terms, countries on a map, art (culture flag), large group discussion, gallery walk

KEY WORDS AND PHRASES
Belief
Country
Culture
Custom
Flag
Language

■ *Anti-Bias Building Blocks: An Elementary Curriculum*

PROCEDURES

1. Begin the lesson by reminding students about the "Groups I Belong To" activity and the pie chart they created about the groups to which they belong. Explain that one type of group people can belong to is groups where they share the same "culture."

2. Ask students, "Do you know what culture is?" Come to a definition of **culture** as parts of daily life that are seen in food, customs, holidays, music and more that a group of people share. Explain that these aspects of culture are often handed down from one generation to the next and they are sometimes connected to the country where people's relatives originally came from. Also, define **custom** as a way of behaving that is usual and traditional among people in a group or place. An example is that in the United States, when adults meet each other, they usually shake hands. In other countries, people bow or kiss each other.

3. Display the world map and ask students, "Does anyone have a connection to another country, either because family members or ancestors lived there or you have discussed or learned about it?" Or, if students are Native American, ask with which tribe or region of the country they identify. As students share countries, point out where this is on the map. [**Optional:** In advance of the lesson, you could choose to have students go home and interview their parents/caregivers about where the family's "roots" are.]

4. Explain to students that they are going to create their own "culture flags." Make sure students know what a flag is and tell them that they are going to make a flag that represents their culture. Remind students about the aspects of culture that were already discussed (food, customs, holidays, music) and ask if they have ideas of others. You can add clothing, arts/crafts, language, religion, housing, beliefs, etc. Be sure to only add those that young children can understand. You will also want to broaden their understanding of culture. Culture can originate from a specific country but it can also come from (1) the region of the U.S. you live, (2) whether you live in a city, suburb or rural setting, (3) aspects of your home and family life, (4) your community or neighborhood, (5) how you celebrate holidays, (6) your religion and (7) words/slang you use and how you say certain things, etc. Have students take a few minutes to share aloud, either in large group or in pairs, the ideas they have about what they will include on their culture flag.

5. Distribute to each student a sheet of construction paper, glue and crayons, markers or colored pencils. Instruct students to write their name at the top of the paper and think through what they want to include in their flag. They can draw pictures, symbols and/

NOTE 3

Be aware that some children will not know where their family/ancestors are from for a variety of reasons including: their parents have not discussed it with them, the situation may have been difficult, they may be undocumented or they are African American and they may not know what country in Africa their ancestors lived before being forcibly brought to the United States.

or words. You may also want to have magazines and a computer with Internet access for additional images to include. 📷◀ Display the culture flag prepared in advance as an example for students. If it is difficult for students to come up with ideas only around culture, they can also go back to their "Groups I Belong To" pie charts and include items from that on their flags.

6. When students have completed their flags, have them glue a popsicle stick to the side so it looks like a flag. Then have them hang them up on a wall in the classroom; all students can then take a gallery walk to look at all of the flags. If time permits, have each student come to the front of the class and explain their flag and what it means about who they are.

7. Engage students in a discussion by asking the following questions:
   - Was it easy or difficult to make your culture flag? How did you feel while creating it?
   - What did you learn about people's cultures and backgrounds from their flags?
   - What did you learn about your own culture in making your flag?
   - Did you notice any similarities between the flags? How about differences?

EXTENSION ACTIVITIES

- Have students work together to prepare a bulletin board (or Pinterest board) entitled, "The United States: A Multicultural Country." Instruct students to use photographs, pictures from the Internet, original drawings, magazine/newspaper cutouts and words to illustrate the diversity of the United States.

- Have students conduct research on different countries in the world, regions of the country and/or Native American tribes in order to learn more about them. They should learn about the group's cultural identity that goes beyond food and holidays and delves into more complex aspects of their culture like family life, beliefs, customs, traditions, etc. Since each of these groups will have differences between and among them, encourage students to explore the differences within a cultural group as well.

- Read aloud and discuss children's books from ADL's Books Matter: The Best Kid Lit on Bias, Diversity and Social Justice at www.adl.org/education-outreach/books-matter/people-identity-culture.html for books about specific cultural groups. Following

FLIPPED CLASSROOM IDEA

Make a short video of you explaining your cultural background, identifying a few aspects of your culture and then sharing your "culture flag," (which you have prepared in advance). Point out how the pictures and words on your flag relate to your cultural identity.

are tips on selecting books about culture:

- Look for books that show people from other cultures in contemporary times with contemporary roles.
- Avoid books that perpetuate stereotypes and those that elevate the status of one cultural group over another.
- Try to balance books you share with students among many cultures, especially those represented in your classroom, but if you can't find books for all cultures, don't avoid the ones you have.

SIMILARITIES AND DIFFERENCES

RATIONALE

The purpose of this activity is for students to consider the similarities and differences about aspects of their identity. This lesson provides an opportunity for students to review what they have explored about their identities, explore their similarities and differences with their classmates and reflect on their feelings about it.

OBJECTIVES

- Students will review all the identity items they have explored thus far.
- Students will consider individual differences and similarities amongst their classmates.
- Students will reflect on their feelings about the similarities and differences.

WHAT'S NEEDED

Handouts and Resources: Who is Similar, Who is Different? (one for each student)

Other Material: Chart paper or board/smart board, markers, pencils or pens

PROCEDURES

1. Begin the lesson by reviewing with students all the ways in which they have explored parts of their identity and began to think about how they are different and similar to each other.
2. Ask students, "What are all the different aspects of who we are, our identity, that we have talked about so far?" Write on chart paper or board/smart board a list of their responses. It should include:
   - Physical Appearance—what they look like
   - Likes and Dislikes—their preferences

Lesson 13

GRADE LEVEL
K–2

TIME
35 minutes

COMMON CORE STANDARDS
Reading, Writing, Speaking & Listening

STRATEGIES AND SKILLS
Review concepts, large group discussion, talking to students and identifying similarities and differences

KEY WORDS AND PHRASES
Differences
Similarities

CHILDREN'S BOOKS

It's Okay to Be Different by Todd Parr

Same, Same But Different by Jenny Sue Kostecki-Shaw

Everybody Brings Noodles by Norah Dooley

Little Blue and Little Yellow by Leo Lionni

■ *Anti-Bias Building Blocks: An Elementary Curriculum*   Unit III.139

- Skills—what they are good at
- Family—structure, how many people, etc. are in their family
- Community—what and who are in their community/neighborhood
- Culture—aspects of their cultural background

3. Explain to students that now they are going to focus on similarities and differences in each of the categories. Make sure students know what the words similar and different mean. Distribute the *Who Is Similar, Who Is Different?* handout. Read it over together. Explain that they will have 10–15 minutes to walk around the classroom and find people in each of the categories who are similar to them and different from them. For example, for the physical appearance category, if they have curly or kinky hair, they will find another student with curly or kinky hair and that student would write their name under "Similar." If they find a student with straight hair, they would write their name under "Different." Or they could focus on height or any other aspect of their physical appearance.

   Make sure everyone understands what to do and what each category means and answer any questions the students have. Explain that they do not have to have every box filled in but they should try to talk to as many other students as possible to find similarities and differences.

4. As students are milling around the classroom completing the sheets, make sure they are circulating around and finding as many similarities and differences as possible. Allow 10 minutes for this process.

5. After the time is up, have students go back to their seats and engage them in a discussion by asking the following questions:
   - How was the activity?
   - Was it easy or difficult to find students with similarities?
   - Was it easy or difficult to find students with differences?
   - How does it feel to be different from someone else?
   - What did you learn by doing this activity?

EXTENSION ACTIVITIES

- Have students think about situations in which they have seen differences between people that led to conflict, bullying or other problems. Brainstorm different situations and have students write a story about their experience, including what happened, how they felt and what they or others did that either helped the situation get better or hurt and made the situation worse.

- Have students create a survey and graph about differences. Together as a group, brainstorm different questions to ask other students in the class. You could start with something simple like: how many people are in your family? Help students understand how to come up with the different possible options/categories for responses, how to collect the "data," and then how to create a graph of the responses, either using post-it notes or drawing a picture of it. Then expand your questions to other areas of difference and have students work in small groups to ask the questions, compile the data and create graphs.

- Read aloud and discuss one or more of the children's books from the list provided in this lesson.

WHO IS SIMILAR, WHO IS DIFFERENT?

[Student Handout]

Student Name: _____

Instructions: Walk around the classroom and find people in each of the categories listed below who are similar to you and different from you. For students who are similar to you in a category, write their name under "Similar. For students who are different than you, write their name under "Different."

Category	Similar	Different
Physical Appearance		
Likes		
Dislikes		
Things I'm Good At		
Family		
Community		
Culture		

Anti-Bias Building Blocks: An Elementary Curriculum

WHAT IS CULTURE?

RATIONALE

The purpose of this activity is to explore the concept of culture and help students identify important aspects of their own cultural identities. Understanding culture and cultural differences is an important aspect of appreciating differences and analyzing bias based on those differences. This lesson provides an opportunity for students to define culture and race, consider what they already know about cultures around the world and their own culture and write an essay that identifies aspects of their identity.

[**NOTE:** While it is important and relevant for students to learn about and discuss different cultures and identities, it also can lead to stereotyping and generalizations. In your discussions about culture, be careful and mindful not to reinforce stereotypes by portraying cultures in a homogeneous way. We know that in any culture, there are similarities as well as many differences and a wide variation of people's interests, identities and backgrounds. In addition, we are all multicultural because we are multi-faceted and often have a variety of cultural backgrounds. Culture is complex and ever changing. This nuance can be challenging to convey to young children but it is essential.]

OBJECTIVES

- Students will define the word culture and identify the elements that make up one's culture.
- Students will reflect on what they know about countries and cultures around the world.
- Students will explore their own individual cultural groups and write an autobiography about different aspects of their identity.

WHAT'S NEEDED

Handouts and Resources: Aspects of Culture and *Autobiography Worksheet* (one of each for each student)

Other Material: World map, board/smart board or chart paper, markers, pens or pencils

Lesson 11

GRADE LEVEL
3–5

TIME
45 minutes

COMMON CORE STANDARDS
Reading, Writing, Speaking & Listening, Language

STRATEGIES AND SKILLS
Brainstorm, define terms, geography (find countries on a map), turn and talk, write autobiography

KEY WORDS AND PHRASES
Ancestor
Autobiography
Beliefs
Country
Culture
Customs
Government
Religion
Values

PROCEDURES

1. Begin the lesson by writing the word "culture" on the board and ask the students to brainstorm what it means to them. Use their responses and examples to come up with a definition as follows:

   Culture refers to the patterns of daily life that can be seen in language, arts, customs, holiday celebrations, food, religion, beliefs/values, music, clothing and more.

2. Explain to students that culture can be handed down from one generation to the next and can be related to racial/ethnic identity and the country or countries where your family or ancestors are from. Culture can originate from a specific country but it can also come from (1) the region of the U.S. you live, (2) whether you live in a city, suburb or rural setting, (3) aspects of your home and family life, (4) your community or neighborhood, (5) how you celebrate holidays, (6) your religion and (7) words you use and how you say certain things, etc. Culture is a dynamic and complex concept.

3. Explain to students that they will be learning about some of the things that are important to various groups of people as well as the ways that groups convey their beliefs, customs and traditions to future generations. Add that many aspects of life influence culture.

4. Distribute the *Aspects of Culture* handout to each student and read it along with them. Ask students, "Based on this list, what are some things that are part of your culture?" Take a few examples from the class but make this brief.

5. Display the world map. Explain to students that, except for Native Americans, everyone who lives in the United States has parents, relatives or ancestors from another part of the world. Ask students to call out the name of the country or for Native Americans, their tribe or region of the country. As students call out names of countries, point out them out on the map.

6. Have students "turn and talk" with a person sitting next to them about cultural groups that they each belong to. Explain that this can include a race or ethnic group (e.g., Latino), a country where ancestors are from (e.g., Jamaica), their religion or belief system (e.g., Catholic), a part of the United States that has a particular culture (e.g., South), a particular culture related to their home life (e.g., Friday night game nights, going to the beach every summer, very connected to their extended family, etc.) or language(s) they speak. They should share with their partners what groups they belong to and anything they know about the history, culture or background of that group.

7. Ask for a few students to share what they discussed in their pairs.

NOTE 5

Be aware that some children will not know the origin of their ancestors because their parents have not discussed it with them, the situation may have been difficult, they are undocumented or they are African American and they may not know what country in Africa their ancestors lived before being forcibly brought to the United States.

FLIPPED CLASSROOM IDEA

Make a short video of you talking with another person, either a student or another teacher, about your culture. You could include what part of the world your ancestors are from, what cultural group(s) you belong to, and what you know about your heritage, special traditions in your home, etc.

Then engage students in a discussion by asking the following questions:

- Does everyone belong to a culture?
- Can a person belong to more than one cultural group? How so?
- How do people learn about their cultures?
- How can people lose part of their culture?

8. Distribute the *Autobiography Worksheet* and explain to students that they will be writing a short essay/autobiography. Explain that an **autobiography** is something written about someone by that same person. Using all the aspects of their identity already discussed (physical characteristics, opinions, skills, interests and talents, family and community), they will complete the worksheet by summarizing those and adding their cultural identities and what they know about them. Then, using the worksheet, they will take the information and turn it into an essay, adding in some key details.

9. Have students share their essays aloud.

EXTENSION ACTIVITIES

- Have students develop interview questions as a class and then go home and interview family members about their culture, heritage, race, geographic location and background. They can also interview relatives who don't live nearby by Skyping with them or emailing them the questions. Students can compile all of the interviews together and share with the class as a presentation or write an essay or poem about their culture based on their family stories and history.

- Set up a pen pal program between your students and a class in another state or country. You can give your students the option of writing letters that go through the regular mail or use email. In the beginning, it will be helpful to give them specific topics to "discuss" with their pen pal and requirements about how often they should write. As the process continues and the relationships develop, you will not need to provide as much structure for the letter writing. Some resources to help you set up a pen pal program include:
  - Friendship Through Education, http://friendshiptougheducation.org/ptpi.htm
  - Amazing Kids Penpals Program, http://amazing-kids.org/get-involved/amazing-kids-penpals-program/

- Read aloud and discuss one or more of the children's books from the list provided in this lesson. In addition to the suggested books, see ADL's Books Matter: The Best Kid Lit on Bias, Diversity and Social Justice at www.adl.org/education-outreach/books-matter/people-identity-culture.html for books about specific cultural groups. Following are tips on selecting books about culture:
  - Look for books that show people from other cultures in contemporary times with contemporary roles.
  - Avoid books that perpetuate stereotypes and those that elevate the status of one cultural group over another.
  - Try to balance books you share with students among many cultures, especially those represented in your classroom, but if you can't find books for all cultures, don't avoid the ones you have.

ASPECTS OF CULTURE
[Student Handout]

Language

Arts (visual, performing, crafts)

Customs and Traditions

Holiday Celebrations

Food Preparation

Religion

Beliefs/Values/Morals

Music

Clothing

Government

Communication styles

Social Interaction and Organization

Housing/Architecture

Work and Careers

Family Roles

AUTOBIOGRAPHY WORKSHEET

[Student Handout]

Student Name: _____

My Physical Characteristics

1. _____ 4. _____ 7. _____
2. _____ 5. _____ 8. _____
3. _____ 6. _____ 9. _____

Some of My Opinions

_____
_____
_____
_____
_____
_____

My Skills, Interests and Talents

1. _____ 5. _____
2. _____ 6. _____
3. _____ 7. _____
4. _____ 8. _____

A Few Things About My Family

1. _____
2. _____
3. _____
4. _____

Anti-Bias Building Blocks: An Elementary Curriculum | Unit III.147

What I Like About My Community

_____
_____
_____
_____
_____

What About My Community Needs Improvement

_____
_____
_____
_____
_____

Cultural Groups I Belong To

1. _____ 4. _____
2. _____ 5. _____
3. _____ 6. _____

What I Like About My Culture

_____
_____
_____
_____
_____
_____
_____

LEARNING ABOUT DIFFERENT CULTURES

RATIONALE

The purpose of this activity is to examine culture more deeply and help students make the connection between country of origin and impact on people's culture. Understanding different cultures is helpful in understanding bias related to culture. This lesson provides an opportunity for students to share what they already know about countries around the world, consider the concept of the United States being a multicultural country and conduct research to learn more about other countries and their cultures.

OBJECTIVES

- Students will reflect on what they already know about the culture of different countries.
- Students will consider the multicultural nature of the United States.
- Students will learn about the culture of several countries by conducting research.

WHAT'S NEEDED

Handouts and Resources: World Map (one for each student), *Aspects of Culture* (see Lesson 11)

Other Material: Large world map, non-fiction books about other countries and cultures, computer and Internet access, board/smart board or projector, chart paper (optional), markers

Advance Preparation:
- Prepare large world map to be posted or displayed on board/smart board or projector.
- Reproduce *World Map* handout as one page. Copy both pages of the handout. Cut off excess white space in left and right margins. Place both pages of the handout side by side so that the map appears to be one complete map. Tape both pages together on the back side of the paper. Copy the map onto 11"x17" paper. Make enough copies for each student.

Lesson 12

GRADE LEVEL
3–5

TIME
45 minutes

COMMON CORE STANDARDS
Reading, Writing, Speaking & Listening, Language

STRATEGIES AND SKILLS
Reading a map, large group discussion, small group work, research, write up research

KEY WORDS AND PHRASES
Continent
Country
Metaphor
Multicultural

FLIPPED CLASSROOM IDEA

Make a short video of you with a world map, pointing out all of the seven continents and then focusing in on a variety of countries either based on where you know your students' families are from or countries you have studied or are interested in. Explain one or two things about each of the countries' cultures.

PROCEDURES

1. Distribute the *World Map* handout to each student.

2. Display a large world map on board/smart board or projector. Point to various countries around the world and ask students what they know about each of the countries. Try to include at least one country in each continent and pay particular attention to countries where you know your students or their family members/ancestors may be from. Explain that each of the countries has a cultural identity and even within that country, there are a variety of cultures by region and within regions.

3. Ask students, "Does the United States have one particular type of food? Way of dressing? Holiday customs?"

4. Write this quote on board/smart board or chart paper and ask a student to read aloud:

   "I see New York as a gorgeous mosaic of race and religious faith, of national origin and sexual orientation."

   This was said by David Dinkins in 1990 when he became mayor. Ask students, "What is a mosaic? Why does David Dinkins compare New York to a mosaic? How are they similar? What is a different metaphor you can use to describe it?"

5. Explain that David Dinkins was describing a multicultural city where there are people who represent many different countries and cultures. Ask students, "What does the word multicultural mean?" Have them split the word apart and define multi (many) and then cultural and come to a definition of **multicultural** as including many different cultures.

6. Explain that the United States is considered a multicultural country because there are people here from many places in the world and with many beliefs and cultural identities. Tell them that some countries around the world are also multicultural and some are not (i.e. they have one major and dominant culture). Also explain there are many people in the United States that are multiracial and within themselves have various cultures because their parents or caregivers' ancestors are from different parts of the world.

7. Have students identify some of the ethnic groups that live in the United States. Your responses will vary depending on where you live and the diversity of that area so it will be important to fill in their responses with your own to paint a more complete picture of our multicultural country. Examples include:

   - Italian
   - Chinese
   - Indian
   - Native
   - American
   - French

Unit III.150 | Understanding and Appreciating Differences

- Jamaican
- Trinidadian
- Pakistani
- Japanese
- Nigerian
- Polish
- Puerto Rican
- African American
- Irish
- Dominican
- Lebanese
- Polish
- Iraqi
- Ghanaian
- Brazilian

8. Explain to students that they are going to learn more about different countries around the world and their cultures by working in small groups. Divide students into six small groups, each representing one of these six (of seven—leave out Antarctica) continents:
   - Asia
   - Africa
   - Australia
   - Europe
   - North America
   - South America

   Explain to students that they are going to work in small groups to learn more about one or more countries in that continent and focus especially about their culture. Provide as much resource information as possible including maps, books about the countries, links to online encyclopedia and Internet with specific websites highlighted. In each of the continent groups, each individual student will undertake one country for further research. After deciding which countries to research, each student will learn and take notes on the country's cultural aspects including food, music, holidays, language, customs, etc. As a reminder, review with students the *Aspects of Culture* handout from the previous lesson.

9. When students have completed their research, they will present what they learned back to the rest of the class. Have students take turns by group to present.

10. Engage students in a large group discussion by asking the following questions:
    - What new information did you learn about a country and its culture(s)?
    - What were some unique cultural aspects you identified?
    - Were there some commonalities/similarities among groups?

EXTENSION ACTIVITIES

- Have students research the history of bread making from the late Stone Age to modern times. Explain that nearly every country and culture in the world makes bread of some kind. Have them learn

---

NOTE 8

Some use websites to highlight are:

Fact Monster: Countries of the World, www.factmonster.com/countries.html

Time for Kids: Around the World, www.timeforkids.com/around-the-world

how areas of the world and countries have different approaches to making bread and how that is influenced by culture and technology.

- If you live in an ethnically diverse area, have your students learn about the different neighborhoods, shops, restaurants and food markets of different cultures. You can take a neighborhood walk to different areas and interview people who have businesses there. You can have your students write up their experiences of the neighborhood walk in essay format or create a photo exhibit or video about the experience.

- Read aloud and discuss one or more of the children's books from the list provided in this lesson. In addition to the suggested books, see ADL's Books Matter: The Best Kid Lit on Bias, Diversity and Social Justice at www.adl.org/education-outreach/books-matter/people-identity-culture.html for books about specific cultural groups. Following are tips on selecting books about culture:
  - Look for books that show people from other cultures in contemporary times with contemporary roles.
  - Avoid books that perpetuate stereotypes and those that elevate the status of one cultural group over another.
  - Try to balance books you share with students among many cultures, especially those represented in your classroom, but if you can't find books for all cultures, don't avoid the ones you have.

WORLD MAP
[Student Handout]

NOTE: Antartica is not displayed in this map.
This map is adapted from VECTORWORLDMAP.COM.
A degree of inaccuracy should be assumed.

■ *Anti-Bias Building Blocks: An Elementary Curriculum* | Unit III.153

WORLD MAP
[Student Handout]

Unit III.154 | Understanding and Appreciating Differences

FEELINGS ABOUT DIFFERENCES

Lesson 13

RATIONALE

The purpose of this activity is for students to review and understand similarities and express their thoughts and feelings about differences. Acknowledging differences, exploring feelings about being different and interacting with difference are steps toward accepting and appreciating differences. This lesson provides an opportunity for students to review aspects of identity, explore differences within the class and reflect on a time they felt different.

OBJECTIVES

- Students will review aspects of identity already covered.
- Students will explore their similarities and differences through a game.
- Students will reflect on a time they felt different through discussion and writing.

WHAT'S NEEDED

Paper and pencils or pens

PROCEDURES

1. Begin the lesson by reviewing with students the areas of identity that they have already discussed: physical appearance, opinions, skills, abilities and talents, families, communities and cultures. Explain that in today's lesson we will be exploring differences and how we feel about them.

2. Place all the chairs in a circle in the middle of the room and instruct all students to sit in a chair in the circle. Explain to students that they are going to do an activity called "The Great Wind Blows" and the goal is for them to discover some of the similarities and differences they share with each other.

3. Explain that one person will stand in the center of the circle and will call out a sentence that begins with, "A great wind blows for everyone who_____." The person in the middle finishes the

GRADE LEVEL
3–5

TIME
45 minutes

COMMON CORE STANDARDS
Reading, Writing, Speaking & Listening

STRATEGIES AND SKILLS
Review aspects of identity, The Great Wind Blows, small group discussion, writing about differences

KEY WORDS AND PHRASES
Differences
Similarities

■ *Anti-Bias Building Blocks: An Elementary Curriculum* Unit III.155

sentence with a description that fits some, many or all of the students in the circle such as "A great wind blows for everyone who wears glasses." After the sentence is called out, everyone who fits that description leaves their seat and finds another in the circle that has been vacated. The person in the center will also take one of the seats, leaving a new person without a seat. The new person without a seat will now stand in the middle and call out a new description. While in the center, students are free to think up their own descriptors to complete the phrase.

Encourage students to consider using some of the identity categories you reviewed at the beginning of the lesson.

4. Ask for a volunteer to start the activity by standing in the center of the circle. Eliminate her/his chair from the circle. If needed, provide suggested descriptors (e.g., "A great wind blows for everyone who is left-handed" or "is an only child" or "speaks Spanish"). Continue this process for ten minutes while interest remains high.

5. After the activity, engage students in a discussion by asking the following questions:

    - What were some of the similarities you discovered in the activity?
    - What were some of the differences you discovered?
    - How did you feel when differences were revealed?
    - Was it difficult or easy to be different than some of your classmates?

6. Divide students into small groups of four. Explain that they are going to talk in small groups about a time they felt different. Tell them that this is a structured and timed activity to help everyone feel safe and able to participate. Remind them of the classroom guidelines.

7. Explain that students will take turns responding to a question and each student gets to talk for one minute without interruption or cross-talk. When you call time, the next person in the group should speak. After each of the four students has spoken, you will move to the next question. Write these three questions on the board so they can refer back to them if they forget.

    - Describe a time you felt different from everyone else. What happened?
    - How did you feel when you felt different? Was it positive or negative?
    - How did the situation turn out? Did you or anyone do anything that made it worse or better?

NOTE 7

Make it clear to students that they can "pass" if they feel like they cannot emotionally handle responding to a particular question. At the same time, encourage as much participation as possible because the most learning is gained by fully participating. In dividing the groups, be aware of interpersonal dynamics between children. Because these are sensitive discussions, it is important that children feel comfortable and safe in their small groups.

8. After all four students in the group have responded to all of the questions, have students come back to the larger group and engage them in a class discussion by asking the following questions:

    - How was it to share about feeling different?
    - How was it to hear others' stories about feeling different?
    - Do differences ever cause problems? What can be done about this?
    - Would anyone like to share their story with the whole class? (Remind them to share only their story, not someone in the group's story.)

9. As a follow-up activity for homework, have students write their story as a narrative essay about their experience of feeling different. They should include everything they discussed in their small groups as well as any additional thoughts or insights they have as a result of the class discussion. They can also write it as a storyboard (graphic novel or cartoon) and include all the relevant details. These can be shared later in class.

FLIPPED CLASSROOM IDEA

Make a video of yourself reading aloud a narrative essay you wrote about a time you felt different, incorporating the three questions from #7.

EXTENSION ACTIVITIES

- Have students develop a social action project that addresses differences. Using some of the ideas and stories shared in the lesson, focus on a common theme or situation that was problematic for students around differences, one that may have led to conflict, bullying or bias. As a class, consider what you can do about it (either at the school or community level) and develop some strategies and an action plan to do something.

- Have students write a story about two people or two groups of people who had differences which caused conflict and how they overcame the differences to get along and maybe even become friends. Consider turning the stories into children's books which can be shared with younger children in a read-aloud.

- Read aloud and discuss one or more of the children's books from the list provided in this lesson.

CHILDREN'S BOOKS

One by Kathryn Otoshi

Sneetches by Dr. Seuss

Two Mrs. Gibsons by Toyomi Igus

UNIT IV. UNDERSTANDING BIAS AND DISCRIMINATION

Changing demographics, economic disparity, segregated communities and schools and societal tensions can foster climates of mistrust, fear and misunderstanding. The potential for conflict, bullying and discrimination is high when prejudice and stereotyping go unchallenged or are ignored. Biased behavior is learned, often at a young age. Left unchecked, biased attitudes can lead to biased behaviors which have the potential to escalate into discrimination, violent acts and systemic injustice.

Educators have the opportunity to affect a different trajectory, because children are not born with prejudice. However, by preschool age, they already have acquired stereotypes or negative attitudes toward those they perceive as "others" (i.e. people different than them). In an attempt to minimize the development of prejudice, sometimes well-meaning adults teach children to ignore differences (e.g., being "colorblind") and focus solely on similarities. Acknowledging and respecting differences is essential to creating a viable and inclusive school and society. By helping young children to view differences positively, and to identify prejudice and discrimination and strategies to combat them, educators can equip young people with the skills and perspective they need to face and thrive in our complex society.

GOALS FOR KINDERGARTEN THROUGH 2ND GRADE

In Unit IV, children in kindergarten through 2nd grade will understand prejudice and stereotypes. They will explore the concept of fairness and learn to make the distinction between unfair and discrimination. Students will reflect on inequality and how it manifests in our society. They will examine the distinction between name-calling/teasing and bullying. Finally, students will consider the cycle of inequality by looking at three examples from the past and present.

GOALS FOR THIRD THROUGH FIFTH GRADE

For third to fifth graders, children will examine different forms of prejudice and stereotyping. They will consider how discrimination happens by reading and analyzing real-world scenarios. Students will discover more about inequality past and present through the specific topic of ableism. They will define bullying and reflect on identity-based bullying. Finally, they will understand the systemic nature of inequality by looking at the three Is of injustice.

WHAT ARE STEREOTYPES?

Lesson 14

RATIONALE

The purpose of this activity is to give students an introduction to stereotypes and generalizations. Students need to understand what stereotypes are in order to understand how prejudice and discrimination operate in our society. This lesson provides an opportunity for students to define stereotype and generalization, explore gender stereotypes and reflect on their personal experiences with stereotypes.

OBJECTIVES

- Students will be able to define stereotype and generalization.
- Students will identify stereotypes about girls and boys.
- Students will reflect on their own experience with stereotypes.

WHAT'S NEEDED

Board/Smart board or chart paper (15–20 pieces), markers

PROCEDURES

1. Begin the lesson by asking students if they agree with the following statements. Read the statements aloud one at a time and have students put a thumbs up if they agree and a thumbs down if they do not agree:
    - All dogs are mean.
    - All cities are dirty.
    - All summers are hot.

2. Ask students, "Did we all agree with these statements? Why or why not?" Introduce students to the word "generalization" and write it on the board/smart board. Explain that a **generalization** is a statement about a group of people or things that is based on only a few people or things in that group.

    Ask students, "What generalization did I make about dogs? What generalization did I make about cities? What generalization did I

GRADE LEVEL
K–2

TIME
35 minutes

COMMON CORE STANDARDS
Reading, Speaking & Listening, Language

STRATEGIES AND SKILLS
Define terms, small group work, large group discussion

KEY WORDS AND PHRASES
Generalization
Stereotype

NOTE 3

Tell students that sharing their ideas of generalizations/stereotypes does not mean they necessarily believe them, just that they have heard these ideas. Some students may feel uncomfortable or reluctant to share stereotypes for fear that others will think they believe those stereotypes. Address that directly by explaining to students that they are sharing stereotypes they have seen or heard and that you know they do not necessarily agree with that belief about the group.

make about summers? Was I correct or incorrect?"

Ask students, "What is helpful about making generalizations? What is harmful about making generalizations?"

3. Introduce students to the word "stereotype." Ask, "Does anyone know what the word stereotype means?" Explain that a **stereotype** is the false idea that all members of a group are the same and think and behave in the same way. Explain that stereotypes are generalizations about groups of people.

   Ask students, "Can you think of any examples of stereotypes that you have heard or thought?" Provide an example if they cannot think of any such as "All old people are slow."

4. Divide students into groups of three and give each group two pieces of chart paper. When they are situated in their groups, explain that you are going to read them two questions about stereotypes of boys and girls. After you read the first question, they will respond to it by writing on the first piece of chart paper. Then you will ask the second question and they will respond to that one, using the second piece of chart paper.

   [NOTE: For kindergarteners, do this activity as a class, with you recording their responses.]

5. Read aloud the first question: "What have you heard people say about how girls should play, think and like to do and what they should wear? What colors are girls supposed to like? What toys are girls supposed to play with? What are girls supposed to like to do? What are the other stereotypes about girls?"

6. In their triads, instruct them to write and/or draw their ideas on chart paper. Give the groups 3–5 minutes to complete the task. Their lists might look something like this:

   <u>**GIRLS**</u>

   Pink

   Purple

   Dolls

   Dance

   Dress Up

   Princesses

7. When the time is up, tell students to stay in their groups. Then ask, "What have you heard people say about how boys should play, think and like to do and what they should wear? What colors are boys supposed to like? What toys are boys supposed to play with? What are boys supposed to like to do? What are the other stereotypes about boys?" Again, have the small groups create

their list (words and/or pictures) on another piece of chart paper and give them 3–5 minutes. It may look something like this:

BOYS

Blue

Action figures

Star wars

Baseball

Green

Video games

Trains

8. When the small groups are done, have each group say out loud what they came up with in their small group. It is likely that they will have some of the same responses on their chart papers so ask students not to repeat responses that have already been mentioned. As each groups reports, compile a list on the board/smart board with two columns: Girls in one column and Boys in the other column.

9. Engage students in a discussion by asking the following questions:
    - How does it make you feel when you look at these lists?
    - Do you think it's true that girls cannot like action figures and the color blue? And do you think all girls like pink and playing dress up?
    - What are some examples of boys and girls who are different than the stereotypes listed above?
    - What is the problem with stereotypes?
    - Have you heard any stereotypes about groups to which you belong? If so, what was the stereotype and how did you feel when you heard it?

10. Summarize the lesson by explaining that stereotypes are hurtful to people. Sometimes people believe the stereotypes about their own group and that can prevent them from exploring their real interests and skills and may limit their opportunities. Also, if you like a lot of different kinds of things (both "boy stuff" and "girl stuff,") and people tell you that is not okay, you might feel bad about yourself. That is why we need to do everything we can to discourage stereotypes.

EXTENSION ACTIVITIES

- Have students look at an assortment of children's books in the classroom and find examples of stereotypes in the books. You can select the books in advance to make sure they have a range of options. They can work in small groups, looking at 4–6 books per group. They should keep track of the stereotype they saw in the book and then report back their findings to the class. In the discussion, ask children how they would portray that character differently in the book to challenge the stereotype.

- Using drawing paper and pictures from magazines, newspapers and the Internet, have students create two collages. They should create one that reinforces stereotypes about boys/men and girls/women and then should create an accompanying collage that challenges and dispels those stereotypes so the pictures and words reflect girls/women and boys/men doing things that are non-stereotypical. They

CHILDREN'S BOOKS

Pirate Girl by Cornelia Funke

Phoebe and Digger by Tricia Springstubb

Little Granny Quarterback by Bill Martin

can also include original pictures of their own.

- Read aloud and discuss one or more of the children's books from the list provided in this lesson.

DISLIKE VS. PREJUDICE

Lesson 15

RATIONALE

The purpose of this activity is for students to understand the concept of prejudice. Prejudice is one of the most important concepts to understand in anti-bias education and serves as the foundation for learning about different forms of prejudice and discrimination. This lesson provides an opportunity for students to define prejudice, distinguish prejudice from dislike and share and reflect on personal experiences with prejudice.

OBJECTIVES

- Students will define prejudice.
- Students will understand the distinction between dislike and prejudice.
- Students will reflect on a personal experience with prejudice.

WHAT'S NEEDED

Board/Smart board or chart paper, construction or drawing paper, markers, crayons

Advance Preparation: Write the definition of prejudice on board/smart board or chart paper

PROCEDURES

1. Begin the lesson by reminding students of the discussion you had about likes and dislikes in Lesson 7. Remind them that there are things, activities, food, etc. they like and dislike, which are based on their experience. Ask for examples of things students do not like.

2. Explain to students that today we are going to talk about prejudice. Ask students, "Does anyone know what prejudice means?" If they have trouble coming up with the definition, have them split the word apart into "pre" (before) and "judge" (to form an opinion about something or someone). Come to a definition of **prejudice** as judging or having an idea about someone or a group of people

GRADE LEVEL
K–2

TIME
35 minutes

COMMON CORE STANDARDS
Reading, Writing, Speaking & Listening, Language

STRATEGIES AND SKILLS
Define terms, turn and talk, large group discussion, draw feelings

KEY WORDS AND PHRASES
Groups
Judge
Prejudice

before you actually know them. Prejudice is often directed toward people in a certain identity group (race, religion, gender, etc.).

3. Post the definition on chart paper or board/smart board and ask for children to read it aloud as well as describe it in their own words. Emphasize the difference between *dislike* and *prejudice*. Explain that it is okay to dislike things and people based on personal tastes, experiences or knowing them. You may not like tacos, swimming, skateboarding or a person you know who is unkind. In these cases, you are basing your dislike on experience. Prejudice is when you form a judgment about someone or something (which is usually negative but not always) before knowing them. Remind students about the previous lesson on stereotypes and explain that often, stereotypes are what lead to prejudice.

4. Read the following quote aloud and explain that it was said by E.B. White, author of *Charlotte's Web* and *Stuart Little*. Ask what the quote means to them.

   "Prejudice is a great time saver. You can form opinions without having to get the facts."

5. Remind students about the "Groups I Belong To" activity where they created a pie chart about different groups they belong to like grade/age, race, culture, gender, religion, family, language spoken, etc. Direct students' attention to the second part of the definition of prejudice. Explain that often (but not always), prejudice is directed toward people of a certain group. As an example, explain that someone could have prejudice about girls and women, thinking they are not strong or fast enough to play sports.

6. Share with students a story about prejudice you have experienced or know about, or share the story below to illustrate what prejudice is:

   Grace is Chinese American. Both of her parents were born in the United States but her grandparents and some other family members still live in China. When she came to school at the beginning of the year, the children did not know anyone who looked like her or who had family members living in another country. They thought she must eat strange food and not speak English. They did not want to play with her and just didn't like her.

7. Engage students in a discussion by asking the following questions. If you provided your own story, be sure to adapt these questions accordingly.

   • How did you feel while listening to the story about Grace?
   • How did the other students in Grace's class feel about her? How do you know?

FLIPPED CLASSROOM IDEA

Make a short video of you introducing the definition of prejudice and talking about an experience you have had with prejudice. Explain what happened, what was said and done, how you felt and how you responded. Or, you can share the story of Grace that is provided.

- In what ways does this story show prejudice?
- Why do you think people are prejudiced?
- How do you feel hearing different stories about prejudice?

8. Distribute construction/drawing paper and markers and crayons. Reflecting on the last question, ask students again, "How does it feel when you hear about prejudice?" Have them draw a picture that illustrates those feelings. At the end of the lesson, have them all hold them up their pictures. End the lesson by explaining that prejudice is harmful and often hurts people's feelings and that later on we will discuss what to do about it.

EXTENSION ACTIVITIES

- Have students write and illustrate a story about prejudice. It can be based on a real life situation (realistic fiction) or completely made up, but it cannot include names of people in their classroom nor should it have details that make it obvious who the story is about.

- Have parents, older siblings, family members or family friends come in and talk about experiences they have had with prejudice in their lives. Be sure you have a range of experiences and that at least some of them have a positive outcome or some way in which the prejudice was addressed and overcome. In advance, have students come up with interview questions that they will ask of their special guest(s).

- Read aloud and discuss one or more of the children's books from the list provided in this lesson.

CHILDREN'S BOOKS

Sneetches and Other Stories by Dr. Seuss

The Berenstain Bears' New Neighbors by Stan Berenstain

Arnie and the New Kid by Nancy Carlson

Yoko by Rosemary Wells

Jacob's New Dress by Sarah Hoffman

UNFAIRNESS AND DISCRIMINATION

RATIONALE

The purpose of this activity is for students to reflect on their experiences of unfairness in order to help them understand the concept of discrimination. This lesson will provide an opportunity for students to define discrimination, reflect on unfairness and personal experiences with discrimination and participate in an activity to help them articulate the difference between prejudice and discrimination.

OBJECTIVES

- Students will define discrimination.
- Students will reflect on situations in which they have experienced unfairness and discrimination.
- Students will understand the distinction between prejudice and discrimination.

WHAT'S NEEDED

Create four signs with the words PREJUDICE, DISCRIMINATION, BOTH and NOT SURE on separate signs.

PROCEDURES

1. Begin the lesson by telling students that you are going to be doing something new today. Explain that you are going to divide the students up by the first letter of their names. All of the students with first names beginning with A–L will sit in the front (or one side, depending on your room set-up) of the classroom—they are Group A. All students whose first names begin with M–Z will sit in the back—they are Group B.

2. Instruct students to switch their seats now. You may need to provide a breakdown of Group A and Group B as follows:

    Group A: Students whose first names begin with A, B, C, D, E, F, G, H, I, J, K, L

    Group B: Students whose first names begin with M, N, O, P, Q, R, S, T, U, V, W, X, Y, Z

Lesson 16

GRADE LEVEL
K–2

TIME
35 minutes

COMMON CORE STANDARDS
Reading, Writing, Speaking & Listening, Language

STRATEGIES AND SKILLS
Define terms, share personal experiences, large group discussion, my opinion is, compare unfair to discrimination

KEY WORDS AND PHRASES
Discrimination
Unfair

■ *Anti-Bias Building Blocks: An Elementary Curriculum*

NOTE 3

This is not a simulation activity. You will simply be verbally stating these rules and explaining them but not actually implementing them. Therefore, Group A will not be receiving these privileges in reality.

3. Explain that these are the new "classroom rules" for the groups.

    a. Group A will be allowed outside for recess; Group B will have to stay in the cafeteria.

    b. Group A will be able to use the bathrooms first; Group B will have to wait until all Group A students have gone.

    c. Group A will have an ice cream party every Friday; Group B will not participate.

4. Give students a few minutes to think about this. Then ask the following questions:

    - How do you feel about the new rules?
    - What did I do?
    - How was I able to do that? (Draw out from students that you have the power/authority to change the rules since you are the teacher and have power.)
    - Can you do anything about it? If so, what can you do?

    Students will most likely say that these new rules are unfair and there is not much they can do about it since you are the teacher and they are the students. They also may suggest that they can tell their parents, complain to the principal or together decide to confront the teacher and "protest" in some way. Explain that what you did was discriminate by using your power and authority as the teacher to change the rules. You discriminated based on the first names of the students, something for which they have no control.

5. Write the word discrimination on the board and ask students, "What does the word discrimination mean?" Come to a definition of **discrimination** as unfair treatment of one person or group of people because of the person or group's identity (e.g., race, gender, ability, religion, culture, etc.). Discrimination is an action that can come from prejudice.

6. Explain that there is a difference between something being unfair and discrimination. For example, if someone cuts in line at the water fountain, that can feel unfair. However, it would be considered discrimination if there was a rule that the girls should always be first in line for the water fountain and all the boys had to stand behind them. Also, make the connection and distinction between prejudice and discrimination. Explain that prejudice is thoughts, feelings, ideas and attitudes (i.e. what is in your head) and discrimination is actions, rules and laws that treat people unfairly.

7. Ask students, "What are some examples of things that are unfair?" (See chart below). If they share an example of discrimination rather than something that is unfair, point that out.

Then say, "For these examples of unfairness, let us think of what might be discrimination in a similar situation." It might look like this:

Unfair	Discrimination
Someone cut me on the lunch line.	White students are allowed to be first on the lunch line.
My cousin who is the same age gets no homework.	Students who do not speak English well have more homework.
I did not get to play hopscotch at recess.	Kids who were playing hopscotch said "No boys allowed."
My friend gets to ride her bike to school and I do not.	Only kids who get good grades can ride bikes to school.

8. Explain to students that the difference between the situations of unfair and discrimination is that for discrimination, someone in authority and with power sets up the rule and the rule itself is unfair. Make sure students understand the distinction, which may be challenging for young children to completely understand. For example, say something like: "The first example where a student cut you in the lunch line is between you and that other person. There was no rule that s/he was allowed to do that. With the discrimination example, someone or the school made the rule that white students are allowed to be first on the lunch line." Share additional examples if necessary. Ask students, "Based on these examples, what is the difference between unfairness and discrimination?" Elicit responses and point out that discrimination almost always includes a rule or a person who has power and control over a situation and can treat that person or group unfairly.

9. Ask if anyone can share an example of discrimination that they heard about or faced themselves. If they cannot think of any, you might share an example from your life to get them thinking. Remind students about what prejudice is. Prejudice is judging or having an idea about someone or a group of people before you actually know them. Prejudice is often directed toward people in a certain identity group (race, religion, gender, etc.). Explain that the difference between prejudice and discrimination is that prejudice is an opinion or attitude and discrimination is when someone or a group (like a school or workplace) acts on those opinions.

10. Explain to students that you are going to make some statements and they will decide whether the statement reflects prejudice, discrimination, both or they are not sure. Post signs around the room that say: PREJUDICE, DISCRIMINATION, BOTH and NOT SURE. Read the words aloud and remind students about the difference between prejudice and discrimination.

11. Read the situation statements below aloud. After each statement is read, have students move to the part of the room with the sign that expresses what they think about the statement. After everyone has chosen their spot, have the students in each group talk with each other about why they have chosen the spot.

    [**NOTE:** The situations below are very specific. If they resonate too closely with children's real-life experience with the potential for strong feelings or singling students out, you may substitute the situations for new ones. However, using examples that students can relate to will make the process easier for them.]

    Situations:
    a. Theo's family is so weird. His father is black and his mother is white."
    b. "Josh can't play Four Square with us because he only speaks Spanish."
    c. "Imami is not allowed to play in the baseball league. Baseball is for boys only—she can play softball."

d. "That food Layla brings for lunch everyday looks disgusting. Is she Muslim?"

12. Have students come back to the large group and engage them in a discussion by asking the following questions:

    - Was it easy or difficult to decide where to stand?

    - If you chose "not sure," did you get some more information that made you sure?

    - How would you describe the difference between prejudice and discrimination?

EXTENSION ACTIVITIES

- Create a class bulletin board entitled "Discrimination in the News." Have students work with their parents/caregivers to use newspaper and magazine headlines or online news articles to find examples of contemporary discrimination. Provide opportunities for students to share their thoughts and feelings about the articles they found and discuss ways that discrimination hurts society as a whole.

- Have students brainstorm what aspects of discrimination they see in their school or community. Think together about what are the most problematic situations and come up a plan to do something about it as a class.

- Read aloud and discuss one or more of the children's books from the list provided in this lesson.

CHILDREN'S BOOKS

White Water by Michael S. Bandy

Grace for President by Kelly DiPucchio

Courtney's Birthday Party by Loretta Long

EQUALITY AND INEQUALITY

Lesson 17

RATIONALE

The purpose of this activity is for students to understand inequality and how it reveals itself in our society. The concept of inequality is broader than personal discrimination and includes how privileges and opportunities are afforded to some but not all. This lesson provides an opportunity for students to review the concepts of prejudice and discrimination, consider what inequality is and provide examples and reflect on what can be done about inequality in our society.

OBJECTIVES

- Students will review the definitions for prejudice and discrimination and understand how they are different.
- Students will be able to define equality and inequality and provide examples of inequality.
- Students will reflect on situations of inequality and possible solutions for addressing them.

WHAT'S NEEDED

Drawing paper (at least two sheets for each student), markers and crayons

PROCEDURES

1. Begin the lesson by reading a children's book that illustrates an example or situation of inequality such as one of the books recommended in this lesson.
2. If that is not possible or in addition, tell students to pretend that one child in the class has a broken arm, another student has a cut on her finger and another child banged his knee and it is swollen. Ask students, "If I give a band-aid to each of these students, will it fix their problems? Why or why not?" Elicit from students that people do not always need the same thing. Each of these students needs something but they need something different. Explain that in our society, people should be treated with fairness which does not necessarily mean that everyone gets or needs the exact same

GRADE LEVEL
K–2

TIME
35 minutes

COMMON CORE STANDARDS
Reading, Writing, Speaking & Listening, Language

STRATEGIES AND SKILLS
Define terms, drawing, class presentation

KEY WORDS AND PHRASES
Benefit
Equality
Inequality
Opportunity

CHILDREN'S BOOKS

A Picture Book of Jackie Robinson by David A. Adler

If a Bus Could Talk by Faith Ringgold

Rainbow Fish and the Big Blue Whale by Marcus Pfister

Let's Hear It For Almigal by Wendy Kupfer

Grace for President by Kelly DiPucchio

■ Anti-Bias Building Blocks: An Elementary Curriculum

NOTE

There is a difference between the terms "equity" and "equality." The example above about the child needing a hearing aid speaks more to equity than equality. However, given the age level of the students, making that distinction is complicated and students will not be able to understand it. For the purposes of this curriculum, the focus should be on equality.

Equality is having the same access and opportunities. In order to maximize opportunities for people who have been the targets of discrimination and injustice in our society-both historic and present-day—additional resources may be needed. Equity includes the resources and support necessary so that people can truly take advantage of that equality. Example: Equality ensures that all children in the United States have equal access to public schooling. Equity works to ensure that students' needs are met when they are in school. Programs such as special education and Title I provide the additional resources students need so that school is equitable.

thing. Explain that one way of being fair is to provide people with equal rights, which we will discuss in this lesson.

3. Ask students, "What does equality mean?" Define **equality** as having the same or similar rights and opportunities as others.

   Ask students, "If there was a student in our class who had a hearing impairment (i.e. partial or full inability to hear) what would that student need?" Explain that she may need a hearing aid and she may need a personal aide in the class who would help her with her work. Is it fair that she gets these things but no one else does? Reinforce the idea that equality provides people with the same opportunities. In this situation, the student deserves the same opportunity to get an education as everyone else and needs a hearing aid to do so.

4. Remind students of the definitions for prejudice and discrimination. Review the distinction by saying that prejudice is thoughts, feelings, ideas and attitudes (i.e. what is in your head) and discrimination is actions, rules and laws that treat people unfairly.

5. Ask students, "What does inequality mean?" Explain that **inequality** is an unjust situation or condition when some people have more rights or better opportunities than other people. Ask students, "Can you think of any examples of inequality?" As students share their examples, write them on the board or smart board. If you read aloud a children's story about inequality at the beginning of the lesson, you can refer to that story. Remind students about what you discussed in the previous lesson, Lesson 16, "Unfairness and Discrimination," and some of the examples shared in the lesson. You can also share other examples such as the following:

   - Some children do not have as many clothes or toys as others because their families are poor (have a lot less money).
   - Overall, men make more money at their jobs than women for doing the same job.
   - Some people who use a wheelchair may not be able to go to a restaurant or store because there is no ramp.
   - In some places, men are not allowed to marry other men and women are not allowed to married other women.
   - Some people do not have homes so they have to live in a shelter.

6. Read aloud all of the examples shared. Explain that each student will choose one of the examples of inequality to think about and develop further. Give students a minute to review the list and make their selection. Write students names next to the statement they selected.

7. Distribute two pieces of construction paper and markers/crayons to the students. Explain to students that they are going to make two pictures: one about inequality and one about an idea they might have for solving it. First, have students write their inequality statement at the top of the first piece of construction paper (for younger students, help them or write it for them). On the second piece of construction paper, have students write: MY SOLUTION (or help them to do so). Have students then draw a picture for each of the papers, both the problem and the solution.

   Share an example such as: "People in wheelchairs can't ride the bus" and say the solution might be: "The bus company should make a ramp on the bus." You might want to create drawings in advance so you can give them an example of how the two drawings go together. Give students 10–15 minutes to work on their pictures. If students have difficulty coming up with solutions, they also can work in pairs.

8. After students have completed their drawings, have them present their statements and drawings to the class. Consider compiling all of the pictures into a class book or take photos of the children with their drawings and make an online photo exhibit.

9. Engage students in a discussion by asking the following questions:
   - What is inequality?
   - How did you feel when you learned about the different kinds of inequality?
   - What kind of solutions did you come up with?
   - What can we do about inequality?

EXTENSION ACTIVITIES

- Have students write persuasive letters that challenge one of the examples of inequality they discussed in class. They should first identify the problem, then consider different solutions to addressing the problem and then think about who the letter should be written to, which could be a public official (mayor, city council, Senator, etc.) or a company that makes a particular product. With younger students, this letter can be written together as a class project.

- As a class, identify examples of inequality (building on the list made during the lesson) and explore how those problems can be addressed. Brainstorm many different ways to work on them, investigate local efforts in your neighborhood or community for the students to learn more about the issues and what is currently being done about them and if appropriate, get them involved in a community service project that addresses the issue.

- Read aloud and discuss one or more of the children's books from the list provided in this lesson.

TEASING, NAME-CALLING AND BULLYING

Lesson 18

RATIONALE

The purpose of this activity is to provide an introduction to bullying and explore the differences between bullying and name-calling and teasing. This lesson provides an opportunity for students to define teasing, name-calling and bullying, understand the similarities and differences between them and reflect on their feelings and experiences with mean behavior.

OBJECTIVES

- Students will define teasing and name calling.
- Students will identify and reflect on their feelings when they have been the target of mean behavior and/or bullying.
- Students will define bullying and make the distinction between teasing, name-calling and bullying.

WHAT'S NEEDED

Index cards or sheets of papers (three per student), colored markers or crayons, puppets (at least three), board or smart board

PROCEDURES

1. Begin the activity by distributing three index cards to each student. Have them draw a different face on each of the cards as follows:

   Card 1: smiley (happy) face ☺

   Card 2: frowny (sad) face ☹

   Card 3: angry face 😠

2. Explain to students what each of the faces means and remind them about what each of the feelings means. Ask students, "What does it mean to feel happy? What does it mean to feel sad? How about angry?" Explain to the students that you are going to make several statements. After each statement, you will ask, "How do you feel?" At that point, they will choose one of their cards based

GRADE LEVEL
K–2

TIME
35 minutes

COMMON CORE STANDARDS
Reading, Writing, Speaking & Listening

STRATEGIES AND SKILLS
Connect feelings with situations, define terms, turn and talk, large group discussion, puppet role plays

KEY WORDS AND PHRASES
Bullying
Bystander
Mean
Name-calling
Teasing

■ Anti-Bias Building Blocks: An Elementary Curriculum

on how they feel. Tell students not to look at anyone else's card before choosing theirs. After you make the statement and ask "How do you feel?" they should hold up the appropriate card.

- Someone grabs my pencil.
- Someone smiles at me.
- Someone shoves me out of the way when we are on line.
- Someone makes a mean face at me.
- Someone laughs at my joke.
- A group of kids don't let me play with them at recess.
- Someone calls me a name.
- Someone makes fun of me and then says, "Kidding!"
- Someone calls my sister a bad name.
- My friend didn't invite me to her party.

3. After the activity, engage students in a class discussion by asking the following questions:
   - How did you figure out which feeling word to choose?
   - Did any of these statements I read ever happen to you?
   - What kinds of behavior were included in the statements I read?

4. Ask students, "What is teasing?" Come to a definition of **teasing** as laugh at and put someone down in a way that is either friendly and playful or mean and unkind. Write the definition on board/smart board Explain to students that sometimes we tease each other and it creates a positive feeling but often we get teased and we do not like it. Ask, "Do kids in our school get teased in a negative way or picked on?" Ask students if they can share an example without giving names of the students involved.

   Next, ask students, "What is name-calling?" Come to a definition of **name-calling** as using words to hurt or be mean to someone or a group. Write the definition on board/smart board. Ask, "Do kids in our school get called names?" Can you think of an example (again, not using specific names)?

5. Have students turn and talk with a person sitting next to them and share about a time they were teased or called a name. If they cannot think of a personal example, they can share one that they observed. They will take one minute per person and then switch when you say "switch." They can share: What happened? How did you feel? Did you do or say anything?

6. Next, have a discussion with students in which you make the distinction between bullying and name-calling/teasing. The discussion about bullying will not be in-depth but will serve to highlight the differences.

7. Ask students, "Does anyone know what the word bullying means? What is bullying?"

   Define **bullying** as when a person or a group behaves in ways—on purpose and over and over—that make another person feel hurt, afraid or embarrassed. Write the definition on board/smart board. Ask students, "How is bullying similar to name-calling and teasing?" Record responses on board/smart board. Then ask, "How is it different?" Make a chart that may look like the following:

   <u>Similar</u>
   Makes you feel bad
   Directed at you or identity group
   Is mean and hurtful

   <u>Different</u>
   Happens over and over again
   Makes you feel bad on purpose
   Is mean and hurtful

Unit IV.178 | Understanding Bias and Discrimination

8. Explain to students that many times when someone gets bullied, they are being called names. Also, sometimes teasing and name-calling can lead to bullying. Excluding people (i.e. leaving someone out on purpose to make them feel bad) is also a form of bullying.

9. Using puppets, create a scenario when one puppet is teasing another one about something, using name-calling. Ask the students to name the puppets, not using any names of people in your class or siblings, etc. Conduct the role play situation for a few minutes, then stop the action and ask, "Why do you think Puppet B is teasing Puppet A? How do you think Puppet A feels? What can Puppet A do to get Puppet B to stop?" Using some of their ideas, continue the role play having Puppet A stop the teasing by using their suggestions. You can also include a third puppet (Puppet C) to act as a bystander, asking students for ideas as to what Puppet C can do to help in the situation.

EXTENSION ACTIVITIES

- Have students write realistic fiction stories about name-calling, teasing and/or bullying. Remind them not to use names of real people nor specific details that would reveal a real-life situation that could be uncomfortable or embarrassing for the involved students. Their story should include descriptions of the characters, the situation as well as dialogue.

- Give students specific situations that include name-calling, teasing and bullying. Using puppets as you did during the lesson, have them act out a role play using that situation. They can brainstorm possible solutions or could use the puppets to come up with realistic solutions. Students can also create their own specific situations and act those out with the puppets as well.

- Read aloud and discuss one or more of the children's books from the list provided in this lesson.

NOTE 9

After discussing issues like bias and bullying, it is natural and understandable for young children to wonder if they can do anything about it. It is important to help them understand that people can and have addressed and confronted bias and bullying. The next unit of this curriculum will focus on ways that individuals, groups and society as a whole can confront and overcome bias and bullying.

CHILDREN'S BOOKS

Each Kindness by Jacqueline Woodson

Jacob's New Dress by Sarah and Ian Hoffman

The Name Jar by Yangsook Choi

Harry and Willy and Carrothead by Judith Caseley

CYCLE OF INEQUALITY

Lesson 19

RATIONALE

The purpose of this activity is for students to understand the cycle of inequality and how it has changed over time. This lesson provides an opportunity for students to understand how stereotypes, prejudice and discrimination work together to create inequality, will learn about past and present issues of the systems of inequality and will reflect on what they can do about it.

OBJECTIVES

- Students will understand about the interconnectedness of stereotypes, prejudice, discrimination and inequality.
- Students will learn about three forms of inequality from the past and present (ableism, racism, weightism).
- Students will reflect on what they can do about inequality.

WHAT'S NEEDED

Board/Smart board, markers

PROCEDURES

1. Review definitions of stereotype, prejudice, discrimination and inequality. Explain the cycle of inequality and how stereotyping and prejudice lead to discrimination which leads to a society of inequality.

2. Ask students, "Do you have the right to be treated fairly in this classroom?" Elicit from the students that they have the right to feel safe, treated with respect and treated fairly. They have the right to have access to the same books, bathroom when they need it, recess time, lunch, etc. Ask, "How would you feel if I favored one group over another? What would you do about it?"

3. Explain that in our country's history (going back many years as well as present day), there have been many examples of inequality, which includes prejudice, discrimination and unfairly treating one group better than another.

GRADE LEVEL
K–2

TIME
35 minutes

COMMON CORE STANDARDS
Reading, Writing, Speaking & Listening, Language

STRATEGIES AND SKILLS
Review terms, history connects to present, writing stories, class presentation

KEY WORDS AND PHRASES
Ableism
Racism
Segregation
Weightism

■ *Anti-Bias Building Blocks: An Elementary Curriculum*   Unit IV.181

NOTE 3

In sharing the provided examples with children, if you think it would be easier for them to understand by simplifying the examples, choose only one of the examples (ableism, racism or weightism) to share or simplify the paragraph on each by only reading part of it. Keep in mind, however, that the advantage of giving a variety of examples is that it conveys the systemic nature on inequality and how people face inequality in a variety of different ways.

Provide three examples of inequality as outlined below. If possible read children's books about each of the topics. Suggestions include: *Arnie and the New Kid* by Nancy Carlson (ableism), *Back of the Bus* by Aaron Reynolds (racism) and *Alley Oops* by Janice Levy (weightism).

Examples of Inequality

Ableism: Before the 1970s, people with disabilities were not able to use public transportation because the trains and buses did not have ramps or elevators like they do today. They were not able to use public telephones and bathrooms. They were often discriminated against when they tried to get a job because of their disabilities. In schools, they did not have services for special needs so children with disabilities had to go to separate schools. In addition, people with disabilities could not get around easily because there were no sidewalk and curb ramps and deaf (hearing impaired) and blind (visually impaired) people did not have technology. People with disabilities were rarely seen on television or movies.

Racial Segregation (Racism): Starting about 100 years ago and continuing until the 1960s, there were laws in the southern states where black people could not eat in the same restaurants, drink out of the same water fountains, watch movies in the same theaters, play in the same parks and go to the same schools as white people. In these cases, the white-only places were usually better quality than the black only (show segregated water fountains as an example). In addition, black people had to sit in the back of buses and streetcars and give up their seats to whites when asked to do so. Signs reading "Colored Only" to mean black people and "White Only" could be seen everywhere.

Weightism: Weightism, which is prejudice and discrimination against people who are obese or overweight, occurs in many different ways. There are a several negative stereotypes of people who are overweight. Children who are overweight get teased and bullied in school more than other children and as a result, these children miss more school. When they are adults, overweight people earn less than non-overweight people in the same jobs, get fewer promotions and can be fired or suspended because of their weight even if they do a good job. Overweight people also reported in a study getting put down by co-workers.

4. Engage students in a discussion by asking the following questions:
    - What do these three examples have in common?
    - How are they different?
    - Do you think things are different today? How so?
    - Do you think there is still inequality for black people and people with disabilities? How so?
    - Can you think of other examples of inequality?

5. Following up on the last question, ask students again, "Can you think of any other examples of inequality?" Record their responses on the board/smart board and ask for examples (if they know of any) where a person or group of people did something about the inequality. Keep this section brief as this concept will be explored in great depth in the next unit.

EXTENSION ACTIVITIES

- Have students identify other examples of inequality in our society and conduct research that explores how the form of inequality has changed over time. They can investigate what happened in the past, how people organized to changes laws and attitudes, what legislation may have been passed to address the inequality and the extent to which things have changed.

- Have students create a class video about how they feel about inequality. First, have each student consider a specific element of inequality that they feel passionate about and if possible, write some words that express what it is, how they feel about it and what can be done. Students can then use what they thought about or wrote about to each make a statement for the creation of a group video, which can be shared with parents, other classes, etc

- Read aloud and discuss one or more of the children's books from the list provided in this lesson.

CHILDREN'S BOOKS

The Soccer Fence by Phil Bildner

Back of the Bus by Aaron Reynolds

Miss Moore Thought Otherwise by Jan Pinborough

PERSPECTIVE AND STEREOTYPES

RATIONALE

The purpose of this activity is for students to understand stereotypes and how they are damaging both to the individual and to society at large. Understanding how stereotypes can lead to prejudice and discrimination is an important part of children's ability to challenge bias. This lesson provides an opportunity to define stereotype, name and reflect on stereotypes they have heard and observed and analyze specific stereotypes.

OBJECTIVES

- Students will be able to define stereotype.
- Students will identify and reflect on stereotypes they have heard about themselves or others.
- Students will examine specific stereotypes, where they come from and information that dispels the stereotype.

WHAT'S NEEDED

Handouts and Resources: Photos #1–3 and *Stereotypes* (one of each for each student)

Other Material: Chart paper or board/smart board, markers, LCD projector

Advance Preparation: Prepare *Photos #1–3* to be displayed or projected so every student can see them

PROCEDURES

1. Begin the lesson by having students sit in a circle. Have them close their eyes and picture two girls, ages 7 and 10, running from a school. The older girl is running very fast and the distance between the two girls begins to widen. The older girl stops, turns around and runs back to grab the seven year old and says, "Hurry up, we have to go!"

2. Give students a few minutes to make up a story in their mind based on the information they just heard as to why the girls were

---

Lesson 14

GRADE LEVEL
3–5

TIME
45 minutes

COMMON CORE STANDARDS
Reading, Writing, Speaking & Listening, Language

STRATEGIES AND SKILLS
Large group discussion, small group work, turn and talk

KEY WORDS AND PHRASES
Counteract
Misinformation
Perspective
Stereotype

running and what happened. Have a few students share their stories out loud. Engage the students in a discussion asking the following questions:

- Are the made-up stories similar in any way? If so, how?
- How are all the stories different from each other?
- Why do you think all of the stories were not exactly the same?
- What influenced the story you made up?

3. Write the word "perspective" on chart paper/smart board. Explain that **perspective** is the way someone sees things and it is often based on what a person expects to happen in a given situation. Ask students, "What things might influence a person's perspective?" Record their responses, which may look like this (add those on the list below that students do not share):

- Personal Experiences
- Family
- Culture
- Media (TV, movies, video games, etc.)
- Teachers and Other Adults
- Commercials and Advertising
- Online Community
- Religion
- Friends
- Books

4. Ask students, "What are some things that people might see differently or have a different perspective about? Based on the list you developed, what are some reasons why people might look at the same thing or hear the same thing but "see" it differently?"

5. Explain that today we are going to discuss stereotypes, which are also related to perspective. Many of the same things and experiences that influence perspective also influence stereotypes.

    Ask students, "What are stereotypes?" Come to a definition of **stereotypes** as the false idea that all members of a group are the same and think and behave in the same way. Share an example of a stereotype such as: "Girls hate sports." Ask students the following questions:

    - Do you think that all girls hate sports?
    - Have you ever known a girl who liked or loved sports?
    - How does this statement make girls feel? How does it make boys feel?
    - What is the problem with stereotypes?
    - How can a stereotype that seems positive like "Boys are good at math" be harmful?

6. Have students think about some of the groups to which they belong: cultural groups, gender, race, age, ethnicity, religion,

---

NOTE 5

Explain to students that while all stereotypes are hurtful and often lead to prejudice and discrimination, some stereotypes are particularly dangerous because they express very negative and destructive things about a group of people. Depending on the maturity level of students, discuss how stereotypes that link groups of people with characteristics like "violent," "lazy," "greedy," among others, perpetuate hateful attitudes and hurt individuals and entire communities. Also, help students think about why and how people who are the targets of such stereotypes may begin to believe them to be true.

country of origin, family, etc. 📷 Ask students to turn and talk with someone sitting near them. With their partner, they will take turns responding to the questions below. Write the questions on board/smart board so everyone can see them while they are talking with their partners:

- Have you ever heard a stereotype about a group to which you belong?
- If so, what was the stereotype?
- How did you feel when you heard this stereotype?

Each person will have one minute to talk, then you will say "switch" and the other person will now share for one minute.

7. Have students come back to the large group and ask if anyone would like to share with the class what they shared with their partner. Then ask, "Where do you think the stereotype came from?" Make a list and point out to students the similarities between this list and the list generated about perspective (above). Also, remind students that prejudice often comes from stereotypes and generalizations about people.

8. Explain to students that they will now have an opportunity to explore some specific stereotypes. Tell them that you are going to share a few pictures of people with them. As they look at the pictures, they will write on a piece of paper descriptive words that come to mind when they see the picture, including stereotypes they or others have about that person. They should not worry about the words being a stereotype because they will write privately and explain that because stereotyping often comes from different aspects of society (media, parents, etc.), it is natural that we will have some stereotypes in our mind.

9. Show Photo #1 and say, "Everyone take a few minutes to write any words, phrases or feelings you have when seeing this person. Include stereotypes you or others may have about this person."

   Repeat this process with Photo #2 and #3.

10. When finished with all three pictures, distribute the *Stereotypes* handout and complete one together as a group. It may look something like this:

Stereotype	Where Stereotype Comes From	What Counteracts Stereotype
Old people are forgetful.	Movies	I have a neighbor who still works.
Old people hate technology.	TV shows	My Grandma has an iPhone.

FLIPPED CLASSROOM IDEA

Make a short video of yourself talking with another person (to model "turn and talk") about a stereotype you have heard about a group to which you belong. Share what the stereotype is and how you felt when you heard it.

11. After working on this as a large group, have students complete the worksheet for at least one of the other groups for which they saw the picture and wrote words. After completing, engage students in a discussion by asking the following questions:

- Was it easy or difficult to come up with stereotypes?
- Do we have a lot of stereotypes? Why or why not?
- How are stereotypes formed? Where do the ideas come from?
- What kinds of things counteracted or challenged stereotypes?
- How are stereotypes harmful?
- What can we do about stereotypes?

EXTENSION ACTIVITIES

- Have students keep a log of stereotypes they see in the media, including billboards, websites, video games, commercials, movies, television, comic books, etc. They will keep the log over several days (or a week) using the *Media Stereotypes Log*. At the end of the designated time period, students will share their observations. As a follow up activity, students can write persuasive letters to some of the companies behind the stereotyping urging them to make changes.

- Have students write their own stories or children's books that challenge stereotypes. First they should decide on the stereotype they want to address, which could be one of the stereotypes discussed in the lesson or another one. They should think through how they are going to portray the person or people in terms of what they say, do and the pictures they use to illustrate the book. Then they will write and illustrate the book and conference with others to get feedback on the book.

- Read aloud and discuss one or more of the children's books from the list provided in this lesson.

CHILDREN'S BOOKS

Grace for President by Kelly S. DiPucchio

10,000 Dresses by Marcus Ewert

Amazing Grace by Mary Hoffman

PHOTO #1: ELDERLY PERSON
[Student Handout]

Anti-Bias Building Blocks: An Elementary Curriculum | Unit IV.189

PHOTO #2: BOY WEARING A YARMULKE

[Student Handout]

Unit IV.190 | Understanding Bias and Discrimination

PHOTO #3: PERSON IN A WHEELCHAIR
[Student Handout]

Anti-Bias Building Blocks: An Elementary Curriculum

STEREOTYPES

[Student Handout]

The identity group is: _____

Stereotype	Where Stereotype Comes From	What Counteracts Stereotype

MEDIA STEREOTYPES LOG

[Student Handout]

Date	Name of Media (TV program, billboard location, movie, etc.)	What did you see? What was the stereotype?	What group was the stereotype about?

Anti-Bias Building Blocks: An Elementary Curriculum | Unit IV.193

FORMS OF PREJUDICE

Lesson 15

RATIONALE

The purpose of this activity is for students to understand what prejudice is, the different forms it takes and how it manifests itself in daily interactions. Understanding prejudice is the foundation for anti-bias instruction. This lesson provides an opportunity for students to define and understand prejudice, reflect on their own experiences with prejudice, identify different forms and manifestations of prejudice and analyze scenarios of prejudice.

OBJECTIVES

- Students will define prejudice and identify ways prejudice is displayed.
- Students will reflect on their own experiences of prejudice.
- Students will understand the different forms of prejudice and analyze and discuss scenarios.

WHAT'S NEEDED

Handouts and Resources: Definitions: Forms of Prejudice and Discrimination and *Prejudice Scenarios* (one of each for each student)

Other Material: Paper and pens or pencils

PROCEDURES

1. Begin the lesson by asking students, "What is prejudice?" If need be, have students break the word into two words "pre" and "judge" and see whether they can determine the meaning. Come to a definition of **prejudice** as judging or having an idea about someone or a group of people before you actually know them. Prejudice is often directed toward people in a certain identity group (race, religion, gender, etc.).

2. Have students write down the definition and ask if they have any questions. Remind them about what stereotypes are (from the previous lesson and ask, "What is the connection between stereotypes and prejudice?" If they do not have a response,

GRADE LEVEL
3–5

TIME
50 minutes

COMMON CORE STANDARDS
Reading, Writing, Speaking & Listening, Language

STRATEGIES AND SKILLS
Brainstorm, semantic web, define terms, small group work

KEY WORDS AND PHRASES
Ableism
Ageism
Anti-Semitism
Attitude
Bullying
Classism
Discrimination
Homophobia
Islamophobia
Prejudice
Racism
Sexism
Slurs
Weightism

■ *Anti-Bias Building Blocks: An Elementary Curriculum* Unit IV.195

explain that often stereotypes about people lead to prejudice.

3. Explain to students that there is a difference between prejudice, which is an attitude (way of thinking) and discrimination, which is an action. Discrimination will be discussed later in this unit. Provide an example by explaining the difference between prejudice ("I don't like girls because they're not good at sports") and discrimination ("Girls aren't allowed to play basketball with us at recess.").

4. With students, create a semantic web about the word prejudice by asking, "What words, phrases and feelings come to mind when you hear the word prejudice?"

5. Engage students in a discussion by asking the following questions:
   - When you look at the words on the web, how do you feel?
   - Do you notice any patterns?
   - How do you feel about prejudice?
   - What do you want to know more about prejudice?

6. Explain to students that there are different ways that people show prejudice. In general, prejudice is thoughts, feelings, attitudes and opinions. Often prejudice is based on stereotypes people have about groups of people.

7. Have students reflect on a time they have either (1) experienced prejudice directed at them, (2) observed prejudice or (3) had feelings of prejudice toward someone or a group. Have them write a quick paragraph (3–5 sentences) explaining what happened during the incident and how they felt. After completing their writing, ask if any student would like to share what they wrote with the class.

8. Distribute the *Definitions: Forms of Prejudice and Discrimination* handout to each student. Using the handout, read each term and share an example for each. Explain again that they will be discussing discrimination (actions) in the next lesson. Tell students that they are going to discuss different kinds of prejudice including:
   - Ableism
   - Ageism
   - Anti-Semitism
   - Classism
   - Homophobia
   - Islamophobia
   - Racism
   - Sexism
   - Weightism

9. After defining and giving an example for each form of prejudice/discrimination, go through the list again and this time, ask students to stand up (or raise their hand) if they have ever seen,

NOTE 8

In some cases and depending on your students, you will likely need to explain what the identity is (e.g., what it means to be Jewish, gay, lesbian, Muslim, etc.) in order for them to understand the form of prejudice/discrimination.

FLIPPED CLASSROOM IDEA

Make a short video of yourself talking about the different forms of prejudice outlined. Go through each word, spell it, define it and give an example.

heard or been the target of each of the forms. For example, "If you have seen or been the target of ableism, stand up" and so on through the list.

10. Distribute the *Prejudice Scenarios* handout to each student. Divide students into groups of four. Working together, have students read each of the scenarios, discuss them in more detail and complete the form by naming the form of prejudice, reflecting on how the person felt and considering what you can say to counteract the prejudice. After students are finished with their small group work, have each group present one of their scenarios and their responses to the questions.

11. Have each student say one new thing they learned today.

EXTENSION ACTIVITIES

- Have students create a survey about prejudice. It can be an anonymous survey that they distribute to classmates, family members and friends. They can survey people about their familiarity with the forms of prejudice discussed in the lesson or about incidences of prejudice they have seen or heard about in life or in media. They should survey at least 10 people and possibly more and compile and share their results.

- Have students write poems or stories about prejudice. They can write a story or poem based on something that has happened to them or something they imagine could happen or happened to someone else. An alternative is to create an acrostic poem with the word PREJUDICE as the format.

- Read aloud and discuss one or more of the children's books from the list provided in this lesson.

CHILDREN'S BOOKS

The Hundred Dresses by Eleanor Estes

The Other Side by Jacqueline Woodson

Allie's Basketball Dream by Barbara E. Barber

One Green Apple by Eve Bunting

DEFINITIONS: FORMS OF PREJUDICE AND DISCRIMINATION

[Student Handout]

Ableism
Ableism is a prejudice and/or discrimination against people because of their physical or mental disabilities.

Ageism
Ageism is a prejudice and/or discrimination against people based on their age.

Anti-Semitism
Anti-Semitism is prejudice and/or discrimination against people who are Jewish.

Classism
Classism is prejudice and/or discrimination against people because of their social class (how much money people or their families have or do not have).

Homophobia
Homophobia is prejudice and/or discrimination against people who are believed to be gay, lesbian or bisexual.

Islamophobia
Islamophobia is a prejudice and/or discrimination against people who are or are believed to be Muslim.

Racism
Racism is a prejudice and/or discrimination against people because of their racial group.

Sexism
Sexism is prejudice and/or discrimination based on a person's gender.

Weightism
Weightism is prejudice and/or discrimination against people because of their weight (overweight or skinny).

PREJUDICE SCENARIOS

[Student Handout]

Instructions: Working together as a group, read each of the following four scenarios, discuss them in more detail and for each scenario write the form of prejudice, how the person felt and suggest what you can say to counteract the prejudice.

1. There is a fourth grader named Emily who is Jewish. The kids in her class think her family must be cheap because they don't buy gifts at holiday time. Every time someone mentions Israel or a Jewish holiday, all eyes are on her.

    Form of prejudice: _____

    How she feels: _____

    _____

    _____

    What you can say: _____

    _____

    _____

2. Jaden, a fifth grade boy, has two Moms and everyone knows. Some of the other kids in the class feel uncomfortable around him and think it is strange.

    Form of prejudice: _____

    How he feels: _____

    _____

    _____

    What you can say: _____

    _____

    _____

3. Mia is in third grade and is overweight. Everyone thinks she eats too much and doesn't exercise and that's why she is fat. They don't like her.

   Form of prejudice: _____

   How she feels: _____

   _____

   _____

   What you can say: _____

   _____

   _____

4. Dylan and Jamal are both black and they often go to the candy store after school. Whenever the store owner sees them, he gets nervous and thinks they are going to steal something.

   Form of prejudice: _____

   How they feel: _____

   _____

   _____

   What you can say: _____

   _____

   _____

Unit IV.200 | Understanding Bias and Discrimination

DISCRIMINATION

Lesson 16

RATIONALE

The purpose of this activity is to give students a deeper understanding of discrimination and how it works in our society. Discrimination is a key aspect of bias and in order for students to do something about it, they need to understand it. This lesson provides an opportunity for students to define discrimination, reflect on their own experiences and how it is manifested in our society and analyze situations in which stereotypes, prejudice and discrimination are involved.

OBJECTIVES

- Students will be able to define discrimination.
- Students will explore different ways discrimination takes place in our society.
- Students will reflect on personal experiences with discrimination.
- Students will analyze scenarios and identify how stereotypes, prejudice and discrimination play a role in each.

WHAT'S NEEDED

Handouts and Resources: Prejudice and Discrimination: Definitions and *Prejudice, Stereotype or Discrimination?* (one of each for each student)

Other Material: Board/Smart board, markers

PROCEDURES

1. Begin the activity by reviewing with students the definition of prejudice. Ask, "Does anyone remember what prejudice means?" If they do not remember, remind them that the definition of prejudice is judging or having an idea about someone or a group of people before you actually know them. Prejudice is often directed toward people in a certain identity group (race, religion, gender, etc.).
2. Ask students, "Has anyone heard the word discrimination? What does it mean?" Come to the definition of **discrimination** as unfair treatment of one person or group of people because of the person

GRADE LEVEL
3–5

TIME
45 minutes

COMMON CORE STANDARDS
Reading, Writing, Speaking & Listening, Language

STRATEGIES AND SKILLS
Define terms, stand up/sit down, turn and talk, small group work, large group discussion

KEY WORDS AND PHRASES
Discrimination
Institution
Vandalize

CHILDREN'S BOOKS

Separate Is Never Equal by Duncan Tonatiah

If a Bus Could Talk: The Story of Rosa Parks by Faith Ringgold

The Harvey Milk Story by Kari Krakow

or group's identity (e.g., race, gender, ability, religion, culture, etc.). Discrimination is an action that can come from prejudice.

3. Write the definitions of prejudice and discrimination on the board/smart board and distribute the *Prejudice and Discrimination: Definitions* handout to each student. Explain that prejudice is thoughts, feelings, ideas, attitudes (i.e. what is in your head) and discrimination is actions, rules, laws that treat people unfairly.

   Share an example of how prejudice and discrimination relate to one another but are also distinct. An example of prejudice is thinking old people are slow and their bodies do not work well. Discrimination against old people would be not letting them participate in the gym.

   Explain that discrimination always involves an element of power and/or rules that may be unfair in some way. In the situation with elderly people and the gym, the owners of the gym are the ones who would have had to create that rule. The people who work out in the gym may not have liked seeing the older people there, but only the people who had power and control in the gym could create the rules that discriminated against the elderly people.

4. Explain to students that you are going to read some sentences about discrimination. You are going to ask students if they know whether this happens and if they do, they will stand up. If they do not, they will stay seated. After reading each statement and having students stand up or not, ask the students who are standing up to say who this happens to and provide an example they know about, heard about, read about or saw on TV/movie, etc. Then everyone sits down and you move to the next statement.

   - Some people are excluded from participating in events.
   - Some people are unfairly paid less for doing the same job.
   - Some people who have committed a crime receive a longer jail sentence than others who committed the same crime.
   - Some people are excluded from jobs, neighborhoods/housing, getting a bank loan, education opportunities, social events and clubs.
   - Some people's homes, places of worship and cemeteries are vandalized.

5. Engage students in a discussion by asking the following questions:
   - Which one of the statements was most familiar to you?
   - Were there examples that you never heard of before?
   - How does discrimination work in our society?

6. Have students turn and talk with someone sitting near them and share about a time they experienced discrimination. If they

FLIPPED CLASSROOM IDEA

Make a short video of you talking about a time that you experienced discrimination or sharing examples of discrimination that have happened in the community. Talk about what happened, how you felt and what, if anything, you did in response to the situation.

cannot think of a personal example, they can share something that happened to someone they know, read in a book and saw on TV or in a movie. Have students take one minute per person and tell them when it is time to "switch" for the second person to begin speaking.

7. After the pairs are done speaking, engage students in a class discussion by asking the following questions:
   - How was it to share an example of discrimination?
   - How did it make you feel?
   - Does anyone want to share with the class?

8. Remind students about the definitions for stereotype, prejudice and discrimination. Have definitions written on board/smart board or chart paper and read out loud.

9. Divide the students into five small groups and distribute the *Prejudice, Stereotype or Discrimination?* handout to each student. Explain that students are going to work in small groups to discuss specific scenarios and identify how each of the concepts (prejudice, stereotype and discrimination) might be playing a role in the situation. They should read each of the scenarios silently and then after reading, go through each of them and determine whether prejudice, stereotyping and discrimination play a role and if so, how. One person can write down their responses on the handout.

10. After doing their small group work, have students come back to the large group and each group will take one of the examples and share their discussion/worksheet. After all the groups have presented, engage the students in a large group discussion by asking the following questions:
    - How did you feel about the scenarios you read?
    - Have you seen situations like this in real life? If so, what did you do?
    - Can you think of any ways we could do anything?

EXTENSION ACTIVITIES

- Have students choose one of the scenarios from the *Prejudice, Stereotype or Discrimination?* handout and write a scene of what might happen next. They can use dialogue as well as narration and write what the target does in the situation and the extent to which anyone else gets involved.

- Have students conduct research projects about discrimination over the course of history. They can choose to look at any of the isms they have already discussed and either choose a time in history where that group was discriminated against and what happened or they can find statistics that show the results of discrimination for that group.

- Read aloud and discuss one or more of the children's books from the list provided in this lesson.

PREJUDICE AND DISCRIMINATION: DEFINITIONS

[Student Handout]

Prejudice

Judging or having an idea about someone or a group of people before you actually know them. Prejudice is often directed toward people in a certain identity group (race, religion, gender, etc.).

Discrimination

Unfair treatment of one person or group of people because of the person or group's identity (e.g., race, gender, ability, religion, culture, etc.). Discrimination is an action that can come from prejudice.

PREJUDICE, STEREOTYPE OR DISCRIMINATION?

[Student Handout]

Instructions: Read each scenario below and determine whether prejudice, stereotyping or discrimination play a role, and if so, indicate by circling the term then explain how it plays a role in the scenario. Select one person in your group to write down your responses on this handout.

1. Belinda is planning her birthday party. She invites all the students in the class except for Hilda. Belinda doesn't want her to come to her party because Hilda just came to the U.S., doesn't speak much English and won't be able to communicate with the other children.

    Prejudice, Stereotyping or Discrimination?

    _____
    _____
    _____
    _____

2. Teams are being formed for a basketball game in physical education class. Each team leader avoids choosing Timothy until he is the only person left. When the team Tim is on loses the game, many of the students start complaining and saying things like, "We should have known we were going to lose with 'fatso' on our team."

    Prejudice, Stereotyping or Discrimination?

    _____
    _____
    _____
    _____

3. A local pizza shop has a sign in the window for part-time jobs. When African-American high school students apply for the job, the owner says he's already found someone for the job. When white students apply for the position, he gives them an application.

   Prejudice, Stereotyping or Discrimination?

4. Miguel has to do a science project for school. His grandfather offers to help him, but Miguel says he can do it himself. Secretly, he is thinking that his grandfather is too old to be able to help him.

   Prejudice, Stereotyping or Discrimination?

5. Sheree is an excellent ice skater who wants to try out for the ice hockey team. When she asks the hockey team coach, she is told that ice hockey is too dangerous for girls to play and she should consider figure skating.

   Prejudice, Stereotyping or Discrimination?

INEQUALITY PAST AND PRESENT

Lesson 17

RATIONALE

The purpose of this activity is to broaden students' understanding of the system of inequality, which includes prejudice, discrimination and unfair opportunities for some and not others. This lesson provides an opportunity for students to define equality and inequality, explore one example of inequality past and present (ableism) and imagine what disabled people experienced before there were laws enacted to protect their rights.

OBJECTIVES

- Students will define equality and inequality.
- Students will learn more about one kind of inequality and will consider solutions to it.
- Students will explore how people with disabilities have been treated in the past and are treated presently and what laws were enacted to protect their rights.
- Students will imagine what life was like for a person with a disability before major laws were enacted.

WHAT'S NEEDED

Handouts and Resources: Equality for People with Disabilities (one for each student)

PROCEDURES

1. Begin the lesson by reviewing the different forms of prejudice from Lesson 15, "Forms of Prejudice." Ask students, "What are the different forms of prejudice that you learned previously?" These can include: ableism, ageism, anti-Semitism, classism, homophobia, Islamophobia, racism, sexism and weightism.

2. Remind students about the distinction between prejudice and discrimination; prejudice is the attitude or belief and discrimination is an action taken. Give an example such as ableism:

   "People in wheelchairs scare me." (Prejudice)

   "I will not hire Frank to work in my store because he uses a

GRADE LEVEL
3–5

TIME
45 minutes

COMMON CORE STANDARDS
Reading, Writing, Speaking & Listening, Language

STRATEGIES AND SKILLS
Define terms, reading background information, large group discussion, writing

KEY WORDS AND PHRASES
Access
Disability
Equality
Hearing impairment
Inequality
Opportunity
Privilege

Anti-Bias Building Blocks: An Elementary Curriculum

wheelchair." (Discrimination)

3. Ask students, "What is equality?" Come to a definition of **equality** as having the same or similar rights and opportunities as others. Explain that "same or similar" means that not everyone needs the same things and therefore, they would not get the exact same treatment. If someone has a hearing impairment, they may need a hearing aid but not everyone would need one.

   Then ask, "What is inequality?" If they do not know, have students consider the definition of **equality** and when there is an "in" prefix, that represents the absence of equality. The definition for **inequality** is an unfair situation when some people have more rights or better opportunities than other people. Ask students, "Can you think of any situations of inequality in our school or community?" If they cannot think of an example, share one of your own to get them thinking. Explain that while discrimination is unfair treatment against a person or group of people because of who they are, the term inequality is broader and includes a system which provides more rights and opportunities for certain groups.

4. Explain to students that they will be reading *Equality for People with Disabilities*, a document with information about the rights of people with disabilities from the past and current day. Ask students, "How do you think people with disabilities were treated 50 years ago? Do you think students or adults with disabilities are treated equally in our society today? Why or why not?" Give students 10 minutes to read the document silently.

   After reading, students should turn and talk with a person sitting next to them and share their reactions to the document as well as any questions they have.

5. Engage students in a class discussion by asking the following questions:
   - What clarifying questions do you have about what you read?
   - What did you learn about disabilities, ableism and people with disabilities rights?
   - Did anything surprise you? If so, what?
   - What do you think life was like for people with disabilities before these laws were passed?
   - What do you think life is like now for people with disabilities?
   - How does what you read connect with the concepts of equality and inequality?
   - What is still needed for people with disabilities to have full access and opportunities similar to people without disabilities?

6. Explain to students that they are now going to write a short

FLIPPED CLASSROOM IDEA

Make a short video of you reading a short 2–3 paragraph essay about someone with a disability before the 1970s, including details about what their life was like.

story (2–3 paragraphs) about a person with a disability pre-1970s. They can make up a name of a person and their particular disability—they might be blind, hearing impaired, have mobile disabilities or cognitive/mental disabilities. The person can be a child or an adult. In preparation for their writing, ask the following questions:

- What is the person's disability?
- What are their physical limitations?
- What are they able to do? Not able to do?
- What do they want to do? Are they able to do it? Why or why not?
- How does the person feel?
- Where do they live?
- How do they get around, communicate with others, have fun, etc.?

7. Have students write their essays and share them with the class.

EXTENSION ACTIVITIES

- Have students work in small groups to research other areas of inequality such as racism, sexism, anti-Semitism, homophobia, etc. They should learn more about how people in that group were treated 50 years ago and compare that to the rights and opportunities today including pointing out rules, laws and procedures that have changed to protect their rights and opportunities.

- Have students think about and design something that is considered "assisted technology," which are devices for people with disabilities to assist them in some way. Have students think about a specific disability, what that person may need and what they can create to help them do the thing they need to do. Then they should construct and/or draw the device according to how it would actually look.

- Read aloud and discuss one or more of the children's books from the list provided in this lesson.

CHILDREN'S BOOKS

Harvesting Hope: The Story of Cesar Chavez by Kathleen Krull

Just As Good: How Larry Doby Changed America's Game by Chris Cowe

Fish for Jimmy by Katie Yamasaki

Gifts from the Enemy by Trudy Ludwig

EQUALITY FOR PEOPLE WITH DISABILITIES

[Student Handout]

Before 1970s—Before major laws were passed beginning in the 1970s to defend the rights of people with disabilities, there were few protections for them. Consider the following:

- People with disabilities were not able to use public transportation (buses, trains), telephones, bathrooms and stores.
- Public services such as parks, recreation centers and libraries were not accessible for people with disabilities.
- Office buildings and worksites with stairs offered no entry for people with disabilities.
- Children with disabilities had to attend special schools and sometimes lived in institutions away from their families.
- People with disabilities were often unable to find jobs because of employment discrimination or because the job itself did not have the equipment needed to do their jobs (e.g., a deaf person could not use the telephone, a blind person could not type, etc.).
- Sidewalks and curb ramps were not accessible for people with mobility disabilities.
- People who were deaf or hearing impaired did not have access to TTY (teletypewriter—used to send a receive messages instead of a telephone and before texting) or closed caption TV.
- People who were blind or visually impaired did not have technology to help them with reading, writing, using a computer and reading a watch.
- People with disabilities were rarely in television and movies and if they were, they were portrayed with negative stereotypes such as being sad, unable to participate in daily life, target/victim of violence or someone to pity.

After 1970s—Starting in the 1970s, major laws were passed including the Americans with Disabilities Act (ADA) in 1990. The goals of ADA were to:

- Eliminate discrimination on the basis of disability in employment, transportation and telecommunications.
- Require businesses to provide "reasonable accommodations" to people with disabilities. An example would be if someone uses a wheelchair, making sure the building and their workspace is wheelchair accessible.
- Mandate that public transportation had to provide accommodations for people with disabilities.
- Require telecommunications services (phone, radio, television, computer) to offer technology for people with disabilities.
- Require public schools to provide services that students with disabilities need.

BULLYING AND IDENTITY-BASED BULLYING

Lesson 18

RATIONALE

The purpose of this activity is to provide an understanding of bullying and in particular, identity-based bullying. This lesson provides an opportunity for students to review and further explore identity, understand what bullying is and how it is related to and is different from teasing and name-calling, share personal experiences and through a writing activity, consider what can be done to address bullying.

OBJECTIVES

- Students will review the concept of identity and connect it to identity-based bullying.
- Students will define bullying and differentiate it from name-calling and teasing.
- Students will share experiences they have had with bullying.
- Students will explore identity-based bullying by writing stories and coming up with ways to address it.

WHAT'S NEEDED

Other Material: Post-it Notes® (at least five per student), board/smart board or chart paper, markers

PROCEDURES

1. Begin the lesson by reminding students about the various activities they have done to explore the parts of their identity, including culture, race, nationality, family, opinions, skills/abilities, physical characteristics and community. Using yourself as an example, share some words that you use to describe your identity such as: "I am a white, Jewish woman who lives in the city." Remind students that many things shape a person's identity.

2. Ask students, "What are the different parts of your identity? What does identity consist of? Who are you?" If you have a smart board, use Wordle to create a graphic illustration of the identities represented in the class that can be done on the spot. If you do

GRADE LEVEL
3–5

TIME
45 minutes

COMMON CORE STANDARDS
Reading, Writing, Speaking & Listening, Language

STRATEGIES AND SKILLS
Brainstorming, define terms, small group discussion, large group discussion, writing

KEY WORDS AND PHRASES
Bullying
Identity
Identity-based bullying
Name-calling
Teasing

■ *Anti-Bias Building Blocks: An Elementary Curriculum*

not have a smart board, record their responses on the board or chart paper and later create a Wordle.

3. Engage students in a discussion about the wordle by asking the following questions:
   - What do you notice about the words on the wordle?
   - Are there some identity words that are missing? If so, what are they?
   - How do you feel when you look at the list?
   - What are the aspects of identity that are most important to you?

4. Explain to students that today we are going to discuss identity-based bullying. Create a semantic web with the word bullying by asking, "What is bullying? How do you feel when you think about bullying? What words and phrases come to mind?" For this web, give students small post-its (at least 5 each) and a marker and have them write the words on the post-its. Have students come up to the front of the room (one table or row at a time) where you have written the word "Bullying" on the board. Have students place their words on the board or wall. After all the words are up, group them together thematically and ask students, "Do we have any other words to add?

    After placing all of the words on the web, engage students in a discussion by asking the following questions:
    - Do you see a pattern or theme looking at the web?
    - How do you feel?
    - Does anything surprise you that you see on the web?
    - Is bullying common or not common?
    - Do we know a lot about bullying?

5. Ask students, "Based on the web and what you know about bullying, what is the definition of bullying?" Come to a definition as **bullying** is when one person or a group behaves in ways—on purpose and over and over—that make someone feel hurt, afraid or embarrassed. Record the definition on board/smart board and have students write it down in their notebooks.

6. Explain to students that there are a lot of different kinds of mean behavior. Name-calling and teasing are also mean behavior but they are not necessarily bullying, although they can be elements of bullying or lead to bullying. Explain that name-calling is using words to hurt or be mean to someone or a group and teasing is to laugh at and criticize someone in a way that is either friendly and playful or cruel and unkind. Emphasize that terms that are related such as name-calling or teasing can start off as playful but lead to cruel behavior and these behaviors are often elements of bullying.

    Ask students "What are the differences between bullying and name calling or teasing?" Elicit from the students.

7. Explain to students that they are going to discuss personal experiences with bullying, either something that happened to them personally or something they witnessed or heard about. Remind the students about your classroom guidelines and the importance of confidentiality. Explain that they will be using a fishbowl strategy to discuss the topic.

8. Ask students "What is a fishbowl?" Explain that this activity is like a fishbowl in that we will make a circle and some students will be inside the circle (i.e. in a fishbowl) and the rest of the students will be observers outside of it.

    Ask for 4–6 volunteers who are willing to sit inside the circle and talk about experiences with bullying (or volunteers to talk about the anonymous essays that the teacher will read). Create a small circle with chairs for those sitting inside the circle. Arrange the other chairs to sit outside this smaller circle. Before discussing the specific ground rules for the fishbowl, review your classroom guidelines, as past experiences and strong feelings may emerge from the fishbowl.

9. Explain the ground rules for the fishbowl:
   - The observers are not allowed to speak. Their job is to listen and learn from the fishbowl students. The observers will have an opportunity to discuss any issues that emerge later.
   - You (the teacher) will facilitate the fishbowl discussion and you will make sure everyone has the opportunity to talk.
   - (Optional) Once the fishbowl discussion has happened for at least 10 minutes and you sense that others want to speak, you can allow a time where if someone in the observer groups wants to join the fishbowl, they can tap the shoulder of someone in the fishbowl and take their place. Use this step at your discretion.

10. Use the following questions to guide the fishbowl and at the same time, allow it to move in the natural direction that the conversation is moving.
    - Share about a time you were bullied or someone you know was bullied—what happened? (This can be substituted with students' writing.)
    - How did you (or the person) feel?
    - What did you (or the person) do or want to do?
    - Did anyone help?

11. After the fishbowl, engage the students in a discussion by asking the following questions:
    - To the observers: Was it difficult to not respond to the comments made during the fishbowl? Why?
    - To the fishbowl students: How did it feel to share your thoughts and feelings about bullying?
    - To everyone: Did you hear anything from the fishbowl that surprised you? What did you learn from the experience? What came out from the discussion about how it feels to be the target of bullying?

Ask students, "Now that you know what identity is and bullying is, what do you think identity-based bullying is?" Explain that **identity-based bullying** is when you bully someone based on an aspect of who they are or are perceived to be: their identity. It can also be called "prejudice-based bullying" because the bullying is

---

NOTE 8

Due to the sensitive nature of these discussions about bullying, you may choose to do this fishbowl activity in a variety of ways. You can either have students who are inside the fishbowl talk about their own experience with bullying or one that they witnessed or observed. Another option is to have students write about experiences with bullying (which will be anonymous) and some of those essays can be shared anonymously in the fishbowl for students to discuss.

FLIPPED CLASSROOM IDEA

Make a short video of you answering the four fishbowl questions, sharing a time you or someone you know was bullied, how you felt and what you did or wanted to do about it.

based on prejudice.

12. Ask students if they can think of any examples of identity-based bullying. Explain that it can be someone who is bullied because students have bias about the fact that the person is overweight, Muslim, is a girl who likes to play with so-called "boy stuff," is a different race, wears clothes that are not seen as "cool," does not speak English well, has a learning disability, etc.

13. Have students draw a storyboard that illustrates a situation of identity-based bullying. A storyboard is a writing format (like a comic book or graphic novel) using boxes placed in a sequence to convey a story. In each box, the writer puts information, pictures, dialogue, symbols or text. While the plot for their storyboard should be a realistic, caution students not to use names of people they know nor details of a real-life situation in which everyone is familiar. In advance of their drawing and writing, they should consider what happened in the identity-based bullying incident(s), how the target (the person who was bullied) felt and what someone did to help and who acted as an ally (could be another student or adult, the school, parent, etc.). Because there is limited time, have students start off with 3–4 boxes to tell their story. If time is available later, they can create more boxes.

14. Ask for volunteers to share their storyboards with the rest of the class. After sharing several, aloud ask, "What can we do as a class about identity-based bullying? How can we be an ally to students who are bullied and what can we do as a class to stop bullying?" Brainstorm ideas.

EXTENSION ACTIVITIES

- Have students talk with younger students in their school (K-1 graders) about bullying, perhaps doing an activity with them, reading them a book about bullying, sharing their personal experiences, etc. They could also write their own children's books and read them to the younger children in the school.

- Have students think of slogans about bullying prevention that they want to share with others, either how bullying is harmful or what can be done about it. After they have refined their slogans so they are memorable, easy to understand and inspiring, they should take the slogans and make signs/posters, bumper stickers or using PowerPoint, or an app like PicCollage, share them electronically.

- Read aloud and discuss one or more of the children's books from the list provided in this lesson.

NOTE 13

It is very important to explain to students that they should never use names of people in their class/school/family or specific situations that would highlight something that actually happened.

CHILDREN'S BOOKS

Confessions of a Former Bully by Trudy Ludwig

One by Kathryn Otoshi

First Day in Grapes by L. King Perez

Wonder by R. J. Palacio*

*This is not a picture book so read aloud over time.

THREE Is OF INJUSTICE

RATIONALE

The purpose of this activity is to help students understand the systemic nature of injustice and how three interrelated forms of injustice reinforce each other. It is important that students understand how injustice manifests itself in ideology, institutions, interpersonal relationships and how people internalize prejudice and stereotypes. This lesson provides an opportunity for students to review terms and learn what injustice means, reflect on the interconnectedness of three faces of injustice and explore the three Is of injustice by going through a small group process to cite examples of each.

[**NOTE:** This is an advanced lesson and it is important to review in advance to assess whether your students will be able to understand the concepts. It is also important to make sure to teach the previous lessons in this section of the curriculum and ideally, all of the lessons preceding this section.]

OBJECTIVES

- Students will review terms and define injustice.
- Students will understand the interconnectedness of the three Is (interpersonal, institutional and internalized) forms of injustice.
- Students will explore the three Is of injustice by considering one ism for each and providing examples.

WHAT'S NEEDED

Handouts and Resources: The Three Is of Injustice and Their Connection and Three Is Worksheet (one of each for each student)

Other Material: Chart paper, markers, pens or pencils

PROCEDURES

1. Start lesson by telling the following story of an imaginary young woman named Kaya.

    Kaya is 19 years old. When she was a young girl, she liked to play with all different kinds of toys—trucks, dolls, trains, dress-up and

---

Lesson 19

GRADE LEVEL
3–5

TIME
45 minutes

COMMON CORE STANDARDS
Reading, Writing, Speaking & Listening, Language

STRATEGIES AND SKILLS
Review and define terms, small group work, large group discussion, class presentation

KEY WORDS AND PHRASES
Injustice
Institutional
Internalized
Interpersonal
Superior

FLIPPED CLASSROOM IDEA

Make a short video of you sharing the story of Kaya and asking the discussion questions.

■ Anti-Bias Building Blocks: An Elementary Curriculum

Legos. She noticed that for birthdays and holiday gifts, her parents and relatives got her mostly pink "girly" toys and never gave her the kind of presents her younger brother received. At school, she got teased for bringing a Star Wars lunchbox to school and for dressing more "like a boy" (i.e. khaki shorts and t-shirts) than a girl. When she was in fifth grade, Kaya got really interested in football and used to watch every game she could on TV. Naturally, she wanted to play football in her town but football was boys only so she played soccer instead. In junior high and high school, Kaya started to notice things about men and women in our society. She noticed there had never been a woman U.S. President and that most of the people in authority positions were men like the principal, manager at the store where she had a part-time job, etc. She also learned that her Dad made a higher salary than her Mom and heard her mother complain about this often. She started to think that maybe women were not as smart as men. She also saw that her mother did all the housework, even though her Mom and Dad both worked outside the home; that also seemed to be true among her group of friends. In school, she liked and did well in Math and Science but when she was applying to colleges, her guidance counselor suggested colleges that emphasized the arts and English. Kaya was very confused about what she should do as a job and career and what she should study in college.

Ask students the following questions:

- What can you tell us about Kaya?
- Do you know anyone like Kaya?
- What messages did Kaya receive growing up about gender?
- What did Kaya believe about what women could do and not do?

2. Review the definitions of prejudice, discrimination and inequality by asking students what each of the words mean and provide an example of each term.

3. Write the word injustice on the board and ask, "What does injustice mean?" Define **injustice** as a situation in which the rights of a person or a group of people are ignored, disrespected or discriminated against. Ask students, "Can you think of any examples of injustice?"

4. Explain that today the class is going to discuss three levels of injustice in our society—each one begins with the letter **I**. Distribute the *The Three Is of Injustice and Their Connection* handout to each student and go over it in detail with the students following along. Explain that within a system of inequality, there are several levels of prejudice and discrimination that lead to injustice: (1) interactions between people expose those prejudices and stereotypes, (2) institutions (like our education system) will

support that prejudicial idea with practices that either discriminate against certain people or give advantages to other people and (3) sometimes the people who are treated unfairly begin to believe the stereotypes and prejudice about themselves. All three of these Is are interconnected. As you explain each of the three Is, ask students for examples of each or provide one of your own if they do not have specific suggestions. Encourage them to think about the story of Kaya for examples. The following are some examples for each "I".

- Interpersonal: Men think that women should do all the housework. Boys tease girls about not being good at soccer.
- Institutional: There are many more men than women represented in politics. Women make less money than men for same job.
- Internalize: Girls don't try out for basketball team. Women become nurses instead of doctors.

5. Engage students in a discussion by asking the following questions:
   - Do these three words make sense?
   - How are the words connected to each other? (Explain that in a system of injustice, all of these work together to make one group feel and behave in a superior manner to another group.)
   - Can you think of any examples that have happened to you?
   - What questions do you have?

6. Explain to students that they are going to work in small groups to create a chart of the three Is of injustice. To help them with this, you will do one together, using sexism as an example.
   - Ableism
   - Ageism
   - Anti-Semitism
   - Classism
   - Homophobia
   - Islamophobia
   - Racism
   - Sexism
   - Weightism

7. Divide students into groups of three. Explain that each group is going to take one of the forms of discrimination and inequality (below) to identify the ways in which the ism takes place in our society in terms of the three Is. You can either assign one of the isms to each group or have them select one of their choosing.

8. Distribute to each group *The Three Is Worksheet*, explaining that they will have 15 minutes to complete their task. They should try to think of as many examples as possible for each of the three Is. Alternately, each group can use a piece of chart paper and markers and recreate the chart so that it is more visible.

9. After the groups have completed their work, have each group come to the front of the classroom and present their *Three Is Worksheet* (project on smart board or chart paper). Provide time for other students to ask questions.

10. Engage students in a discussion by asking the following questions:
    - What were some of the similarities between the different forms of injustice?
    - What were some of the differences?
    - What did you learn by doing this activity?
    - What can we do about individual, institutional and internalized injustice?

EXTENSION ACTIVITIES

- Have students explore institutional injustice on a deeper level by choosing one institution, like the media, and brainstorming all the ways in which the media perpetuates injustice and in different ways (sexism, racism, anti-Semitism, etc.). Students could do research, find statistics, survey friends, talk to adults and as a culmination, create a PowerPoint presentation to share with others.

- Have students write a story similar to the story of Kaya but about a different ism. They should choose the time period and research how that ism was playing out in our society during that time. In the story, they should include all three of the elements of injustice—interpersonal, institutional and internalized and make the story believable.

- Read aloud and discuss one or more of the children's books from the list provided in this lesson.

CHILDREN'S BOOKS

A Place Where Sunflowers Grow by Amy Lee-Tai

From North to South by René Colato Laínez

The Bus Ride by William Miller

THE THREE Is OF INJUSTICE AND THEIR CONNECTION

[Student Handout]

Interpersonal: The idea that one identity/societal group is better than another gives permission for people to disrespect or mistreat individuals in the other group (jokes, slurs, stereotypes, threats, physical assaults, bullying).

Institutional: The idea that one identity/societal group is better than another gets rooted in the institutions—the laws, legal system, police, education/schools, hiring, housing, media images, political power so that they implement discriminatory or unequal practices.

Internalized: The idea that one identity/societal group is better than the other gets internalized so that people start to believe the stereotypes, prejudice and negative messages about themselves (that they are weak, not smart or competent).

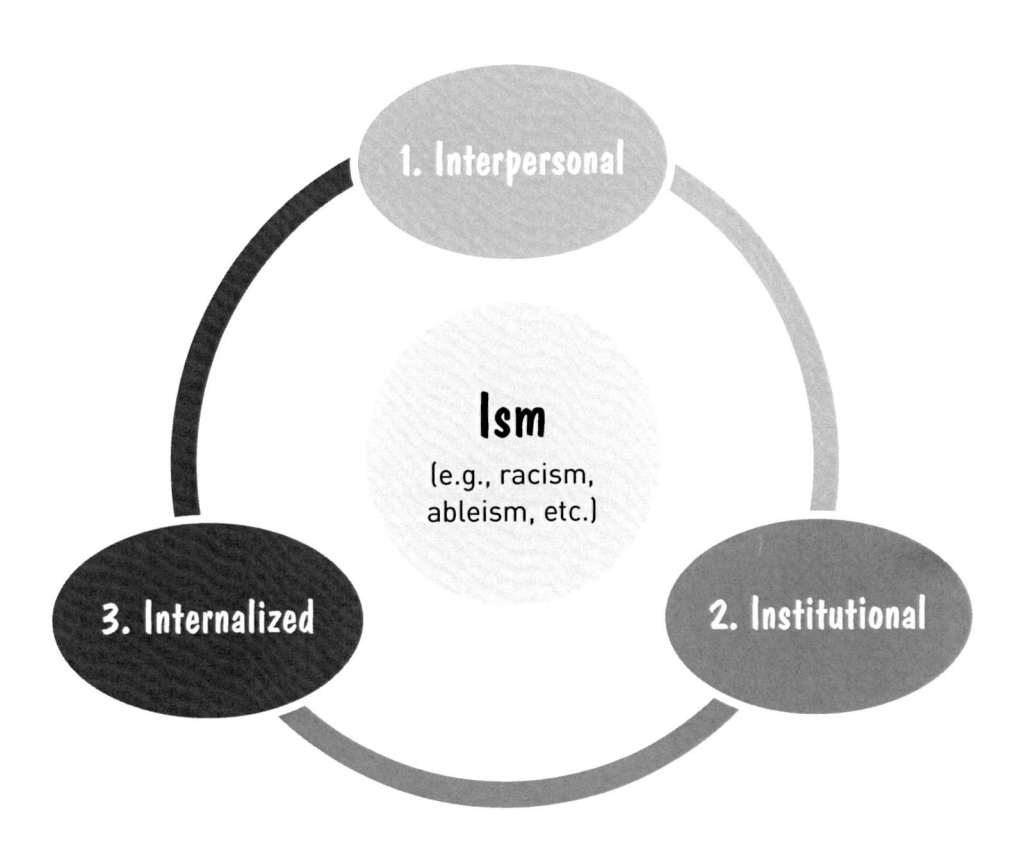

1. Interpersonal

2. Institutional

3. Internalized

Ism (e.g., racism, ableism, etc.)

THE THREE Is OF INJUSTICE WORKSHEET

[Student Handout]

Instructions: Write in the middle circle the "ism" chosen or provided to you. Work together in your group to identify the ways in which the ism takes place in our society in terms of the three Is and write them in the corresponding circle.

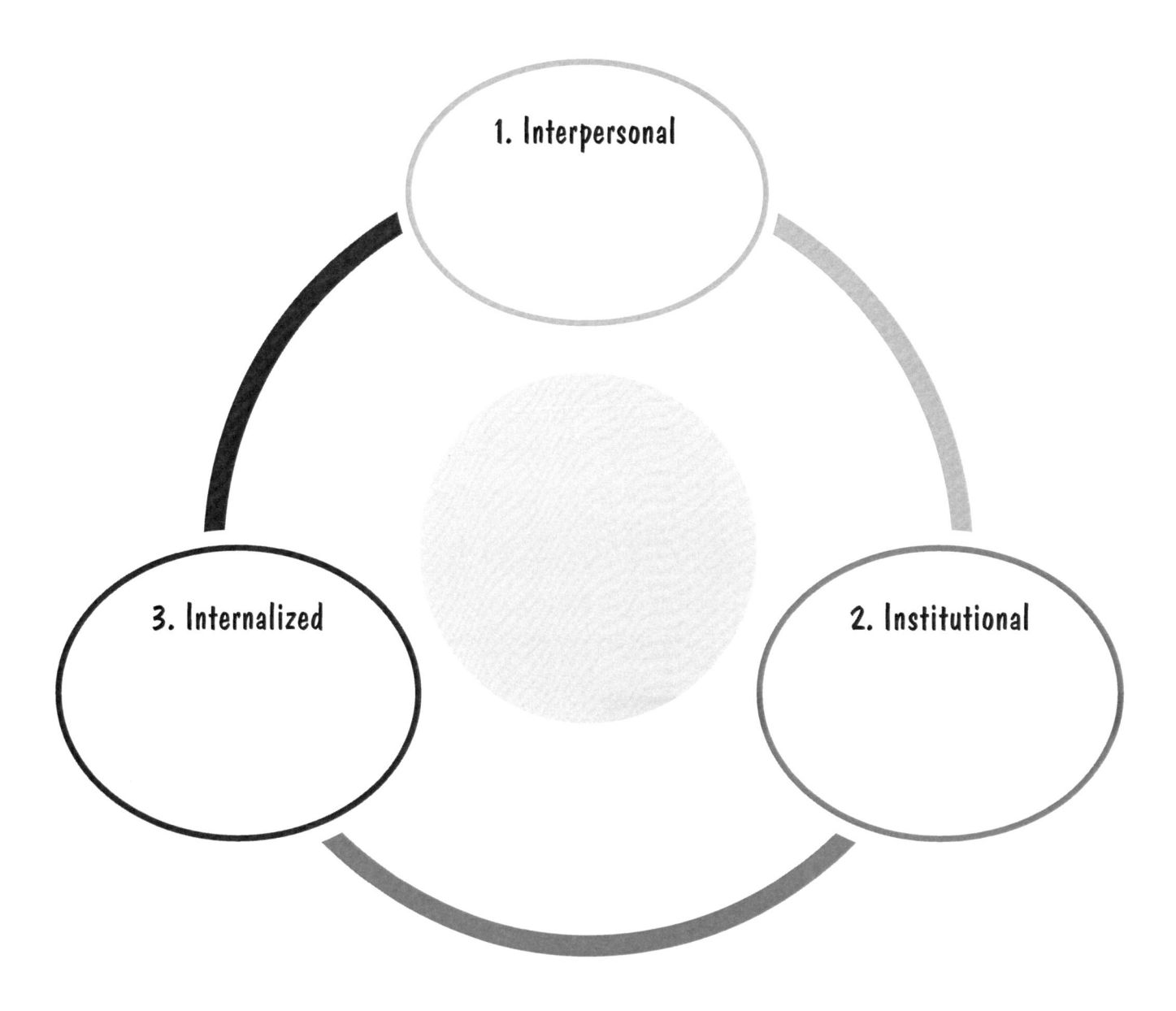

1. Interpersonal

2. Institutional

3. Internalized

Unit IV.220 | Understanding Bias and Discrimination

UNIT V. CONFRONTING/CHALLENGING BIAS AND BULLYING

When faced with bias, bullying and discrimination, it is crucial that children feel empowered to do something about it. Making a difference in their classroom, on the playground, in their community and within the larger society is not only an important lifelong skill; it is an important perspective that children should develop. Building on their communication skills and knowledge of bias and bullying, students are now ready to address and challenge the stereotypes, prejudice, discrimination and bullying they face. In realistic and developmentally-appropriate ways, children can learn how to be an ally, both on an individual level and by working with others to stand up for themselves and each other in order to make positive change in their world.

GOALS FOR KINDERGARTEN THROUGH 2ND GRADE

In Unit V, children in kindergarten through 2nd grade will learn different ways to respond to bullying and teasing situations. Students will understand that there are different ways to make change and working with others makes a difference. They will explore an example in our country's history for insight into how groups of people have enacted change. Finally, children will use their skills and understanding to take on a school project in order to make a difference.

GOALS FOR THIRD THROUGH FIFTH GRADE

For third to fifth graders, children will examine the different roles that are played in bias and bullying situations and will learn how to be ally. They will explore different strategies to challenge prejudice and discrimination and will analyze how strength in numbers can have a deeper impact. Students will consider social change movements throughout history and will identify and implement a social action project based on the problems and needs in their community.

RESPONDING TO BULLYING AND TEASING

RATIONALE

The purpose of this activity is for students to explore the different roles people play in a bullying or bias situations and to reflect on their own experiences. Understanding different roles will help empower them to make more proactive decisions when faced with these situations. This lesson provides an opportunity for students to review bullying terminology, understand different roles through watching a puppet role play and consider their own experiences taking on different roles.

OBJECTIVES

- Students will review definitions for teasing, name-calling and bullying.
- Students will analyze a role play in order to understand the roles of target, ally, aggressor and bystander.
- Students will reflect on their own experiences with playing one of these roles.

WHAT'S NEEDED

Handouts and Resources: Roles in Bullying and Prejudice (one for each student)

Other Material: Puppets (at least 3), drawing paper, markers, crayons, colored pencils

PROCEDURES

1. Review definitions and concepts for bullying, name-calling and teasing, reminding students of these definitions:

   Bullying: When a person or a group behaves in ways—on purpose and over and over—that make someone feel hurt, afraid or embarrassed.

   Name-Calling: Using words to hurt or be mean to someone or a group.

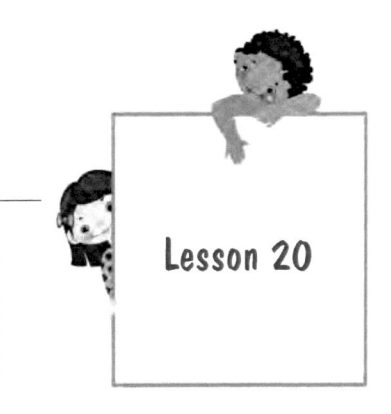

Lesson 20

GRADE LEVEL
K–2

TIME
35 minutes

COMMON CORE STANDARDS
Reading, Writing, Speaking & Listening, Language

STRATEGIES AND SKILLS
Role play, define terms, analyzing role play, turn and talk

KEY WORDS AND PHRASES
Aggressor
Ally
Bystander
Target

Teasing: To laugh at and put someone down in a way that is either friendly and playful or mean and unkind.

2. Take out three puppets and have students name them, reminding students to not use names of anyone in their class or school. After you have come up with the names, make sure everyone knows each of their names. Make sure at least one of them is a boy. For the purpose of the role play, refer to Puppets A, B and C with the names chosen by the students. Ask for a few students to stand near where the role play is happening and explain to them that they are in the story by watching what is happening. Act out the following role play. Please note that you can change the role play but just be certain that all the elements and roles are covered:

   Puppet A: "Hey, why do you bring that Hello Kitty lunch box to school?"

   Puppet B (boy): "Um, because I like it and my Mom got it for me."

   Puppet A: "But that's a girly lunchbox. Only girls like Hello Kitty."

   Puppet B: "I like Hello Kitty and I'm a boy."

   Puppet A: "Are you really? Are you sure? You also play four square with the girls at lunch. What's up with that? And look at those sneakers—so girly!"

   Puppet B: Looks down, sadly.

   Stop the action and ask:
   - What's happening here?
   - What is Puppet A (you can call by name) doing?
   - How do you think Puppet A (call by name) feels?
   - How do you think Puppet B (call by name) feels?
   - If you were observing this conversation, what would you do?

   Continue the action, introducing Puppet C:

   Puppet C: "Hey, what's happening?"

   Puppet B: (Head down) "Nothing."

   Puppet A: "Can you believe he has a Hello Kitty lunchbox? That's so wrong."

   Puppet C: "What's wrong with that?"

   Puppet A: "Only girls like Hello Kitty. Puppet B (use name) acts so girly sometimes."

   Puppet C: "Just leave him alone. He can like whatever he wants."

   Stop the action.

3. Distribute the *Roles in Bullying and Prejudice* handout to each student or project on smart board. Read each of the definitions for target, aggressor, ally and bystander out loud and after each definition is read, ask the following questions:
   - Who is the target in the situation we just watched? How?
   - Who is the aggressor in the situation we just watched? How?
   - Who is the ally in the situation we just watched? How so?
   - Who are the bystanders in the situation we just watched? How so? (Explain that everyone "watching" is a bystander.)

4. Engage students in a discussion by asking the following questions:
   - What could Puppet A have done differently?
   - What could Puppet B have done differently?
   - What did Puppet C do and how do you think that made Puppets A and B feel?
   - What could the bystanders have done?

   Next to each of the four roles, ask and record as the students respond: How many people were the target? (Write down "1") How many were the aggressor? (Write down "1") How about the ally? (Write down "1") How many bystanders were there? (Explain that all of the children watching were bystanders.) At this point, point out the difference in numbers and ask, "Since there are so many bystanders, what could they do?"

5. Ask students, "Can you think of a time you were in a situation like this and if so, what "role" (aggressor, ally, bystander, target) did you play?" Ask them for details about the situation without including anyone's name, especially if it involved someone in the class.

6. End the lesson by having students draw a picture of someone being an ally.

EXTENSION ACTIVITIES

- Have students make their own puppets and then create and act out role play scenarios that involve bullying or prejudice. Depending on their writing skills, students can write out some of the dialogue (or talk about what they would say and then paraphrase) for each character and then act out the role play according to the "script" they write. Make sure students do not use names of classmates or use real-life situations that have happened in school or at home. As a culmination, they can act out their role plays for younger children in the school (e.g., second graders to kindergarteners or first graders with Pre-K students) or for a presentation to parents/guardians.

- Watch the two early childhood videos on the stopbullying.gov website at www.stopbullying.gov/kids/webisodes/index.html. Have students either view them at home or watch together in class and discuss them afterwards, asking students: (1) What happened? (2) What roles did each of the characters play? (3) How was bullying involved in the video and (4) How did it end?

- Read aloud and discuss one or more of the children's books from the list provided in this lesson.

CHILDREN'S BOOKS

Stand Tall, Molly Lou Melon by Patty Lovell

Simon's Hook: A Story About Teases and Putdowns by Karen Gedig Burnett

Each Kindness by Jacqueline Woodson

ROLES IN BULLYING AND PREJUDICE

[Student Handout]

Target
Someone who is bullied or treated in hurtful ways by a person or a group on purpose and over and over.

Aggressor
Someone who says or does hurtful things.

Ally
Someone who helps or stands up for someone who is being bullied or the target of prejudice.

Bystander
Someone who sees bullying or prejudice happening and does not say or do anything.

BEING BRAVE AND STANDING UP

Lesson 21

RATIONALE

The purpose of this activity is to explore ally behavior. It is important that children do not feel powerless in the face of bullying and prejudice and know that there is something they can do about it. This lesson provides an opportunity for students to reflect on what it means to be brave, define and think about different ways of being an ally and hear or read and analyze scenarios about bullying and bias.

OBJECTIVES

- Students will reflect on what it means to be brave.
- Students will define ally and consider different ways to be an ally.
- Students will analyze situations of teasing, bullying or bias and explore different ally behaviors.

WHAT'S NEEDED

Handouts and Resources: Be An Ally Scenarios #1–4

Other Material: Drawing paper, crayons, markers, colored pencils

PROCEDURES

1. Begin the lesson by asking students: What does it mean to be brave? Elicit stories, words, feelings and ideas from them. Together, define **brave** as doing something you would not normally do that may be hard physically or emotionally (you will need to explain what physical and emotional means in this case, perhaps with an example).

2. Distribute paper and drawing materials. Explain to students that they are going to remember a time they felt brave and then are going to draw a picture. Have them close their eyes (if they feel comfortable doing so) and ask them to think about a time they felt brave. Say something like, "Let's remember a time we felt brave, when we did something that we would normally not do that may have been hard. When you felt brave that time, where were you? What were you doing? Do you remember any sounds? What

GRADE LEVEL
K–2

TIME
35 minutes

COMMON CORE STANDARDS
Reading, Writing, Speaking & Listening, Language

STRATEGIES AND SKILLS
Brainstorm, turn and talk, drawing, define terms, small group discussion, gallery walk

KEY WORDS AND PHRASES
Ally
Brave

were you wearing? What happened? Who else was there? What did you do that made you feel brave? How did you feel afterwards?" Ask as many of these questions as feel appropriate. Then say, "OK, now everyone, let's open our eyes."

3. Explain to students that now they will draw a picture of what they imagined in their minds. They can include as much or as little detail as possible. They can choose to write words on the page or not. Give them 10 minutes to draw, working individually, with you circulating around the room checking in with students. After students have completed their drawings, ask for volunteers to come to the front of the room and explain their pictures. Have as many students present as possible. After, hang the drawings on a wall and make sure to have a time later when students can do a "gallery walk."

4. Remind students about the discussion in the previous lesson on the different roles in bullying and prejudice and specifically the role of ally. Ask students, "Does anyone remember what it means to be an ally?" Define **ally** as someone who helps or stands up for someone who is being bullied or the target of prejudice. Share an example from your own life about being an ally. Then ask students, "What does it mean to help someone who is being bullied? What does being brave have to do with being an ally? What are the different ways we can be allies to people who are the target of bullying or prejudice?" Create a list that looks like this:

    Being an Ally
    - Ask the person (target) to play with me at recess.
    - Be extra nice to the target.
    - Tell a teacher about what happened.
    - Ask the person (aggressor) why they did that.
    - Tell the person (aggressor) to stop.
    - Compliment the target.
    - Don't join in on the bullying.
    - Ask an older child or adult what I should do.

5. Divide students into groups of three. Distribute a different *Be An Ally Scenario* to each group (you will have more than one group with the same scenario). When students get into their groups, have one person read the scenario aloud (or read for them) and then have them brainstorm at least 2–3 ways to be an ally in that situation. Give students 10 minutes to complete this task. For kindergarten students, read aloud one of the scenarios and ask students how they can be an ally in that situation.

6. Have students come back together and one student from each group will explain or read their scenario and one idea they came up with for being an ally. Add their ideas to the list created earlier. As a way to end the lesson, have a few students share something new they learned about being an ally.

EXTENSION ACTIVITIES

- Have students practice being an ally but first sharing a situation that involves name-calling, teasing or bullying. Then have them either (1) share aloud their ideas for being an ally, (2) role-play an ally behavior or (3) use puppets to act out an ally behavior. You can start with the scenarios in the lesson or make ones up of your own but be sure that they do not hit too close to home and potentially cause emotional distress for your students.

- Have students write or draw a story about a time they were an ally. They should include what happened, what they did, what others did, how they made the decision to be an ally and how the story ended. They can illustrate the story and share with the class.

- Read aloud and discuss one or more of the children's books from the list provided in this lesson.

CHILDREN'S BOOKS

The Juice Box Bully by Bob Somson

Spaghetti in a Hot Dog Bun by Maria Dismondy

Maddi's Fridge by Lois Brandt

BE AN ALLY SCENARIO #1

[Student Handout]

Maribel is new to the school and the town. She wants to be friends with Hannah and Hannah's friends but Hannah is not nice to Maribel. She makes fun of Maribel's clothes and tells her other friends not to play with Maribel at recess. You don't think Maribel should be treated this way.

What are some ways you can be an ally to Maribel?

1. _____

2. _____

3. _____

Unit V.230 | Confronting/Challenging Bias and Bullying

BE AN ALLY SCENARIO #2

[Student Handout]

Oscar gets teased all the time for being overweight. There are several kids who often call him "fat" and "porker." He does not have many friends and spends most of his time alone. You want to invite him to your birthday party but you might get teased if you do.

What are some ways you can be an ally to Oscar?

1. _____

2. _____

3. _____

■ *Anti-Bias Building Blocks: An Elementary Curriculum* | Unit V.231

BE AN ALLY SCENARIO #3

[Student Handout]

Sebastian wears a hearing aid and has a special adult in the classroom to help him with his work. Most of the kids think he is deaf and can't hear at all, but that isn't true. At recess, Sebastian never gets asked to play with other kids and today, a group of children are trying to pull out his hearing aid. You watch this happen and want to stop them.

What are some ways you can be an ally to Sebastian?

1. _____

2. _____

3. _____

Unit V.232 | Confronting/Challenging Bias and Bullying

BE AN ALLY SCENARIO #4

[Student Handout]

Ruby loves to draw. During free time, she draws a picture of her Mom. Jackson, the boy who sits at her table, makes fun of her drawing. He says that skin isn't yellow and the picture looks really bad. Another student at the table joins in to making fun of her picture. You are also at the table and want to do something but don't know what to do.

What are some ways you can be an ally to Ruby?

1. _____

2. _____

3. _____

■ *Anti-Bias Building Blocks: An Elementary Curriculum* | Unit V.233

ONE, SOME, MANY, ALL— STANDING UP TO PREJUDICE

Lesson 22

RATIONALE

The purpose of this activity is for students to understand that there are many ways to help and stand up to prejudice and discrimination. They will learn that there are different ways to make a difference— one person, a small group or a larger part of our society. This lesson provides an opportunity for students to understand and identify the many different ways people can and do stand up to prejudice and discrimination.

OBJECTIVES

- Students will distinguish between one, some, many and all.
- Students will identify ways that one, some, many and all people can stand up to prejudice and understand the different impacts of each.
- Students will express different ways to stand up to prejudice by drawing pictures and writing slogans.

WHAT'S NEEDED

Chart paper (4–8 pieces), markers, crayons, colored pencils and drawing paper (one sheet for each student)

PROCEDURES

1. Begin the lesson by reviewing the definitions for:

    Prejudice: Judging or having an idea about someone or a group of people before you actually know them.

    Discrimination: Unfair treatment of one person or group of people because of the person or group's identity; discrimination is an action that can come from prejudice.

    Ally: Someone who helps or stands up for someone who is being bullied or the target of prejudice.

2. Ask students if they remember some of the ways to be an ally discussed in the previous lesson (Lesson 21). They should include:
    - Reach out to the target.

GRADE LEVEL
K–2

TIME
35 minutes

COMMON CORE STANDARDS
Reading, Writing, Speaking & Listening, Language

STRATEGIES AND SKILLS
Define terms, small group brainstorm, drawing, large group discussion

KEY WORDS AND PHRASES
Aggressor
All
Change
Impact
Many
One
Some

CHILDREN'S BOOKS

Allie's Basketball Dream by Barbara E. Barber

Aunt Harriet's Underground Railroad in the Sky by Faith Ringgold

The Story of Ruby Bridges by Robert Coles

■ *Anti-Bias Building Blocks: An Elementary Curriculum* Unit V.235

- Be extra nice to the target.
- Tell a teacher.
- Ask the aggressor why they said/did that.
- Tell the aggressor to stop.
- Don't join in.
- Ask an older child or adult for help.

Explain that most of these ally actions start with one individual person doing something. Tell students that today we are going to discuss different ways to stand up to prejudice and discrimination that involve groups of people and that we are also going to discuss the impact of different numbers of people standing up together.

3. Ask students, "How much is 'one'? How much is 'some'? How much is 'many'? How much is 'all'?" After being clear about each of these terms, divide students into four groups, assigning one group "one," one group "some," one group "many" and the last group "all." If there are too many children in the small groups, divide them into eight groups.

4. Explain to children that they are going to make a list of items or people of which their group(s) is assigned (one, some many or all). Share an example of each such as: one (bicycle), some (siblings), many (rocks or anything they collect) and all (the whole class). Give students 10 minutes to brainstorm their list of things and make sure there is someone to record their responses on chart paper and someone who will report back to the rest of the group. Younger children who are not writing can draw pictures or generate a list as a whole group.

   After students finish this task, have each group (with one person reporting) share their list.

5. To continue the concept of one, some, many and all, ask one student to stomp their feet (or say the word "yes" loudly). Then ask some (2–3) students to do that, then many (10–12) and then the whole class. Engage students in a class discussion by asking the following questions:
   - How did it sound when one person stomped their feet?
   - How about some? Many? All?
   - What experience do you have when one person takes your side or stands up for you? How about when many people do? How do you feel?

6. Explain to students that with prejudice and discrimination, sometimes if one person helps or stands up it makes a difference and that is what is needed for change to happen. And sometimes, more people get involved and that makes a really big difference. Ask if anyone can share a story or example of this (or you can provide a story/example).

7. Explain to students that as we discuss ways to stand up to prejudice and discrimination, it is helpful to think about one, some, many and all. Share the following scenario with students:

   One of your classmates is constantly being teased and called names because of her size—she is overweight. Kids giggle about her and don't really hide it. She always get picked last for sports and projects.

8. After explaining the situation, ask students these questions:
   - What could <u>one</u> person do to help or stand up for her?
   - What could <u>some</u> students do to help or stand up for her?
   - What could <u>many</u> people do to help or stand up for her?

- What could <u>all</u> (everyone in the class or lunchroom) do to help or stand up for her?
9. Engage students in a discussion by asking the following questions:
    - In this case, do you think one person standing up for her will make a difference? Why or why not?
    - Do you think increasing the numbers will increase the impact? Why or why not?
    - If you stood up for her, how would you feel?
    - Have you ever worked together with others to stand up to prejudice and discrimination? How did that feel?
10. Explain to students that they are going to each create a drawing and write a slogan for each of the four ways (one, some, many and all) to stand up to prejudice and discrimination. Some students will create drawings about one person standing up, some, many and all. Have students count off by 4's: 1, 2, 3, 4, 1, 2, 3, 4 etc. and assign all #1s to "one," #2s to "some," #3s to "many" and #4s to "all." Instruct students to either draw a picture based on the examples shared earlier or create something new. After the drawing, they will come up with a slogan about how what they drew makes a difference. Give students 15 minutes to draw their pictures and when completed, ask for a few volunteers to share their drawings and slogans with the class.
11. Hang up all the drawings and slogans and have students to do a "gallery walk" to see all of them.

EXTENSION ACTIVITIES

- Have students interview parents or family members about their experiences with standing up to prejudice. Create a list of questions in advance by brainstorming ideas with the students and then they can use the questions to interview their parents or other family members. You can have them record the interview (audio or video) or take notes and then later play the recording or have them write up the questions and answers and create a class book with all of the interviews.

- Have students write a realistic fiction story about someone standing up or helping someone out who is the target of prejudice. The story can use an example of one, some, many or all people challenging prejudice and should include what happened, who stood up and why and the impact it made. Students can illustrate the stories as well.

- Read aloud and discuss one or more of the children's books from the list provided in this lesson.

TOGETHER WE CAN MAKE A DIFFERENCE

Lesson 23

RATIONALE

The purpose of this activity is to give students a sense that they can make a difference on a larger scale on issues of prejudice and discrimination, beyond individual actions. This lesson provides an opportunity for students to explore the pros and cons of working with others, reflect on a real-life story that involves a large group of people making a difference and identify characteristics of being an ally through a small group art activity.

OBJECTIVES

- Students will explore what it's like to work with others.
- Students will consider how real people can and have made a difference.
- Students will identify characteristics of an ally through creating an ally art project.

WHAT'S NEEDED

Handouts and Resources: Pros and Cons of Working with Others and *Boy Allowed to Bring 'My Little Pony' Backpack Back to School* (one of each for each student)

Other Material: Picture of a My Little Pony backpack, board/smart board, chart paper (at least one sheet per 4–5 students), old magazines, scissors, markers, pens or pencils

PROCEDURES

1. Begin the lesson by reminding students, from the previous lesson ("One, Some, Many All"), about the different ways to be an ally and stand up to prejudice and discrimination. Remind students that one person can make a difference and many people together can make a difference.

2. Distribute a pen or pencil and the *Pros and Cons of Working with Others* handout to each student. Have students discuss the pros and cons of working with others by turning and talking with a

GRADE LEVEL
K–2

TIME
35 minutes

COMMON CORE STANDARDS
Reading, Writing, Speaking & Listening, Language

STRATEGIES AND SKILLS
Turn and talk, large group discussion, small group art work

KEY WORDS AND PHRASES
Facebook
Forbid
Hashtag
Impact
Superintendent
Twitter

person sitting next to them. Give them two minutes to come up with three things that are positive (pro) about working with a group on something and three things that are difficult (cons) about working with others. Have them record their ideas on the handout. After completing their work, have students share some of the pros and cons and record on the board/smart board.

3. Share an example of the impact of more people standing up by explaining this story:

   A nine-year old boy named Grayson Bruce, who lives in North Carolina, was told he could no longer bring his My Little Pony backpack to school. Kids in the school were teasing and bullying Grayson for carrying the backpack. His Mom said that the bullying got so bad that one morning Grayson did not want to get out of the car because kids were being really mean. She tried to get the school counselors involved but it did not help. The principal told her that Grayson should not bring the backpack to school any more to stop the bullying.

   At this point, stop telling the story and ask the children the following questions:
   - Why do you think the kids were teasing and bullying Grayson?
   - How do you feel about what you heard so far?
   - Do you think the principal did the right thing by telling Grayson he could not bring the backpack to school? Why or why not?
   - What else could have been done?

4. Continue with the story by sharing the following:

   Grayson's Mom, Noreen, did not agree with forbidding Grayson from bringing the backpack to school and she was determined to change that. Grayson's story made national news and his mother started a Facebook page about the incident. More than 65,000 Facebook members supported Grayson by using the #SupportForGrayson hashtag and thousands of followers from around the world posted photos of My Little Pony products and supportive comments. (At this point explain the words Facebook and hashtag or you can just tell students that Grayson got a lot of support on the Internet.) After all of that support was expressed for Grayson, the superintendent met with Grayson's Mom and said he could bring the backpack to school and that the district would organize a parent advisory council on bullying.

5. Distribute the article "Boy Allowed to Bring 'My Little Pony' Backpack Back to School" and read it aloud while students follow along.

6. Engage students in a discussion by asking the following questions:
   - What happened?
   - Why do you think the superintendent changed his mind?
   - What did Grayson's mother do that made a difference?
   - Do you think the same thing would have happened if Grayson hadn't gotten all that support from people all over the country and world? Why or why not?
   - What did you learn from this story?

7. Explain that Grayson's mother acted as an ally by standing up for Grayson. Ask students, "How did she stand up for Grayson? What qualities and characteristics might a person need to be an ally in order to stand up to prejudice and discrimination?" Record their responses on the board/smart board which may include: bravery, compassion, strength, knowledge, people skills, etc.

8. Explain that students are going to work in small groups to create a collage that includes qualities, attitudes and skills of being an ally. Divide students into small groups of 4–5 students. Give each

group a piece of chart paper (or larger pieces of butcher paper) and markers, magazines and scissors. Instruct students to cut out pictures from the magazine and write words or draw pictures on the paper that include characteristics they feel are important for a person fighting prejudice and discrimination to have (e.g., a big heart). Encourage students to think about what happened to Grayson Bruce and the My Little Pony backpack. They can also use some of their brainstormed list of ally characteristics. Then they should work together to represent those characteristics on the paper. In addition to words or pictures to describe qualities, older students can also include quotes of things they think allies might say.

9. After students have finished their projects, have each group share its picture and ideas with the class, explaining what they have identified as important characteristics of an ally. Display the pictures around the room.

EXTENSION ACTIVITIES

- Have students write a letter to Grayson Bruce in which they express how they felt about his story and what ended up happening. They can start by writing their thoughts and feelings on a piece of paper and then turn that into a letter with at least five sentences including: (1) how they felt hearing the story, (2) what made a difference and (3) what they learned from the story. (Grades 1–2).

- Have students create a storyboard on what happened to Grayson. They can start with thinking about the beginning, middle and end of the story, making an illustration for each part. They can then include a sentence or two for each storyboard that describes in their own words what happened and can include dialogue that they imagine was said.

- Read aloud and discuss one or more of the children's books from the list provided in this lesson.

CHILDREN'S BOOKS

Stone Soup by Jon Muth

Brave Girl: Clara and the Shirtwaist Makers' Strike of 1909 by Michelle Markel

Side By Side: The Story of Dolores Huerta and Cesar Chavez by Monica Brown

PROS AND CONS OF WORKING WITH OTHERS

[Student Handout]

What is positive about working with others?

1. _____

_____

2. _____

_____

3. _____

_____

What is difficult about working with others?

1. _____

_____

2. _____

_____

3. _____

_____

BOY ALLOWED TO BRING 'MY LITTLE PONY' BACKPACK BACK TO SCHOOL

[Student Handout]

ASHEVILLE, N.C., March 21 (UPI) -- A North Carolina woman said school officials lifted the ban on her 9-year-old son's "My Little Pony" backpack and are introducing new anti-bullying measures.

Noreen Bruce of Asheville said she met with Buncombe County Schools administrators Thursday and they agreed to allow her son, Grayson, to resume using his "My Little Pony" backpack, which they had earlier told him not to bring to school because it "triggers bullying," the Asheville Citizen-Times reported Friday.

"We are considering all options for getting Grayson back in school," Bruce said Thursday. "We are pleased the school system is working closely with us. All of the options include Grayson taking his My Little Pony bag to school."

Bruce said she felt "much better" after her talk with superintendent Tony Baldwin and director of student services David Thompson.

"We had a real heart-to-heart talk," Bruce said. "I strongly feel we can work together to make things better for Grayson and all the students in our school system."

Bruce said she and Thompson talked about forming a parent advisory council to help the schools deal with bullying-related issues.

Buncombe County Schools administrators released a statement Thursday saying Bruce would be involved in creating "a safety transition plan and an allowance for Grayson to bring the bookbag to school."

"We have appreciated the opportunity to meet with the Bruce family and discuss the issues. We sincerely regret that the issue of being told to leave the bookbag at home was perceived as blaming Grayson. While that was not the intent, the perception became reality. We support Grayson bringing the bookbag to school." the statement said.

Article reprinted by permission of the United Press International (UPI), http://upi.com/2924915. © UPI. All rights reserved.

STANDING UP TO INEQUALITY

Lesson 24

RATIONALE

The purpose of this activity is to help students understand that throughout history, people have worked together to create change in their communities and society. It is important that children understand that social change has come about by people standing up to injustice and working together to challenge it. This lesson provides an opportunity for students to learn about and reflect on the case of Sylvia Mendez and school desegregation as an example of how people can work together to fight discrimination.

OBJECTIVES

- Students will learn about the case of Sylvia Mendez and school desegregation.
- Students will reflect on the case as an example of how people can work together to fight injustice.
- Students will consider the parts of the story that are most meaningful to them and express them in drawing.

WHAT'S NEEDED

Handouts and Resources: Sylvia Mendez and Segregated Schools in California and Sylvia Mendez Photos (one of each for each student); *Separate Is Never Equal: Sylvia Mendez and Her Family's Fight for Desegregation* by Duncan Tonatiuh

Other Material:
- Board/Smart board, drawing paper, markers, crayons and colored pencils
- (Optional) *Voices of History: Sylvia Mendez* video (2 mins., *Education Week*, www.youtube.com/watch?v=SIMWdfSxoh8#t=13)
- (Optional) *Mendez v. Westminster: Desegregating California's Schools* video (8 mins., PBS/WGBH, www.pbslearningmedia.org/resource/osi04.soc.ush.civil.mendez/mendez-v-westminster-desegregating-californias-schools/)
- Internet Access, LCD Projector

GRADE LEVEL
K–2

TIME
35 minutes

COMMON CORE STANDARDS
Reading, Writing, Speaking & Listening

STRATEGIES AND SKILLS
Reading aloud, large group discussion, drawing

KEY WORDS AND PHRASES
Enroll
Lawsuit
Segregated
Separate
Shack

PROCEDURES

1. Begin the lesson by explaining to students that throughout our country's history, people have stood up to prejudice, discrimination and injustice and it has made a difference. Ask students, "Can you think of anything we have already talked about or that you know of where people have worked together to fight prejudice, discrimination and inequality?"

2. Ask students, "Does anyone know what the word segregation means?" Come to a definition of **segregation** as the practice of keeping people of different races, religions, etc., separate from each other. Ask if they know of any examples of segregation in our country. Explain that we will be talking about segregation in this lesson.

3. Read aloud to students the book *Separate Is Never Equal: Sylvia Mendez and Her Family's Fight for Desegregation* by Duncan Tonatiuh. If you do not have the book, distribute the handout *Sylvia Mendez and Segregated Schools in California* to each student and have them follow along as you read.

4. After reading the book or the handout, you may also want to show the students the video *Voices of History: Sylvia Mendez*, where Sylvia Mendez talks about her life and the segregation in the schools during that time or watch PBS/WGBH's 8-minute video *Mendez v. Westminster: Desegregating California's Schools*. You can also show the photos included on the *Sylvia Mendez Photos* handout.

5. After reading about Sylvia Mendez and sharing the photos and video, engage students in a class discussion by asking:

    - How do you feel about what happened to Sylvia and her family?
    - How was this story an example of discrimination?
    - Why did the Mendez family get other families involved?
    - Did that make a difference?
    - How do you think it was to go to the school after it was integrated (white and Latino children all going to the school)?
    - What part of the story stands out for you?

6. Following up on the last question, ask again, "What part of the story stands out for you?" Explain that the most meaningful part of the story does not have to be a positive part or their favorite part but something that meant something to them, positive or negative. Have students share these parts of the story and record them on the board/smart board.

7. Read the list aloud and explain to students that they are now going to pick one part of the story that they most connect to, draw that scene(s) and write a caption for their drawing. Give students 10–15 minutes to create their drawings and captions and then have students share their drawings with the class. When all are complete, create a class story board with all the drawings and captions together. Consider creating a photo exhibit of all of the pictures and captions and posting them in the school or online.

EXTENSION ACTIVITIES

- Have students go home and interview their parents/family members about what they know about school segregation. Prior to the interviews, engage students in developing interview questions including questions about school segregation in general and about Sylvia Mendez and her family's story. Encourage the students to share the story with their family members if they don't know about Sylvia Mendez. Students should either take notes during the interview or video or audiotape the interview.

- Have students learn about other people who have fought against discrimination by either doing research or reading a book. Then have them do a report, either written or oral, about what that person did and how it made a difference.

- Read aloud and discuss one or more of the children's books from the list provided in this lesson.

CHILDREN'S BOOKS

Separate Is Never Equal by Duncan Tonatiuh

Through My Eyes by Ruby Bridges

A is for Activist by Innosanto Nagara

SYLVIA MENDEZ AND SEGREGATED SCHOOLS IN CALIFORNIA

[Student Handout]

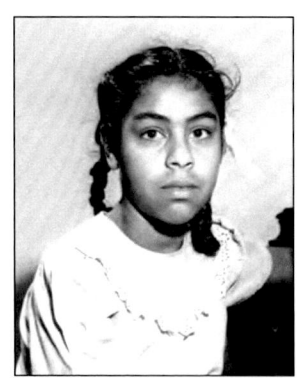

Sylvia Mendez, 11 years old

Sylvia's parents

In the 1940s, most schools in the south and southwest were segregated which means that white, black and Latino children had to attend separate schools. They were not allowed to go to school together and usually the all-white schools were much better schools.

In 1944, Sylvia Mendez was in third grade and her family had just moved from the city of Santa Ana, California to a farm in nearby Westminster, California. When Sylvia, her two younger brothers and cousins went to 17th Street Elementary School on the first day to enroll (accompanied by her Aunt), she and her brothers were told they could not attend the school and had to attend the "Mexican school." Her cousins, who had light skin, were told they could enroll in the school but her Aunt refused to enroll them if Sylvia and her brothers could not attend. Sylvia and her family were American and spoke perfect English and they did not understand why they could not attend the school.

Sylvia's parents were very upset about what happened at school that day. The next day, her father went to school and met with school officials to find out why she and her brothers could not attend the school. No one could give him an answer as to why his children could not attend the 17th Street Elementary School. He was told that Sylvia and her brothers had to attend Hoover Elementary, which was known as the "Mexican school." Hoover Elementary was a two-room shack in the middle of the city's Mexican neighborhood and the books and education were not as good as the all-white school.

Sylvia's father, Mr. Mendez, talked with coworkers, friends and other parents who had also been told they could not attend the 17th Street Elementary because they were Mexican. They all wanted the best for their children and they didn't feel the other school would prepare them for high school and college. Over the next several years, Mr. Mendez worked with other parents to file a lawsuit in order to allow Latino children to attend their neighborhood school. They fought their case in the courts and the case was called *Mendez v. Westminster*. In 1947, they won the right of Mexican-American children to attend white schools.

SYLVIA MENDEZ PHOTOS

[Student Handout]

Westminster School (17th Street Elementary School), 1944

Hoover (Mexican) Elementary School, 1944

Hoover School, 1944
Fourth & Figh Grade Classes

Unit V.250 | Confronting/Challenging Bias and Bullying

Sylvia Mendez
2010 Presidential Medal of Freedom Recipient

MAKING A DIFFERENCE IN MY SCHOOL

RATIONALE

The purpose of this activity is to give students a real-life experience with social action by identifying something unfair/unjust in their school that they want to change. This lesson provides an opportunity for students to consider how to make the world more fair and just, identify what personal characteristics they have that have contributed to helping others and develop and implement a project to make their school more equal or fair.

OBJECTIVES

- Students will reflect on something they have done (or want to do) to make the world a better place and what personal characteristics have contributed to their helping others.

- Students will envision the characteristics of an ideal school and identify what needs to change in order to finish this statement

- Students will brainstorm and select a project to make their school more equal or fair.

WHAT'S NEEDED

Drawing paper, crayons, markers, index cards (at least one per student)

PROCEDURES

1. Begin the activity by having students think about everything they have learned so far about identity, prejudice, discrimination and inequality. Ask students, "If you could do one thing about inequality in our school or community, what would it be?" Have students write a few words on an index card to express what they would do. Shuffle the index cards and hand out one card to each student and have them read aloud the words on the card they received.

2. Have students think about something they have done to make their school or community a better place. It can be something large or small (e.g., listened to a friend when they were upset;

Lesson 25

GRADE LEVEL
K–2

TIME
35 minutes

COMMON CORE STANDARDS
Reading, Writing, Speaking & Listening

STRATEGIES AND SKILLS
Turn and talk, visioning, drawing, brainstorming

KEY WORDS AND PHRASES
Ideal

Anti-Bias Building Blocks: An Elementary Curriculum | Unit V.253

gave up their seat on the bus or train for a person with a disability; helped out at a soup kitchen or homeless shelter).

After they have thought of what they did or would want to do, they will talk with a person sitting near them and respond to this question: "What personal quality do you have that helped make a difference?" Instruct them to think about two or three qualities that they will share with their partner. You may want to provide an example. Remind them that as one of them is sharing the qualities, their partner should listen and not comment. After, have students share aloud some of what they shared with their partner and record those qualities on the board or chart paper.

3. Explain to students that now they are going to envision their ideal school. Ask them to close their eyes. If some students are not comfortable doing so, they can keep their eyes opened but should focus on the questions and the activity. When everyone is ready, say the following to students:

   I want you to think about a perfect or ideal school. You love coming to this school every day. You can't wait to step in the building in the morning. Imagine what your classroom looks like. How do students talk to each other? Now think about the hallways and the other places in school like the cafeteria, gym and auditorium. What do you see? What are some of the sounds that you hear? How do teachers talk to students? How do students talk to teachers? Is there bullying and prejudice? How do students feel about what they are learning? What are they excited about?

4. After doing the visioning exercise, immediately hand out drawing paper and materials and have students draw a picture of what they saw in their minds. They can either draw the classroom they envisioned or the whole school. They should include students and some dialogue of how people in the building (kids, teachers, other adults) talk to each other. Give student 5–10 minutes for this task.

5. Ask students, "What is getting in the way of us having our ideal school? What needs to change in our classroom or school in order for it to be a safe, productive and equal place?" Brainstorm ideas of what they can do to make the school better and solve problems. Create a list which might look like the following:

   - Stop name calling and bullying.
   - Students should have a say in things that matter in the school.
   - Schoolyard should be cleaner.
   - Lunch should taste better.
   - There will be a lot less yelling.
   - There will be more activities to play at recess.

6. After brainstorming a list of ideas, work together to come up with one project idea that you can take on as a class. You can then divide students into smaller task-oriented groups and work on the details to fully realize the project. Manageable projects might include: doing a school-wide assembly on bullying, developing a clean-up crew for the playground, starting a student government committee with a few representatives from each grade, etc.

EXTENSION ACTIVITIES

- Have students create posters and signs to publicize their chosen project to the rest of the community. The posters should include an engaging picture or photo, a catchy slogan or title for the project, why it is important (what problem the project is trying to solve) and what others can do to help.

- Invite a local elected official (school board member, town/city council member, State Assembly person) into the classroom to speak to the children about community action projects. Get children involved in writing a letter to the person to invite them to their school, developing interview questions, asking the questions during the interview, taking a photo and writing something up about what the person said.

- Read aloud and discuss one or more of the children's books from the list provided in this lesson.

CHILDREN'S BOOKS

One Love by Cedella Marley

Yertle the Turtle and Other Stories by Dr. Seuss

Those Shoes by Maribeth Boelts

ROLES WE PLAY IN BULLYING AND BIAS

RATIONALE

The purpose of this activity is for students to learn about the different roles that are played in a bullying and/or bias incident and understand that we all play different roles at different times. Through the process of reflecting on roles, students will be more intentional and thoughtful when faced with these situations. This lesson provides an opportunity for students to define the different roles played in bullying and bias, reflect on their own experiences with the roles and consider various ways to be an ally.

OBJECTIVES

- Students will review what bullying is and explore how they see it in their school.
- Students will define roles in a bullying/bias situation they read: target, aggressor, bystander and ally.
- Students will reflect on their own experiences playing the four roles.
- Students will consider ways to be an ally.

WHAT'S NEEDED

Handouts and Resources: The New Girl and The Roles We Play (one of each for each student)

Other Material: Index cards (one for each student), pens or pencils

PROCEDURES

1. Begin the lesson by explaining that in the previous section, students learned about and examined forms of bias and bullying and that now we will focus on ways that individuals and groups of people can challenge and confront bias and bullying. Do a quick brainstorm of how people can do this but keep this brief. Ask students, "How can we challenge bullying and prejudice in our lives?"

Lesson 20

GRADE LEVEL
3–5

TIME
45 minutes

COMMON CORE STANDARDS
Reading, Speaking & Listening, Language

STRATEGIES AND SKILLS
Define terms, small group discussion, large group discussion

KEY WORDS AND PHRASES
Aggressor
Ally
Bystander
Challenge
Confront
Target

2. Ask students, "Have you ever moved to a new place and had to meet new people and attend a new school where you did not know anyone? Did you ever join a new club or sports team where you did not know anyone? What happened and how did that feel?"

3. Explain to students that they are going to read a story about someone in a similar situation. Explain that as they read the story, they should think about some of things they studied earlier (stereotyping, prejudice, bullying, etc.). Distribute a copy of the story *The New Girl* and have students read it silently or project the story on the smart board and read aloud.

4. Engage students in a class discussion by asking the following questions:
   - How did you feel while reading (or listening) to the story?
   - Do you think something like this really happened or could? How so?
   - In the story, we learned that Hilda felt like her classmates treated her as if she were "invisible." What do you think she meant by this?
   - Does the story include examples of stereotyping or prejudice? If so, explain.
   - Was there bullying taking place in the story?

5. Review the definition of bullying: Bullying is when one person or a group behaves in ways—on purpose and over and over—that make someone feel hurt, afraid or embarrassed. Ask students, "In our school, what are some identity characteristics that tend to be the basis for bullying?" Brainstorm a list and record on the board/smart board. The list might look something like this:
   - Weight/size
   - Gender (boys "acting" like girls, girls "acting" like boys)
   - Not speaking English well
   - Having gay or lesbian parents
   - Being Jewish or Muslim
   - Having special needs

6. Distribute *The Roles We Play* handout to each student. Have students silently read the definitions for target, aggressor, bystander and ally. Ask the following questions:
   - Who was the target in the story we read together? How so?
   - Who was the aggressor in this story? How so?
   - Who were the bystanders in this story? How so?
   - Who was an ally in this story? How so?

7. Ask students to silently reflect on the four roles. Ask, "Do you think that you have been in each of these roles at one time or another?" Explain to students that they will have 10 minutes to think and write about the different roles they play at different times. Explain that they will have time to think about each of the roles in the boxes and write some notes (either words to remind them or full sentences) about a time they played each of these roles and they can also include a picture if time permits. Encourage students to complete all four squares but if they have no experience with one of the roles, they may leave it blank. They can think about experiences at school, at home, in clubs or sports activities, in their neighborhood, etc.

8. 📷 After they have written notes in the boxes, divide students into groups of five. Explain that each student in the group will share one of her or his words and pictures from one of their boxes and they will choose which box to share. Explain that students should explain enough about the situation so that the other group members will understand the event and the student's role in it. Review classroom guidelines and emphasize good listening.

9. After the small groups have finished sharing, engage students in a whole class discussion using the following questions:

   - Was it difficult or easy to come up with a story for each role? How so?
   - How did you feel sharing a story with your classmates?
   - How did you feel listening to other people's experiences?
   - Which square did you choose to talk about with your classmates? (Read aloud each one and have students raise hands.)
   - Which square was the easiest to talk about and why? Which was the most difficult to talk about and why?
   - Did you notice any similar themes in the stories that were told in your group?
   - Why do you think people sometimes stand by when unfairness, bullying or other hurtful acts occur?
   - Why do you think some people decide to be an ally?

10. Close the lesson by distributing index cards and have students think of one way they can be an ally. Their ideas could be based on *The New Girl* story or one of the experiences they shared. They can write the word or sentence on the card. Collect the cards, shuffle them and then read aloud some of their suggestions. Hold onto these cards for the next lesson.

EXTENSION ACTIVITIES

- Have students interview a parent, family member, neighbor or older sibling about their experience with the four roles. Ask them to write or talk about situations in their lives where they have played each of the roles and then have students write a story about the person and the roles they have played.

- Have a discussion with students about cyberbullying. Ask students if they know what cyberbullying is and whether they have seen examples of it. Explain that cyberbullying is the bullying that uses technology (such as computers, video games, cell phones or

FLIPPED CLASSROOM IDEA

Make a short video of you completing the *Roles We Play* handout and you talking about at least one of the roles you have played and giving details about the situation.

CHILDREN'S BOOKS

Confessions of a Former Bully by Trudy Ludwig

My Secret Bully by Trudy Ludwig

Say Something by Peggy Moss

other electronic devices) to hurt other people and seek examples from them that they have seen. Talk with them about the different roles played in cyberbullying and talk about ways to be an ally online.

- Read aloud and discuss one or more of the children's books from the list provided in this lesson.

THE NEW GIRL

[Student Handout]

Hilda was in fourth grade and new to Central Elementary School. Her family had recently moved into the area and they didn't know anyone. Her mother worked as a cashier and her Dad was a day laborer, which meant he got work on a daily basis and usually was gone for many hours each day. Hilda had been "the new girl" other times, but even so it was always hard to meet new friends and get new teachers and fourth grade seemed different. Everyone already had their friends.

As Ms. Robertson introduced Hilda to the class, some students in the back of the room giggled. One student whispered loud enough for others to hear except for the teacher, "Look at that outfit! Does this girl get her clothes from charity or what?" Others joined in the laughter. Hilda had been teased many times before so she was used to it but it still hurt. She knew the kids laughed at her clothes and sneakers because they weren't the latest style and when she began to speak, they made fun of her accent. It had all happened before. Ms. Robertson paused for a moment while the giggling stopped and then continued by saying, "Let's all make Hilda feel welcome."

As the day continued, Hilda felt worse and worse and did not feel welcomed at all. There was a group of kids who laughed every time they looked her way and when it was time to divide into small groups to work on an assignment, no one in the group even talked to her. In fact, everyone acted as if she was invisible. When it was lunchtime, everyone began making their way to the cafeteria. Another student brushed past her and said, "Hope she knows there's no free lunch at this school." Everyone laughed at this comment except one girl named Lily who said, "C'mon, give her a break. It's her first day and she hasn't done anything to us."

THE ROLES WE PLAY

[Student Handout]

BOX A: TARGET Someone who is bullied or treated in hurtful ways by a person or a group on purpose and over and over.	**BOX B: AGGRESSOR** Someone who says or does hurtful things.
BOX C: BYSTANDER Someone who sees bullying or prejudice happening and does not say or do anything.	**BOX D: ALLY** Someone who helps or stands up for someone who is being bullied or the target of prejudice.

BEING AN ALLY

Lesson 21

RATIONALE

The purpose of this activity is for students to explore the different ways of being an ally and give them tools in being able to be an ally. This lesson provides an opportunity to students to expand their thinking around what is ally behavior, explore the ways in which they have and have not been an ally in the past and explore ally behavior by writing realistic fiction.

OBJECTIVES

- Students will consider ways to be an ally.
- Students will reflect on the ways they have been and not been an ally.
- Students will explore ally behaviors by writing a realistic fiction story about being an ally.

WHAT'S NEEDED

Handouts and Resources: Being an Ally Self-Reflection (one for each student)

Other Material: Pens or pencils

PROCEDURES

1. Begin the lesson by reminding students about the different roles that are played in bullying and prejudice situations. Focus on the ally role and ask students to define **ally** as someone who helps or stands up for someone who is being bullied or the target of prejudice. From the previous lesson, read aloud the index cards students wrote with ideas about how to be an ally.

2. After hearing some of those ideas, ask students, "What are some ways to be an ally when you see a situation of bullying or prejudice?" Come up with a list that looks like the following and for each, ask for examples:
   - Support the target (e.g., include the target in an activity, be

GRADE LEVEL
3–5

TIME
45 minutes

COMMON CORE STANDARDS
Reading, Writing, Speaking & Listening

STRATEGIES AND SKILLS
Large group discussion, self-reflection in writing, fishbowl, realistic fiction writing

KEY WORDS AND PHRASES
Ally
Never
Often
Self-reflection
Sometimes

■ *Anti-Bias Building Blocks: An Elementary Curriculum*

extra nice to the target, ask them if they want to talk about what happened).

- Don't participate in the bullying or prejudice.
- Tell the aggressor to stop.
- Tell an adult you can trust.
- Get to know people before judging them.
- Be an ally online.

3. After coming up with the list, distribute the *Being An Ally Self-Reflection* handout to each student. Explain to students that they will reflect on how many of the ally behaviors they use and how often by checking often, sometimes or never. You may need to define those terms. They will also answer a few other questions. Give students 10 minutes to complete the handout.

4. Engage students in a discussion by asking the following questions:
   - Are some of these ally behaviors more difficult than others? Why or why not?
   - Are there some ally behaviors you do more than others or not at all? Please explain.
   - In addition to being an ally for someone else, can you use these ally behaviors to stand up for yourself?

5. Explain to students that they will be doing a fishbowl activity. Remind them about the fishbowl activity they did in a previous lesson. Ask, "What is a fishbowl?"

6. Explain that this activity is like a fishbowl in that we will make a circle and some students will be inside the circle (i.e. in a fishbowl) and the rest of the students will be observers outside of it. Ask for 4–6 volunteers who are willing to sit inside the circle and talk about their experiences with bullying and prejudice. Create a small circle with chairs for those sitting inside the circle. Arrange the other chairs to sit outside this smaller circle. Before discussing the specific ground rules for the fishbowl, review your classroom guidelines as past experiences and strong feelings may emerge from the fishbowl.

7. Explain the ground rules for the fishbowl:
   a. The observers are not allowed to speak. Their job is to listen and learn from the fishbowl students. The observers will have an opportunity to discuss any issues that emerge later.
   b. You (the teacher) will facilitate the fishbowl discussion and you will make sure everyone has the opportunity to talk.
   c. (Optional) Once the fishbowl discussion has happened for at least 10 minutes and you sense that others want to speak,

---

FLIPPED CLASSROOM IDEA

Make a short video of you talking about the *Being An Ally Self-Reflection* handout. You should fill out the form and verbally share what your responses are including the four questions at the end.

NOTE 6: FISHBOWL OPTIONS

Due to the sensitive nature of these discussions about bullying and prejudice, you may choose to do this fishbowl activity in a variety of ways. You can have students who are inside the fishbowl talk about their own experience with bullying, prejudice and being an ally or talk about one that they witnessed or observed. Another option is to have students write about experiences related to the questions below (which will be anonymous) and some of those essays can be shared anonymously in the fishbowl for students to discuss.

you can allow a time where if someone in the observer groups wants to join the fishbowl, they can tap the shoulder of someone in the fishbowl and take their place. Use this step at your discretion.

    d. Use the following questions to guide the fishbowl discussion and at the same time, allow it to move in the natural direction the conversation is moving.

- Have you ever been the target of bullying? What happened? How did you feel?
- Have you ever been the target of prejudice or discrimination? What happened? How did you feel?
- In the situations you described, did you try to help or stand up for yourself?
- In the situations you described, did anyone act as an ally to you? What happened? How did you feel?
- Have you ever been an ally to someone? If so, what happened? How did you feel?

8. After the fishbowl, engage the whole class in a discussion by asking the following questions:
   - To the observers, was it difficult to not respond to the comments made during the fishbowl? Why?
   - To the fishbowl students, how did it feel to share your feelings about bullying, prejudice and being an ally?
   - Did you hear anything from the fishbowl that surprised you?
   - What did you learn from the experience?
   - What came out from the discussion about being an ally?

9. Have students begin to write a realistic fiction story in which there is bullying or prejudice/discrimination and an ally gets involved. They can use class time to outline the story and then complete it for homework. Explain or remind them that realistic fiction is a story that *could* happen in real life and whose characters are fictional (i.e. made up) but are true to life. Make sure that they use fictional names (i.e. no one in the class or school) and not use specific details of a real-life situation that students in the class are familiar with. For the outline, have them include the following details:
   - characters (main character, supporting characters and be sure to include target, aggressors, bystanders and ally)
   - background information—do not just start with the incident, help us get to know the characters a little
   - the incident that requires an ally
   - the overall plot
   - setting (where does the story take place?)
   - theme or "message" the story will convey

10. When stories are complete, have students read their stories aloud for the rest of the class.

EXTENSION ACTIVITIES

- Watch some of the videos in Cartoon Network's Speak Up Campaign at www.cartoonnetwork.com/video/stopbullying/episodes/. As a class, explore how you might join with Cartoon Network by speaking up. Brainstorm ideas for a project (either as a whole class or small groups), work out all the details and make it happen.

CHILDREN'S BOOKS

Gifts from the Enemy by Trudy Ludwig

One by Kathryn Otoshi

My Name is Bilal by Asma Mobbin-Uddin

- Have students do research projects on famous people who stood up to bullying, prejudice or discrimination. First, brainstorm a list of people they may already know. Then have students go home and interview family members and others about allies in history. Then narrow down the list and have students engage in research projects to learn more about the person, what the issue was, how they acted as an ally and the extent to which it made a difference.

- Read aloud and discuss one or more of the children's books from the list provided in this lesson.

BE AN ALLY SELF-REFLECTION

[Student Handout]

Instructions: For each of the following ally behaviors indicate how often you have been an ally in that way by checking often, sometimes or never.

I have been an ally by...	Often	Sometimes	Never
Supporting the target	( )	( )	( )
Not participating in the bullying or prejudice	( )	( )	( )
Telling the aggressor to stop	( )	( )	( )
Telling an adult I trust	( )	( )	( )
Getting to know people before judging them	( )	( )	( )
Be an ally online	( )	( )	( )

Complete the following statements.

1. I am most comfortable being an ally by _____

2. I am least comfortable being an ally by _____

3. To be an ally more often, I need to _____

4. My goal for being an ally is _____

CHALLENGING PREJUDICE AND DISCRIMINATION

Lesson 22

RATIONALE

The purpose of this activity is for students to understand that being an ally can mean standing up for yourself or someone else individually, in a group or as part of a larger context or movement. This lesson provides an opportunity for students to learn different strategies for confronting prejudice and discrimination, reflect on how people can make a difference and identify individual, group and national/global actions for challenging prejudice and discrimination.

OBJECTIVES

- Students will learn several strategies for confronting prejudice and discrimination and identify examples.
- Students will reflect on how people can make a difference individually, as a group or as part of a larger movement.
- Students will consider individual, group/community, and national/global actions to stand up to prejudice and discrimination.

WHAT'S NEEDED

Handouts and Resources: Strategies to Challenge Prejudice and Discrimination and Addressing Different Levels of Prejudice and Discrimination Worksheet (one of each for each student)

Other Material: Drawing paper and markers, colored pencils

Advance Preparation: Write on board/smart board or chart paper the quote "Never doubt that a small group of thoughtful, committed citizens can change the world; indeed, it's the only thing that ever has." —Margaret Mead

PROCEDURES

1. Begin the lesson by reviewing what being an ally is. Ask students to define the term: Someone who helps or stands up for someone who is being bullied or the target of prejudice.
2. Reflect on the previous lesson by asking students if they remember

GRADE LEVEL
3–5

TIME
45 minutes

COMMON CORE STANDARDS
Reading, Writing, Speaking & Listening

STRATEGIES AND SKILLS
Review terms, large group discussion, small group work

KEY WORDS AND PHRASES
Challenge
Community
Confront
Global
Intention
Strategy
Support

CHILDREN'S BOOKS

Grace for President by Kelly DiPucchio

Shin-chi's Canoe by Nicola Campbell

A Picture Book of Harriet Tubman by David Adler

■ Anti-Bias Building Blocks: An Elementary Curriculum

👆 **NOTE 2**

It is important to talk with students about the potential risks/consequences of being an ally. They should understand and assess the risks involved in any particular situation before choosing the best way to respond. If they are unsure if it is safe to get directly involved, they should seek the help of a trusted adult.

FLIPPED CLASSROOM IDEA

Make a short video of you reading aloud the scenario below (or you can create your own) and then select one or two strategies from the *Strategies to Challenge Prejudice and Discrimination* handout and give examples of what you would say and how you would say it.

Scenario: *There is a new student in your school who speaks with a different accent than the other kids and wears a hijab (head covering). She also eats different food from the rest of the kids and students tease her at lunch. One time, someone threw her food in the garbage saying it was "gross." The students seem to know she is Muslim but don't really know what that means. A few students called her a terrorist.*

the different ways one can be an ally. The list might look something like this:

- Support the target (e.g., include the target in an activity, be extra nice to the target, ask them if they want to talk about what happened).
- Don't participate in the bullying or prejudice.
- Tell the aggressor to stop.
- Tell an adult you can trust.
- Get to know people before judging them.
- Be an ally online.

3. 📷 Distribute the *Strategies to Challenge Prejudice and Discrimination* handout to each student. Go over the sheet in the following ways:

    - Have one student read one of the strategies.
    - After the strategy is read, ask for an example of that strategy.
    - After an example is shared, ask a student to stand up and say/act out the example.
    - Next to "for example" on the handout, have students write out what the student said or include their own original example.

4. After completing the handout together, engage students in a discussion by asking the following questions:

    - Was it easy or difficult to think of examples for some of the strategies?
    - Have you ever tried any of these strategies?
    - Do any of these feel easier to do than others? Why or why not?
    - Are there other strategies you use to help or stand up to someone?
    - What are the possible consequences for being an ally?
    - Are you likely to use some of these in the future? Please explain.

5. Explain to students that the last strategy on the list is about seeking help from others and involving more people. Ask students, "Can someone read the last strategy aloud again? ("Look for support.") What does it mean to look for support?" On the board/smart board, project the following quote:

    "Never doubt that a small group of thoughtful, committed citizens can change the world; indeed, it's the only thing that ever has."
    —Margaret Mead

Ask students, "What do you think this quote means?" Explain that many social change movements started with one person or a small group of people wanting to make a difference in the world and it spread to other people. Explain that in subsequent lessons, we will learn more about times in our history where this occurred.

6. Distribute the handout *Addressing Different Levels of Prejudice and Discrimination Worksheet* each students. Divide students into small groups of 4–5 students each. Remind students about the different forms of prejudice/discrimination discussed in previous lessons as a guideline for coming up with examples.

   - Sexism
   - Ableism
   - Homophobia
   - Anti-Semitism
   - Racism
   - Islamophobia
   - Ageism
   - Weightism
   - Classism

7. Have students work in small groups to complete the worksheet and come up with 2–3 examples for each level. After completing the sheet, they will choose one of their examples and draw a picture to go along with it. The picture may also include dialogue.

8. When students complete their worksheet and pictures, have them hang up the pictures and hold onto their handouts. Each group will present at least one example to share.

9. After groups have presented one of their examples, engage students in a group discussion by asking the following questions:
   - What are the benefits of being an ally?
   - How is taking individual action, community action and national/global action similar and different from each other?
   - Have you ever acted as an ally on any of these levels?

EXTENSION ACTIVITIES

- Have students learn about social change movements in history by interviewing parents/family members, conducting Internet research and reading books. Ask them come up with at least three social change movements they can identify by naming the movement and articulating what the movement's goals.

- Have students take one of their examples from the *Strategies to Challenge Prejudice and Discrimination* handout and write a realistic fiction story that begins with what the act of prejudice/discrimination was and then the student should develop the story by giving details about what happened, what the person (or they themselves, if the story is from the first person perspective) did or said to challenge prejudice, how the person reacted and what happened next. Explain that challenging prejudice and discrimination does not always have a positive outcome so they can choose to make the story end on a positive note or not.

- Read aloud and discuss one or more of the children's books from the list provided in this lesson.

STRATEGIES TO CHALLENGE PREJUDICE AND DISCRIMINATION

[Student Handout]

Challenging prejudice and discrimination, either as a target or as an ally, can be difficult but it becomes easier with practice. Read the strategies below and where there is a blank, fill in what you might say.

1. *Explain how you feel.*
   Try to help the person who said or did something understand how it felt to you or others who heard or saw what happened. Use "I" statements not "you" statements.
   I might say _____

2. *Don't assume people mean harm or hurt.*
   Many people who say or do hurtful things do so because they don't know it is hurtful. Because they don't mean harm, they often assume no harm was done. Explaining how someone was hurt by a person's words or actions can help the person learn how to get along with others better.
   I might say _____

3. *Talk to the person alone.*
   By speaking with someone privately (one-on-one), you don't embarrass the person publicly. He or she may be more open to listening and hearing what you are saying one-on-one than in a group.
   I might say _____

4. *Help people rethink their stereotypes.*
   Whenever possible, give information that helps the other person learn new information and rethink stereotypes and generalizations they have learned.
   I might say _____

5. *Tell the person to stop.*
   Sometimes it is important to simply interrupt the comment or action and not explain. You may not feel comfortable or ready to have a discussion but you want to let the person know their comments and/or actions are not okay.
   I might say _____

6. *Model fairness and respectful behavior yourself.*
   People who challenge prejudice and discrimination must demonstrate fairness and respect in their daily life.
   I might say _____

7. *Look for support.*
   Often, others may not like things that are being said and done. Sometimes they don't speak up but want to. Remind friends, peers and classmates that if you work together, the message will be more effective than if one of you is always confronting bias alone.
   I might say _____

ADDRESSING DIFFERENT LEVELS OF PREJUDICE AND DISCRIMINATION

[Student Handout]

Form of Prejudice: _____

Individual Action (Example: Interrupt a joke.)

School Action (Example: Hold a school-wide meeting about stopping bullying.)

Community or National Action (Example: Attend a town or state rally about racial injustice.)

STRENGTH IN NUMBERS

RATIONALE

The purpose of this activity is to help students understand the complexity of ally behavior and the power and strength in numbers when addressing prejudice and discrimination. Using an example of the burning of thirty African-American churches in 1995 and 1996, this lesson provides an opportunity for students to learn about those incidents, analyze ally behavior by reading letters written by concerned citizens and create slogans about being an ally.

OBJECTIVES

- Students will learn about the predominantly African-American churches that were burned down in 1995 and 1996.
- Students will analyze the different ways people chose to be allies by reading letters written in response to an advertisement about those incidents.
- Students will create slogans and accompanying pictures/logos about being an ally.

WHAT'S NEEDED

Handouts and Resources: Advertisement: *The Fire of Hate Consumes Us All* and *Letters to Burned Churches* (one of each for each student)

Other Material: Chart paper (one piece per 4-5 students), markers, colored pencils

PROCEDURES

1. Begin the lesson by reviewing Lesson 22, "Challenging Prejudice and Discrimination." Ask students for examples of how to stand up to prejudice and discrimination and encourage them to consider individual as well as group actions. Explain to students that beyond their schools and communities, unjust and unfair things also happen outside their communities—in the larger society or world. Often these acts of unfairness are a result of stereotypes, prejudice or discrimination and they can be hateful or violent.

Lesson 23

GRADE LEVEL
3-5

TIME
45 minutes

COMMON CORE STANDARDS
Reading, Writing, Speaking & Listening, Language

STRATEGIES AND SKILLS
Reading aloud, large group discussion, turn and talk, small group art work

KEY WORDS AND PHRASES
Advertisement
Bigotry
Citizen
Congregation
Consumes
Cowardly
Impact
Outraged

When such situations occur, people must decide to either ignore what is happening or to act.

2. Explain to students that an example of a hateful act in our country was the intentional burning of more than thirty churches with predominately African-American congregations, between January 1995 and May 1996. Two civil rights organizations, the Anti-Defamation League (ADL) and the National Urban League, placed advertisements in newspapers across the country, including major ones such as *The New York Times, The Washington Post* and the *Atlanta Journal-Constitution*. The ad told about the churches being burnt down by people who did not like African Americans and encouraged people to write letters of support and send donations to help rebuild the churches. The advertisement was called "The Fire of Hate Consumes Us All: Help Put It Out Now."

FLIPPED CLASSROOM IDEA

Make a short video of you reading the advertisement aloud. After reading the advertisement and explaining a little of the background, ask a few of the discussion questions provided for students to reflect upon.

3. Project the advertisement on the board (or distribute copies to each student) and engage students in a discussion by asking the following questions:

   - What does the advertisement say? How does it convey its point?
   - Why do you think that these two organizations placed ads in the newspaper? What was their goal?
   - How do you think people reacted upon hearing about the burned churches?
   - What do you think concerned citizens might do?

4. Tell students that as a result of the advertisements, thousands of people responded. Distribute the *Letters to the Burned Churches* handout to each student. Working in pairs, have students read each of the letters and verbally respond to the following questions for each letter:

   - What stands out for you in the letter?
   - What kind of ally behavior was exhibited?
   - Why do you think the person decided to do something?
   - Do you think it had an impact and if so, what?

NOTE 4

If the language in the *Letters to the Burned Churches* is too difficult for your students to read independently, instead of having students read the letters in pairs, read aloud together and paraphrase and define words for the students so the meaning is clear. After that have students get into pairs and discuss the questions provided.

5. After working in pairs, have students come back to the larger group and ask for a few volunteers to each share one of the letters and their response to it.

6. After reading the letters, engage students in a large group discussion by asking the following questions:

   - How did you feel listening to the letters that people wrote?
   - What are some of the things people might have done to show they were allies?
   - How does being an ally, even to people you don't know,

strengthen communities?

- Do you think this also had an impact on the people who wrote the letters? How so?

- What might happen in communities when people don't speak out against prejudice, discrimination and hate?

7. Explain to students that now they are going to work in small groups to develop a slogan and logo or drawing about acting as an "ally." Ask students, "What is a slogan?" If they do not know, define **slogan** as a short, memorable and catchy phrase used in advertising or to promote an idea. Ask if anyone can share an example and if not, share an example such as: "M&M's melts in your mouth, not in your hands." Also, point to the advertisement about the burning of the churches, "The Fire of Hate Consumes Us All: Help Put It Out Now."

8. Divide students into small groups of 4–5 each. In the small groups, instruct students to think together about a slogan that will help develop allies in their school or community. Give them 15 minutes to (1) agree on a slogan that promotes acting as an ally, (2) decide on a drawing or logo that goes along with the slogan and (3) decide how to present it to the rest of the class.

9. After students have finished their slogans, have each group share its picture and ideas with the class, explaining their slogan and how they came up with it as a group.

EXTENSION ACTIVITIES

- After all the groups have presented their slogans (from the lesson), have students vote on the one they like best. Then, as a class, create a campaign to spread the slogan around the school. Think together about all the strategies to do this and then implement the plan.

- Have students go home and interview their parents or family members about the African-American church burnings and ask them what they already know about it. If they are not familiar with the incident, explain to students that they should tell their parents/family members about it, sharing the advertisement with them and any other information they remember. Have they come back to school and reflect on their reactions either by writing a paragraph about their conversation or sharing their thoughts in class.

- Read aloud and discuss one or more of the children's books from the list provided in this lesson.

CHILDREN'S BOOKS

Ellie McDoodle, New Kid in School by Ruth McNally Barshaw

Harvesting Hope: The Story of Cesar Chavez by Kathleen Krull

Nelson Mandela by Kadir Nelson

ADVERTISEMENT: THE FIRE OF HATE CONSUMES US ALL

[Student Handout]

The Fire of Hate Consumes Us All

Help Put It Out Now

Far more than the men, women and children of the more than 30 burned Black Churches have been hurt by the cowardly acts of prejudice that burned their places of worship.

We have all been hurt by these acts of hate.

They have defaced the values that affect each of us. They have violated our American guarantees of freedom regardless of race, religion or ethnicity.

At the Anti-Defamation League and the National Urban League, we know all too well that people of good will must never be silent in the face of bigotry. The consequences of silence are deadly.

You can — indeed you must — do something to stop these vicious hatemongers from succeeding. Speak out. Tell the victims they are not alone. Show the perpetrators that their acts of hate enrage all good Americans.

Show your support by writing letters to the members of the burned churches. Mail them to us and we will forward them to the appropriate addresses. And, if you are able, please contribute as much as you can to help rebuild these houses of worship.

Send your check, made out to *ADL-Rebuild the Churches Fund*, and mail to the address below. All contributions to this fund will be distributed for the rebuilding of these churches.

ADL and the Urban League will stand together to combat hatred, bigotry, intolerance and discrimination. We will join to develop programs to battle the bigots, to champion laws against crimes of hate and to urge our fellow Americans to reject the ugly messages of the haters who plague our world.

Edmund Burke said it best, "All that is necessary for the triumph of evil is for good men to do nothing."

David H. Strassler
National Chairman

Abraham H. Foxman
National Director

ADL Anti-Defamation League®

Hugh B. Price
President

Reginald K. Brack, Jr
Chairman of the Board of Trustees

National Urban League, Inc.

Rebuild the Churches Fund, Anti-Defamation League, 823 United Nations Plaza, New York, NY 10017   www.adl.org

LETTERS TO THE BURNED CHURCHES

[Student Handout]

The letters below are excerpts from some of the thousands of letters sent to the ADL—Rebuild the Church Fund following the burning of more than three dozen African-American churches between January 1995 and May 1996.

...

Dear Fellow Human Beings,
We are shocked and outraged by the burnings of your churches. We are so sorry this has happened to you. We must all stand together. This is an outrage against humanity. We have enclosed a check to help with the rebuilding.

...

Dear Church Members,
I am writing to express my sorrow and outrage over the burning of black churches across our Southern states. These are clearly acts of prejudice that hurt all of us, black and white. As white parents raising a black son, we are especially aware of the fear and anger these incidents cause for the majority of all Americans. I have called my U.S. Senator to express my outrage and demand a continuing investigation about these burnings.

...

Dear New Friend,
Let me know how we can help. In our day school we have 250 children and our Sunday school for public school students has 100 children. Many of them are eager to become pen pals to new friends, to build bridges of friendship that cannot be burned down. I may have pictures that would work for a Christian education program and our teachers may have resources that can help you get back on your feet again. If you send me a contact name and address, I'll go to work.

...

Dear Fellow Americans,
We want you to know that we elderly residents of Florida detest the cowardly acts of hatred that resulted in the senseless burning of your churches, and that we are enraged that such bigotry exists in America. We hope your church will be rebuilt. We do not have the strength and skill to come with hammers and saws, but we want to assist the only way we can—by sending checks as concerned individuals.

...

To the Members of the Burned Churches,
I am sorry for your loss. This is why I have written to you. To let you know that you are not alone. These cruel acts must be and will be stopped and those responsible punished for them. If there is anything I can do from NYC, please let me know. I am not afraid of speaking out for what I believe. Speaking out is the only thing that keeps all of us alive. I will do what I can, as a writer and an activist, to help you. I will write to President Clinton and insist that he make this a priority—for the White House and for the country. I will write to my local newspapers. I will get others to write. You are not alone.

...

Dear Church Members,
As we put our two young children to bed each night lately, we challenge ourselves to make sure that they understand that the racism that is still so prevalent in our society must not be tolerated. We will speak out to condemn these burnings, and also to condemn racism and bigotry whenever we learn of it.

From *An American Testament: Letters to the Burned Churches,* Anti-Defamation League, 1996

EXPLORING SOCIAL CHANGE MOVEMENTS

RATIONALE

The purpose of this activity is to introduce students to social change movements throughout history. Through this process, they will come to appreciate that much change in our society has come about by people standing up to injustice together. This lesson provides an opportunity for students to explore social activism during the civil rights movement of the 1950s and 1960s and to undertake a research project of their own about a social change movement in our country's history.

OBJECTIVES

- Students will learn more about the civil rights movement and how people worked together to bring about change.
- Students will define social change and identify other social change movements throughout history.
- Students will explore one social change movement by doing a research paper and presentation.

WHAT'S NEEDED

Handouts and Resources: Segregation Photos; Activism During the Civil Rights Movement and *Steps in Writing and Presenting a Research Project* (one of each for each student); *The Montgomery Bus Boycott* video (2 mins., PBS, www.youtube.com/watch?v=1QZik4CYtgw)

Other Material: Computer, Internet access, LCD projector

Advanced Preparation: Prepare *Segregration Photos* to be projected

PROCEDURES

1. Begin the activity by asking, "Who is Martin Luther King, Jr.?" Explain that Martin Luther King, Jr. was a major leader in the Civil Rights Movement of the 1950s and 1960s. Explain that even though he was a leader in the movement and there were many other leaders, things would not have changed without ordinary people organizing for social change.

Lesson 24

GRADE LEVEL
3–5

TIME
45 minutes

COMMON CORE STANDARDS
Reading, Writing, Speaking & Listening, Language

STRATEGIES AND SKILLS
Brainstorming
Research
Writing
Presenting

KEY WORDS AND PHRASES
Citizens
Desegregation
Injustice
Protest
Social change

■ *Anti-Bias Building Blocks: An Elementary Curriculum* | Unit V.281

2. With the students, view *The Montgomery Bus Boycott* video.

   Video Synopsis: This clip begins with Reverend Martin Luther King, Jr. describing the events that led to the boycott, including the arrest of Rosa Parks, followed by footage of empty buses and African Americans walking to work. Then Reverend Ralph Abernathy is shown addressing a church meeting about the boycott.

3. Engage students in a discussion by asking the following questions:
   - What is Martin Luther King, Jr. talking about?
   - What is the protest that he talks about and what percentage of people were participating?
   - Why were they protesting?

4. Explain to students that you are going to share some information about the Civil Rights Movement in the 1950s and 1960s, showing how people worked together to bring about change. Then, students will work on their own research projects to learn more about another social change movement. Ask students, "What is social change?" Help students come up with a definition of **social change** as when elements of a society are altered or changed in some way, including the changes in society's institutions, behaviors, rules or social relationships.

5. Explain that during the Civil Rights Movement in the 1950s and 1960s, African-American people fought in a variety of ways to have the same rights as white people. Display the *Segregation Photos*. As you advance through each picture, explain that during this period, there were some regions of the country where blacks and whites were segregated by law; there were "white" and "colored" domains and in most cases, the "colored" domains were inferior. Also, laws were passed that made it more difficult for black people to vote. When these laws were passed, the number of black voters dropped dramatically which meant that they were not able to participate in the process of electing their representatives. Explain that during the Civil Rights Movement, there were organized activities and strategies aimed at overturning or changing these laws, often called "activism."

6. Distribute the handout *Activism During the Civil Rights Movement* and read together as a class, having students read parts aloud.

7. After reading the handout, engage students in a discussion by asking the following questions:
   - For each of the examples what was the civil right for which the person or people were fighting?
   - How did they go about trying to obtain those rights?

FLIPPED CLASSROOM IDEA

Make a short video of you explaining the Civil Rights Movement and reading the information in the *Activism During the Civil Rights Movement* handout or explaining and sharing that information in your own words. At the end, ask aloud the discussion questions provided in #7.

ALTERNATIVE

Do a jigsaw activity where students are divided into groups of three and each member of the group reads one of the examples and shares with others in their group.

- What do all three of these examples have in common?
- How did people work together to bring about change?

8. Explain that students will be doing a research project on another social change movement in our country's history. With the students, brainstorm other social change movements they know or have heard about. Remind them what social change is. If students do not have any ideas or they do not mention the following, add these to the list:

   - marriage equality
   - anti-bullying
   - animal rights movement
   - disability rights
   - anti-Apartheid
   - labor movement
   - anti-nuclear movement
   - environmental/climate change
   - anti-war
   - LBGT movement
   - Occupy movement
   - women's rights
   - women's suffrage
   - Immigrant rights movement
   - prohibition movement

9. Explain to students that each of them will work alone or with one other person to learn about a social change movement in history. Using the *Steps in Writing and Presenting a Research Project*, go over the steps involved in writing and presenting a research project. Provide deadlines for each step in the process and allow some class time (as well as homework assignments) to complete the project. With students, brainstorm creative ways to present the research (some are listed in the document). The projects will take a few weeks to complete.

10. When students have completed their research projects, invite parents and family members to class and have each student present their project or coordinate a "share fair" where their projects are placed around the room for other students and family members to provide feedback.

11. Engage students in a discussion about what they learned by asking the following questions:

    - What did you learn about social change movements?
    - What were some strategies that people in these movements engaged in that made a difference?
    - Did the people in the movements ever make any mistakes?
    - In reflecting on yours and other students' projects, was there anything they all had in common?
    - Were there always leaders in the movement?

NOTE 8

As students begin to do their research, be aware that unfortunately, hate groups have published hateful content about some of social justice activists and students might find these sites while searching. For example, the Web site www.martinlutherking.org is operated by Don Black, a white supremacist, who created the website to attract people to his ideology. Therefore, it is important that students are aware of possible hate on the Internet and learn to analyze information found on the Web. You may also want to find some "safe" websites from which they can conduct their research.

- What was the role of the leaders and what was the role of ordinary citizens?

EXTENSION ACTIVITIES

- As a class, choose one of the social change movements and learn more about some of the statistics and numbers impacting the issues on that topic. For example, in looking at the immigrant right's movement, have students research information about how many immigrants live in this country currently, the United States' history of immigration patterns, how many and what percentage of immigrants are "undocumented" and what percentage of young people are potentially impacted by the DREAM Act.

   [For more information about the DREAM Act, visit www.whitehouse.gov/blog/2010/12/01/get-facts-dream-act.]

- As a class, interview someone who was alive and active during the Civil Rights Movement or one of the movements that the students researched. In advance, have students share with each other about the purpose of the movement and from that, develop interview questions. After the interview, have students write up their notes in essay form.

- Read aloud and discuss one or more of the children's books from the list provided in this lesson.

CHILDREN'S BOOKS

Sit-In: How Four Friends Stood Up by Sitting Down by Andrea Davis Pinkney

That's Not Fair: Emma Tenayuca's Struggle for Justice by Carmen Tafolla

You Wouldn't Want to Be a Suffragist: A Protest Movement That's Rougher Than You Expected by Fiona MacDonald

SEGREGATION PHOTOS
[Student Handout]

Tourist cabins near a highway sign in South Carolina advertising "Cabins for Colored," June 1939. Photo courtesy of Library of Congress, LC-USF34-051945-D.

A black man standing under a "Colored Waiting Room" sign at a bus stating in Durham, NC, May 1940. Photo courtesy of Library of Congress, LC-USZ62-125806.

White people waiting for the bus at the Memphis, TN terminal near the white waiting room area, September 1943. Photo courtesy of Library of Congress, LC-USW3-037974-E.

A rest stop for Greyhound bus passengers with separate dining accommodations for colored passengers, September 1943. Photo courtesy of Library of Congress, LC-USF34-051945-D.

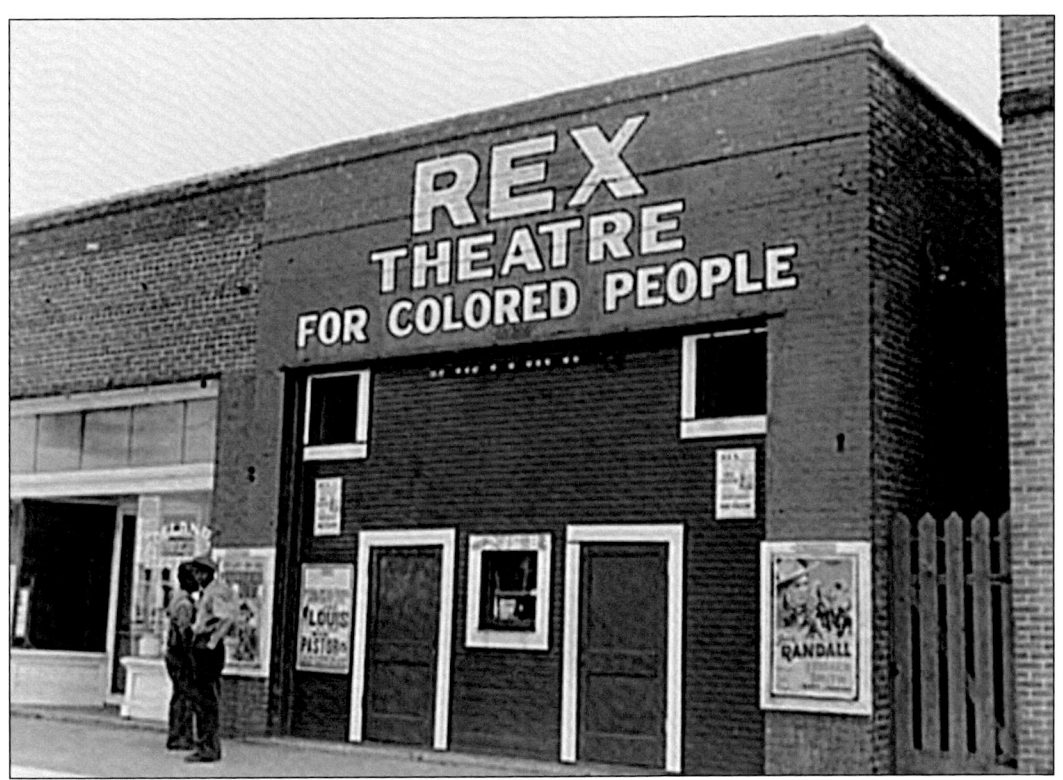

Rex Theatre for colored people in Leland Mississippi, November 1943. Photo courtesy of Library of Congress, LC-USF34-052508-D.

First-nighters posing outside the Warners' Theatre, August 6, 1926. Photo courtesy of National Archives and Records Administration, 535750.

Drinking fountain on the county courthouse lawn for colored people, North Carolina, April 1938. Photo courtesy of Library of Congress, LC-USZ62-100414.

Black man drinking at "Colored" water cooler in streetcar terminal in Oklahoma City, OK, July 1939. Photo courtesy of Library of Congress, LC-USZ62-80126.

ACTIVISM DURING THE CIVIL RIGHTS MOVEMENT

[Student Handout]

Montgomery Bus Boycott

On December 1, 1955, Rosa Parks refused to give up her seat to a white man on a Montgomery bus. She was arrested and fined. The boycott of public buses by blacks in Montgomery began on the day of Parks' court hearing and lasted 381 days. Instead of riding buses, black people walked, took cabs, drove their own cars, rode mules or traveled on wagons pulled by horses. The Montgomery Bus Boycott, in which blacks refused to ride city buses in Montgomery, Alabama, to protest segregated (separate) seating, took place from December 5, 1955 to December 20, 1956, and was the first large demonstration against segregation in the United States. The U.S. Supreme Court finally ordered Montgomery to integrate its bus system, and Martin Luther King, Jr., one of the leaders of the boycott, emerged as a prominent national leader of the American Civil Rights Movement in the wake of the action.

Woolworth's Lunch Counter

On February 1, 1960, four black college students sat down at a "whites-only" lunch counter at a Woolworth's in Greensboro, North Carolina, and politely asked for service. The staff refused to serve them, but they stayed until closing time. The next morning they came with twenty-five more students. On the third day, sixty-three students joined their protest. Their peaceful sit-in demand helped begin a youth-led movement to challenge racial inequality throughout the South. In Greensboro, hundreds of students, civil rights organizations, churches and members of the community joined in a six-month-long protest. This led to the desegregation of the F. W. Woolworth lunch counter on July 25, 1960.

Ruby Bridges Desegregates Elementary School

In November 1960, a six-year-old girl named Ruby Bridges became the first black child to desegregate an elementary school. When Ruby was in kindergarten, she was one of several black students in New Orleans who were chosen to take a test to determine whether or not she could attend a white school. She lived five blocks from an all-white school, but attended kindergarten several miles away at an all-black segregated school. In 1960, Ruby's parents were told that she was one of only six other black children to pass the test and would attend the William Frantz School, near her home. Although she only lived a few blocks from school, federal marshals had to take Ruby to school because of angry groups of white people who did not want her to attend the school. For a whole year, she was the only student in her class because white parents would not allow their children to attend the school.

Left: Rosa Parks on a Montgomery Bus on December 21, 1956 after public transportation was legally integrated.

Right: Ruby Bridges being escorted by U.S. Marshals from William Frantz Elementary School, New Orleans on November 14, 1960.

STEPS IN WRITING AND PRESENTING A RESEARCH PROJECT

[Student Handout]

1. **Choose a topic**
   - Decide what social change movement you want to learn more about.
   - Ask yourself, "Am I interested in this topic? What does it mean to me?"

2. **Narrow your topic**
   - Decide on what aspect of that movement you want to research by asking yourself, "What do I want to know about this social change movement?"
   - To narrow your topic, write three questions you want your research project to answer.

3. **Gather information from different sources**
   - Books
   - Magazines and newspapers (online or paper)
   - Internet research
   - People who may know something about the social change movement
   - Learn about organizations who are addressing your topic
   - Videos, DVDs
   - Online encyclopedias (www.kids.britannica.com or www.factmonster.com)

4. **Plan and organize information**
   - Take notes on notecards or *Post-it Notes*®.
   - Sort all your notes and put them in a logical order.
   - Create an outline or graphic organizer in order to plan the writing.

5. **Write a rough draft**
   - Do some pre-writing based on your outline (a sketch of what you want to say).
   - Share these ideas with a writing partner or teacher and get their feedback.
   - Write a rough draft and include your unanswered questions or areas where you need more research.

6. **Revise and edit**
    - Share rough draft with classmates and get feedback.
    - Incorporate student and teacher feedback.
    - Correct grammatical and spelling errors.
    - Neatly write or type your final draft.

7. **Publish/Present**
    - Submit final draft.
    - Cite sources.
    - Decide on how you will present your information to class:
        - Video
        - Photos
        - Poster board presentation
        - Dramatization or play/role play
        - Diary/journal entry of person involved in the movement
        - Storyboards
        - PowerPoint presentation
    - Evaluate the project by asking yourself and writing/sharing:
        - How well was my project organized and presented?
        - Did I have reliable information?
        - What did I learn?
        - Am I proud of my project?

SOCIAL ACTION PROJECTS

RATIONALE

The purpose of this activity is to empower students to take on an issue of injustice that is important to them and to do something about it. This is a critical step in the process to give students real-life experience with how it feels to make a difference. This lesson provides an opportunity for students to learn about the context of Rosa Parks' actions during the Civil Rights Movement, identify problems in their own community and devise an action plan for solving them.

OBJECTIVES

- Students will reflect on what they already know about Rosa Parks and will learn more about the context of Rosa Parks' actions during the Civil Rights Movement.
- Students will identify problems or concerns in their community and possible solutions to those problems.
- Students will work in small groups to devise an action plan for solving one of the identified problems.

WHAT'S NEEDED

Handouts and Resources: A Case Study in Community Activism and *Group Action Plan* (one of each for each student)

Other Material: Board/Smart board, markers, index cards (one per student)

PROCEDURES

1. Begin this activity by explaining to students that while individuals often work alone to confront unfairness or to educate others about problems, there are also many times when a group of people work on a problem together. Ask for examples or provide one of your own.
2. Write the name Rosa Parks on the board and ask students to share everything they know about her, how they know it and what else they could learn about Rosa Parks. The chart might

Lesson 25

GRADE LEVEL
3–5

TIME
45 minutes

COMMON CORE STANDARDS
Reading, Writing, Speaking & Listening, Language

STRATEGIES AND SKILLS
Large group discussion, small group work, presentation

KEY WORDS AND PHRASES
Activism
Civil rights
Social change

FLIPPED CLASSROOM IDEA

Make a short video of you talking about Rosa Parks and how she worked with others to organize the Montgomery Bus Boycott, reading aloud parts of *A Case Study in Community Activism* and asking aloud some of the discussion questions provided in #3.

look something like this:

What I Know	How I Know	What Else I Can Learn
Involved in Civil Rights movement	Books	Why she made that decision
Wouldn't give up seat on the bus	Movies	Who else helped Rosa Parks
	School	What else Rosa Parks did

3. Engage students in a discussion by asking the following questions:
   - Did most of you know the same basic information about Rosa Parks?
   - Where do most people get their information about famous people like Rosa Parks?
   - Do you think that people always get the complete story when they learn about famous people and historical events? Explain your thinking with an example.
   - How does not telling or knowing all the details about a story impact what people know and think?

4. Explain to students that they are now going to learn more about Rosa Parks and her role in the Civil Rights movement. Distribute *A Case Study in Community Activism* to each student and read aloud together or have students read silently for 10 minutes. As you read it together or silently, have students highlight the ways in which Rosa Parks worked with others to achieve goals. After reading, engage students in a discussion by asking the following questions:
   - How did you feel as you read the information?
   - Was there anything that surprised you or that you had never heard before?
   - Share something new you learned about Rosa Parks that you didn't know before today.
   - How was Rosa Parks' work a continuation of work that was already underway across the United States?
   - Rosa Parks' story is often told as though one day she got tired physically on the bus and tired of discrimination and decided to start the Montgomery Bus Boycott. Why do you think the story has come to be told this way?

5. Tell students that together we are going to develop a community action plan to do something about a problem in our community that needs to be addressed. Review the word community with students from Lesson 10, "What Is Community?" and define **community** as a group of people who live in the same area such as a city, town or neighborhood or who share common characteristics or interests. Explain that for some people, community may be the city or town where they live, while others may view community as a neighborhood, subdivision, block or apartment complex.

6. Distribute an index card to each student. Take a few minutes to have students reflect upon their dreams for *themselves* (e.g., I want to be a doctor), their *family* (e.g., I hope my Aunt can become a U.S. citizen), their *community/neighborhood* (e.g., I wish there were less stray dogs in my neighborhood) and ultimately their *world*. In addition to thinking about their dreams, have them think about what gets in the way and what problems need to be solved to realize their dreams. Ask them to consider if they could rid the world of discrimination and hate, what would it look like? They can take notes on index cards.

7. Divide students into small groups of 4–5. For this exercise, it will be helpful to decide on the groups beforehand and make sure to group students according to their ability to work well together as they

will be potentially working on this project for several weeks. As a group, they will name their community and identify problems or areas of concern in their communities. At this point, they should not consider how these problems can be solved, but simply identify what they see as problems or concerns.

8. After completing the task, engage students in a class discussion by asking the following questions:
   - What kind of problems or concerns did you identify in your group?
   - Which problems, if any, were concerned with fairness, discrimination and how people are treated?
   - What are some things the group should consider as group members decide how to address the problem? (e.g., skills and resources of group members, time available to work on the project, etc.)
   - Are there already solutions or ideas in place to solve this problem in the community?

9. Distribute the *Group Action Plan* handout to each student and review as a whole group first, explaining that they will get back into their small groups and complete the following four tasks:
   a. Students will decide about problem or concern their group will address (consensus or majority vote).
   b. Students will brainstorm a list of possible ways to address this problem. Challenge them to be realistic about whether this is something they have the resources and ability to do.
   c. Based on the interest, skills and resources of group members, students will decide on one of the best ways to address this problem.
   d. Students will complete the *Group Action Plan* handout by identifying specific tasks that will need to be completed by group members.

10. Give students 15 minutes to complete this task, circulating around the room to offer help and to make sure students are on task. Explain that this is a "mock" action plan designed to give them practice in identifying tasks and matching people with their skills. If students intend to implement the plan, it will also be necessary to include dates for task completion.

11. After all groups have completed their action plans, provide time for each group to make a presentation to the class, which includes: (1) explanation of the problem or concern, (2) the way the group decided to work on the problem and (3) some of the key steps in the action plan. At the end of the presentation, encourage students

NOTE 10

It is strongly suggested that you find time during the school year for students to implement their action plans. It will give them firsthand experience in working with others to solve a problem in our society and the confidence and understanding that they can make a difference.

to ask questions about the action plan or make suggestions about other things that the group might want to consider.

12. After presentations, engage students in a discussion by asking the following questions:

    - What is the purpose of developing an action plan?
    - Do you think you would be able to implement your plan? Why or why not?
    - How did you work together to come up with your plan?
    - How likely is your group to attempt to implement the plan?
    - What do you need to get started?
    - What is the likely outcome of your actions?

13. End the lesson by having students consider the following quotation by Rosa Parks:

    "I would like to be known as a woman who is concerned about freedom and equality and justice and prosperity for all people."

    Do a go round where each student says what they hope to be known for one day.

EXTENSION ACTIVITIES

- Have students learn about (reading books, doing Internet research, etc.) other African-American leaders who have worked on behalf of civil rights. Students can present the information they learned in a variety of ways including: a short biographical summary of the person and their work, journal entries, a sculpture or drawing of the person with a short caption about their life, etc.

- Have students read books that are set in the South during segregation and write several diary entries from the point of view of the main character about what it was like living in that time period.

    [**NOTE:** ADL provides an online bibliography of the best kid literature on bias, diversity and social justice. Visit Books Matter at www.adl.org/books-mattter.]

- Read aloud and discuss one or more of the children's books from the list provided in this lesson.

CHILDREN'S BOOKS

The Kids Guide to Social Action Projects by Barbara Lewis

Real Kids, Real Stories, Real Change: Courageous Actions Around the World by Garth Sundem

Malala Yousafzai: Warrior with Words by Karen Leggett Abouraya

The Streets Are Free by Kurusa

A CASE STUDY IN COMMUNITY ACTIVISM

[Student Handout]

SEGREGATION AND "JIM CROW LAWS"

Following the Civil War, during a period called Reconstruction (1865-1875), several amendments to the Constitution seemed to pave the way for an end to discrimination against African Americans. The Thirteenth Amendment officially ended slavery in all states. The Fourteenth Amendment stated that all persons born in the United States and subject to its laws, were citizens of the United States. The Fifteenth Amendment declared that the right to vote could not be denied on the basis of "race." Many African Americans expected that they would enjoy all the rights of American citizens. As time passed however, interest in rebuilding the South and protecting the rights of African Americans faded. Northern states, which had begun to focus on industrialization, did not see rebuilding the South as their responsibility, and, in fact, many Northerners didn't believe in "racial" equality any more than Southerners did. By 1875, Federal troops that had been sent to the South to enforce the new amendments were withdrawn and Reconstruction was declared over.

Once Reconstruction was over, Whites fought to regain the power they felt they had lost following the Civil War. Their efforts were supported by the U.S. Supreme Court, which began to strike down the few advancements that African Americans had been able to make. A turning point was the Plessy v. Ferguson Supreme Court case. In 1890, Louisiana passed the "Separate Car Law," which claimed to ensure passenger "comfort" by directing railroads to provide "equal but separate" cars for Blacks and Whites. It was illegal for anyone to occupy seats used by the other "race." In 1891, a group of African-American citizens formed a committee to test whether this law was constitutional. The committee hired a lawyer and then had Homer A. Plessy, an African-American man, sit in a "white-only" railroad car. When Plessy refused to move, he was arrested. The state argued that separating the "races" was legal, as long as the service provided to each was equal. In 1896, the Supreme Court agreed that "separate but equal" facilities were legal. This decision paved the way for segregation across the South.

By 1914, every Southern State had passed laws that created two societies—one Black and one White. "Jim Crow" laws, as they were called, ordered "racial" separation in every area of life. Schools, parks, playgrounds, pools, restaurants, hotels, public transportation, theaters, hospitals, prisons, orphanages, restrooms and so on were all segregated. African Americans could no longer serve on juries. In Atlanta, Georgia, a black person could not even "swear to tell the truth" on the same Bible used by white witnesses. In North Carolina, factories were separated into black and white sections. Schools and other facilities were rarely, if ever, equal. Schools for African-American children, for example, were often small, unheated rooms without plumbing, textbooks, paper or other teaching supplies. In some Alabama towns it was against the law for Blacks and Whites to play cards, checkers or dominoes together. In Washington, DC, black people could not bury their dead dogs or cats in the same pet cemeteries used by Whites. White taxi drivers could not carry black passengers; black taxi drivers could not accept white passengers. There were separate elevators for Blacks and Whites in office buildings. In movie theaters, black people had to sit in the balcony, well apart from any white people. White nurses could not treat a black person and even a dying black person would not be admitted to a "white" hospital. The goal was to keep Blacks separate from Whites from birth to even after death in separate cemeteries.

Other states besides those in the South also had laws, some written and some implied, that kept Blacks and Whites separate. In New Mexico, for example, there were separate rooms in schools for white and black students. In Wyoming and Arizona, intermarriage between Blacks and Whites was illegal. In Northern cities, it was understood that Blacks and Whites did not live in the same neighborhood; African Americans were forced to live in only certain neighborhoods, which soon became overcrowded and run-down. African Americans living in the South following Reconstruction lived not only in poverty, but also in fear. The Ku Klux Klan, a secret society that believed African Americans were inferior, brutalized, terrorized and murdered thousands of African Americans and Whites who were sympathetic to their cause. Lynchings and mob violence against African Americans became common. According to Ida B. Wells-Barnett, an African-American teacher, journalist and one of the founders of the NAACP, African Americans were being lynched at the rate of two per week in the South between 1890 and 1899. In 1893, she wrote, "In the past ten years over a thousand black men and women and children have met this violent death at the hands of a white mob. And the rest of America has remained silent."

THE NATIONAL ASSOCIATION FOR THE ADVANCEMENT OF COLORED PEOPLE (NAACP)

The NAACP started with a lynching 100 years after the birth of Abraham Lincoln, in the city, Springfield, Illinois, that was Lincoln's long-time residence. William English Walling, a white Southerner, dramatized the gruesome happening and a group of people, both black and white, who were committed to social justice formed a committee. A conference was held in 1909 in New York. Among those who attended the first meeting were scientists, philanthropists, social workers and journalists. The main goal of the NAACP was and is today to ensure the political, educational, social and economic equality of "minority" group citizens of the United States and eliminate racism.

Some of the early work of the NAACP included publishing a magazine, *The Crisis*, which told what life was like for African Americans. The magazine, edited by W.E.B. Du Bois, built up a large readership amongst black people and white sympathizers and by 1919, was selling 100,000 copies a month. In addition to publishing a magazine, the NAACP campaigned against the film *Birth of a Nation* (1915), which glamorized the Ku Klux Klan and further perpetuated stereotypes and prejudices against African Americans. Later, the NAACP promoted voter registration campaigns, worked for school desegregation, fought for fair housing and brought important lawsuits to the courts to force segregation to end. While the NAACP attorneys were busy challenging segregation in the courts, the NAACP's Youth Council, which was primarily young adult college students, was organizing sit-ins, marches and voter registration campaigns across the South.

ROSA PARKS

Rosa Louise McCauley was born on February 4, 1913, in Tuskegee, Alabama. Her father was a carpenter and her mother was a teacher. Rosa McCauley attended a liberal private school as an adolescent and after briefly attending Alabama State University, she married Raymond Parks, a barber and activist, in 1932. The couple settled in Montgomery, Alabama, where Rosa Parks worked as a seamstress and housekeeper. Rosa Parks believed that segregation was wrong and did what she could in her daily life to take a stand against the injustices that African Americans faced. She would walk up and down stairs rather than take elevators marked "colored" and often walked a mile to work rather than ride the segregated buses. Rosa Parks also became involved in several African-American organizations, including the NAACP, the Montgomery Voters League, the NAACP Youth Council and other civic and religious groups.

Over the years, Rosa Parks learned about previous challenges to segregation, including another bus boycott in Montgomery, fifty years earlier; a bus boycott in Baton Rouge, Louisiana; and the arrest of two young women in Montgomery (Claudette Colvin in March, 1955 and Mary Louise Smith in October 1955) who refused to give their seats to white passengers. As secretary for the Montgomery branch of the NAACP, Parks was involved in discussions between organizations like the NAACP and the Women's Political Council who were considering a legal challenge to the segregation laws as they pertained to public transportation. Rosa Parks also attended a ten-day training session at Tennessee's labor and civil rights organizing school, the Highlander Folk School. This center, founded in 1932 by Myles Horton, a social activist, helped potential leaders learn ways to bring about social change through collective action. Individuals were taught how to think about problems in new ways and then apply the information to local issues that they chose to address.

On December 1, 1955, Rosa Parks and three other black passengers were asked to vacate an entire row of seats just behind the "White Only" section of the bus so that one white man could sit down. Parks recognized the bus driver as the same one who, 12 years earlier, had evicted her from his bus for boarding through the front door. At first, the black passengers all remained seated. When the bus driver told them again to move, all stood except Parks. Two police officers boarded the bus and arrested Rosa Parks and took her to jail where she was fingerprinted, booked and jailed. Jo Ann Robinson and other Women's Political Council members immediately made copies of thousands of leaflets calling for a one-day boycott of the city's buses on Monday, December 5, the day of Rosa Parks' trial, and distributed them throughout the community. Dr. Martin Luther King, Jr. and other African-American ministers announced the one-day boycott from their pulpits on Sunday morning. On the morning of Rosa Parks' trial, empty buses could be seen all over the streets of Montgomery, Alabama. Rosa Parks was found guilty and fined $14.00. Later the same day a group of 18 black leaders organized under the name the Montgomery Improvement Association (MIA) and agreed to continue the boycott of Montgomery buses indefinitely. For the next 381 days, the majority of the African-American community refused to use public transportation. Ordinary citizens organized carpools, while other people walked. There were even instances of people riding donkeys around the city.

On November 13, 1956, the Supreme Court declared that Alabama's state and local laws requiring segregation on buses were unconstitutional, and on December 20th, Montgomery was forced to enforce the Court's ruling on public transportation. Violence erupted in the city over the next few weeks as snipers fired at the buses and black churches were bombed. Ministers from 11 Southern states met and decided the civil rights struggle needed to continue in a nonviolent manner. They formed the Southern Christian Leadership Conference (SCLC) and elected Dr. Martin Luther King, Jr. as its president. Bus boycotts were organized in other southern cities.

For her role in the anti-segregation movement, Rosa Parks earned the title "Mother of the Civil Rights Movement;" however, she and her family paid a big price, which included both Rosa Parks and her husband losing their jobs and numerous threats on Rosa Parks' life. In 1957, Rosa and Raymond Parks, along with her mother, moved to Detroit. There they founded the Rosa and Raymond Parks Institute for Self-

Development, which prepares young African Americans for leadership positions in the workplace and community. A subdivision of the Institute, called Pathways to Freedom, allows groups of teens to follow the Underground Railroad and visit the historic sites of the Civil Rights Movement.

References

Gamerman, K., ed. 1969. *Seperate and Unequal 1865-1910.* Vol. 3 of *Afro-American History Series.* Chicago, IL: Encyclopedia Britannica Education Corporation.

Igus, T. 1991. *Great Women in the Struggle.* Vol. 2 of *Books of Black Heroes.* East Orange, NJ: Just Us Books, Inc.

Lucas, E. 1996). *Civil Rights: The Long Struggle.* Springfield, NJ: Enslow Publishers, Inc.

McKissack, P., and F. McKissack. 1991. *The Civil Rights Movement in America from 1865 to Present.* Chicago, IL: Children's Press.

Myers, W. D. 1991. *Now is Our Time: The African American Struggle for Freedom.* New York, NY: HarperTrophy.

Robinson, J. G. ed. 1987. *The Montgomery Bus Boycott and the Women Who Started It: The Memoir of Jo Ann Gibson Robinson.* Knoxville, TN: The University of Tennessee Press.

Sandifer, J. A. ed. 1969. *The Afro-American in United States History.* New York, NY: Globe Book Company.

Wells-Barnett, I. B. 1991. *Selected Works.* New York, NY: Oxford University Press.

GROUP ACTION PLAN
[Student Handout]

Names of Group Members: _____ Date: _____

The problem that our group is going to address is _____

The way we decided to address this problem is _____

ACTION STEPS (What needs to be done?)	PEOPLE (Who will do this?)	TIME LINE (When will task be started and completed?)		RESOURCES What is needed to complete this task?	ADDITIONAL PEOPLE Who else can help?
		Start	Complete		

Anti-Bias Building Blocks: An Elementary Curriculum | Unit V.303

APPENDIX. CORRELATION OF LESSONS TO THE COMMON CORE LEARNING STANDARDS

UNIT I. CREATING A SAFE AND COMFORTABLE CLASSROOM ENVIRONMENT

Content Area/Standard	Grades K–2 L1	L2	L3	L4	L5	Grades 3–5 L1	L2	L3	L4	L5
Reading										
R.1: Read closely to determine what the text says explicitly and to make logical inferences from it; cite specific textual evidence when writing or speaking to support conclusions drawn from the text.	X	X	X	X	X	X	X	X	X	X
R.2: Determine central ideas or themes of a text and analyze their development; summarize the key supporting details and ideas.	X	X	X	X	X	X	X	X	X	X
Writing										
W.1: Write arguments to support claims in an analysis of substantive topics or texts, using valid reasoning and relevant and sufficient evidence.						X				
W.3: Write narratives to develop real or imagined experiences or events using effective technique, well-chosen details and well-structured event sequences.			X		X		X	X	X	
W.4: Produce clear and coherent writing in which the development, organization, and style are appropriate to task, purpose, and audience.									X	X
W.7: Conduct short as well as more sustained research projects based on focused questions, demonstrating understanding of the subject under investigation.										X
Speaking and Listening										
SL.1: Prepare for and participate effectively in a range of conversations and collaborations with diverse partners, building on others' ideas and expressing their own clearly and persuasively.	X	X	X	X	X	X	X	X	X	X
SL.3: Evaluate a speaker's point of view, reasoning, and use of evidence and rhetoric.		X		X						

Content Area/Standard	Grades K–2					Grades 3–5				
	L1	L2	L3	L4	L5	L1	L2	L3	L4	L5
SL.4: Present information, findings, and supporting evidence such that listeners can follow the line of reasoning and the organization, development and style are appropriate to task, purpose and audience.		X			X				X	
SL.5: Make strategic use of digital media and visual displays of data to express information and enhance understanding of presentations.	X	X		X	X		X			
Language										
L.4: Determine or clarify the meaning of unknown and multiple-meaning words and phrases by using context clues, analyzing meaningful word parts, and consulting general and specialized reference materials, as appropriate.				X					X	
L.5: Demonstrate understanding of figurative language, word relationships and nuances in word meanings.		X		X	X	X	X	X	X	X
L.6: Acquire and use accurately a range of general academic and domain-specific words and phrases sufficient for reading, writing, speaking, and listening at the college and career readiness level; demonstrate independence in gathering vocabulary knowledge when considering a word or phrase important to comprehension or expression.									X	

UNIT II. UNDERSTANDING MY STRENGTHS, SKILLS AND IDENTITY

Content Area/Standard	Grades K–2					Grades 3–5				
	L6	L7	L8	9	L10	L6	L7	L8	L9	L10
Reading										
R.1: Read closely to determine what the text says explicitly and to make logical inferences from it; cite specific textual evidence when writing or speaking to support conclusions drawn from the text.	X	X	X	X	X	X	X	X	X	X
R.2: Determine central ideas or themes of a text and analyze their development; summarize the key supporting details and ideas.	X	X	X	X	X	X	X	X	X	X
R.9: Analyze how two or more texts address similar themes or topics in order to build knowledge or to compare the approaches the authors take.		X								
Writing										
W.1: Write arguments to support claims in an analysis of substantive topics or texts, using valid reasoning and relevant and sufficient evidence.						X	X			
W.2: Write informative/explanatory texts to examine and convey complex ideas and information clearly and accurately through the effective selection, organization, and analysis of content.	X									X
W.3: Write narratives to develop real or imagined experiences or events using effective technique, well-chosen details and well-structured event sequences.					X	X		X	X	
W.4: Produce clear and coherent writing in which the development, organization, and style are appropriate to task, purpose, and audience.						X	X		X	X
W.5: Develop and strengthen writing as needed by planning, revising, editing, rewriting, or trying a new approach.						X				
Speaking and Listening										
SL.1: Prepare for and participate effectively in a range of conversations and collaborations with diverse partners, building on others' ideas and expressing their own clearly and persuasively.	X	X	X	X	X	X	X	X	X	X
SL.3: Evaluate a speaker's point of view, reasoning, and use of evidence and rhetoric.					X	X	X		X	X

■ Anti-Bias Building Blocks: An Elementary Curriculum | 307

Content Area/Standard	Grades K–2					Grades 3–5				
	L6	L7	L8	9	L10	L6	L7	L8	L9	L10
SL.4: Present information, findings, and supporting evidence such that listeners can follow the line of reasoning and the organization, development and style are appropriate to task, purpose and audience.		X	X			X	X	X	X	X
SL.5: Make strategic use of digital media and visual displays of data to express information and enhance understanding of presentations.	X	X		X	X	X		X	X	X
Language										
L.3: Apply knowledge of language to understand how language functions in different contexts, to make effective choices for meaning or style, and to comprehend more fully when reading or listening.							X	X		X
L.4: Determine or clarify the meaning of unknown and multiple-meaning words and phrases by using context clues, analyzing meaningful word parts, and consulting general and specialized reference materials, as appropriate.								X		
L.5: Demonstrate understanding of figurative language, word relationships and nuances in word meanings.						X				

UNIT III. UNDERSTANDING AND APPRECIATING DIFFERENCES

Content Area/Standard	Grades K–2 L11	Grades K–2 L12	Grades K–2 L13	Grades 3–5 L11	Grades 3–5 L12	Grades 3–5 L13
Reading						
R.1: Read closely to determine what the text says explicitly and to make logical inferences from it; cite specific textual evidence when writing or speaking to support conclusions drawn from the text.	X	X	X	X	X	X
R.2: Determine central ideas or themes of a text and analyze their development; summarize the key supporting details and ideas.	X	X	X	X	X	X
Writing						
W.2: Write informative/explanatory texts to examine and convey complex ideas and information clearly and accurately through the effective selection, organization, and analysis of content.				X		
W.3: Write narratives to develop real or imagined experiences or events using effective technique, well-chosen details and well-structured event sequences.				X	X	X
W.6: Use technology, including the Internet, to produce and publish writing and to interact and collaborate with others.				X		
W.7: Conduct short as well as more sustained research projects based on focused questions, demonstrating understanding of the subject under investigation.	X	X			X	
W.8: Gather relevant information from multiple print and digital sources, assess the credibility and accuracy of each source, and integrate the information while avoiding plagiarism.	X				X	
Speaking and Listening						
SL.1: Prepare for and participate effectively in a range of conversations and collaborations with diverse partners, building on others' ideas and expressing their own clearly and persuasively.	X	X	X	X	X	X
SL.2: Integrate and evaluate information presented in diverse media and formats, including visually, quantitatively, and orally.				X	X	
SL.3: Evaluate a speaker's point of view, reasoning, and use of evidence and rhetoric.				X	X	X
SL.4 Present information, findings, and supporting evidence such that listeners can follow the line of reasoning and the organization, development and style are appropriate to task, purpose and audience.	X	X	X	X	X	X
SL.5: Make strategic use of digital media and visual displays of data to express information and enhance understanding of presentations.	X	X	X		X	
Language						
L.4: Determine or clarify the meaning of unknown and multiple-meaning words and phrases by using context clues, analyzing meaningful word parts, and consulting general and specialized reference materials, as appropriate.	X	X		X	X	

Content Area/Standard	Grades K–2			Grades 3–5		
	L11	L12	L13	L11	L12	L13
L.5: Demonstrate understanding of figurative language, word relationships and nuances in word meanings.	X				X	
L.6: Acquire and use accurately a range of general academic and domain-specific words and phrases sufficient for reading, writing, speaking, and listening at the college and career readiness level; demonstrate independence in gathering vocabulary knowledge when considering a word or phrase important to comprehension or expression.		X		X		

UNIT IV. UNDERSTANDING BIAS AND DISCRIMINATION

Content Area/Standard	Grades K–2						Grades 3–5					
	L14	L15	L16	L17	L18	L19	L14	L15	L16	L17	L18	L19
Reading												
R.1: Read closely to determine what the text says explicitly and to make logical inferences from it; cite specific textual evidence when writing or speaking to support conclusions drawn from the text.	X	X	X	X	X	X	X	X	X	X	X	X
R.2: Determine central ideas or themes of a text and analyze their development; summarize the key supporting details and ideas.	X	X	X	X	X	X	X	X	X	X	X	X
Writing												
W.1: Write arguments to support claims in an analysis of substantive topics or texts, using valid reasoning and relevant and sufficient evidence.				X			X					
W.3: Write narratives to develop real or imagined experiences or events using effective technique, well-chosen details and well-structured event sequences.		X		X			X	X	X	X	X	X
W.5: Develop and strengthen writing as needed by planning, revising, editing, rewriting, or trying a new approach.							X					
W.6: Use technology, including the Internet, to produce and publish writing and to interact and collaborate with others.											X	
W.7: Conduct short as well as more sustained research projects based on focused questions, demonstrating understanding of the subject under investigation.					X				X	X		X
W.8: Gather relevant information from multiple print and digital sources, assess the credibility and accuracy of each source, and integrate the information while avoiding plagiarism.			X									

Content Area/Standard	Grades K–2						Grades 3–5					
	L14	L15	L16	L17	L18	L19	L14	L15	L16	L17	L18	L19
Speaking and Listening												
SL.1: Prepare for and participate effectively in a range of conversations and collaborations with diverse partners, building on others' ideas and expressing their own clearly and persuasively.	X	X	X	X	X	X	X	X	X	X	X	X
SL.3: Evaluate a speaker's point of view, reasoning, and use of evidence and rhetoric.		X	X									
SL.4: Present information, findings, and supporting evidence such that listeners can follow the line of reasoning and the organization, development and style are appropriate to task, purpose and audience.	X								X	X		X
SL.5: Make strategic use of digital media and visual displays of data to express information and enhance understanding of presentations.	X	X		X		X				X	X	X
Language												
L.4: Determine or clarify the meaning of unknown and multiple-meaning words and phrases by using context clues, analyzing meaningful word parts, and consulting general and specialized reference materials, as appropriate.							X	X				
L.5: Demonstrate understanding of figurative language, word relationships and nuances in word meanings.			X		X		X				X	X
L.6: Acquire and use accurately a range of general academic and domain-specific words and phrases sufficient for reading, writing, speaking, and listening at the college and career readiness level; demonstrate independence in gathering vocabulary knowledge when considering a word or phrase important to comprehension or expression.	X	X	X	X		X	X	X	X	X	X	X

UNIT V. CONFRONTING/CHALLENGING BIAS AND BULLYING

Content Area/Standard	Grades K–2						Grades 3–5					
	L20	L21	L22	L23	L24	L25	L20	L21	L22	L23	L24	L25
Reading												
R.1: Read closely to determine what the text says explicitly and to make logical inferences from it; cite specific textual evidence when writing or speaking to support conclusions drawn from the text.	X	X	X	X	X	X	X	X	X	X	X	X
R.2: Determine central ideas or themes of a text and analyze their development; summarize the key supporting details and ideas.	X	X	X	X	X	X	X	X	X	X	X	
R.3: Analyze how and why individuals, events, or ideas develop and interact over the course of a text.					X							
R.6: Assess how point of view or purpose shapes the content and style of a text.										X		
R.7: Integrate and evaluate content presented in diverse media and formats, including visually and quantitatively, as well as in words.					X					X	X	
Writing												
W.1: Write arguments to support claims in an analysis of substantive topics or texts, using valid reasoning and relevant and sufficient evidence.				X								
W.2: Write informative/explanatory texts to examine and convey complex ideas and information clearly and accurately through the effective selection, organization, and analysis of content.						X				X	X	
W.3: Write narratives to develop real or imagined experiences or events using effective technique, well-chosen details and well-structured event sequences.	X	X						X	X			X

Anti-Bias Building Blocks: An Elementary Curriculum

Content Area/Standard	Grades K–2						Grades 3–5					
	L20	L21	L22	L23	L24	L25	L20	L21	L22	L23	L24	L25
W.7: Conduct short as well as more sustained research projects based on focused questions, demonstrating understanding of the subject under investigation.					X			X			X	X
Speaking and Listening											
SL.1: Prepare for and participate effectively in a range of conversations and collaborations with diverse partners, building on others' ideas and expressing their own clearly and persuasively.	X	X	X	X	X	X	X	X	X	X	X	X
SL.2: Integrate and evaluate information presented in diverse media and formats, including visually, quantitatively, and orally.	X				X			X				
SL.3: Evaluate a speaker's point of view, reasoning, and use of evidence and rhetoric.		X	X		X	X	X		X	X	X	X
SL.4: Present information, findings, and supporting evidence such that listeners can follow the line of reasoning and the organization, development and style are appropriate to task, purpose and audience.		X	X	X	X		X	X	X	X	X	X
SL.5: Make strategic use of digital media and visual displays of data to express information and enhance understanding of presentations.	X	X	X	X	X	X			X	X		
Language											
L.4: Determine or clarify the meaning of unknown and multiple-meaning words and phrases by using context clues, analyzing meaningful word parts, and consulting general and specialized reference materials, as appropriate.	X			X			X			X	X	
L.5: Demonstrate understanding of figurative language, word relationships and nuances in word meanings.	X		X									

Content Area/Standard	Grades K–2						Grades 3–5					
	L20	L21	L22	L23	L24	L25	L20	L21	L22	L23	L24	L25
L.6: Acquire and use accurately a range of general academic and domain-specific words and phrases sufficient for reading, writing, speaking, and listening at the college and career readiness level; demonstrate independence in gathering vocabulary knowledge when considering a word or phrase important to comprehension or expression.		X					X				X	

BIBLIOGRAPHY

BOOKS

Alexander, Michelle. *The New Jim Crow: Mass Incarceration in the Age of Colorblindness.* New York: The New Press, 2012.

Au, Wayne, Bill Bigelow, and Stan Karp. *Rethinking Our Classrooms: Teaching for Equity and Justice*, Vol. 1. Milwaukee: Rethinking Schools, 2007.

Ayers, William, Jean A. Hunt, and Therese Quinn, eds. *Teaching for Social Justice: A Democracy and Education Reader.* New York: The New Press, 1998.

Banks, James A. *Educating Citizens in a Multicultural Society*, 2nd ed. New York: Teachers College Press, 2007.

Bigelow, Bill, Brenda Harvey, Stan Karp, and Larry Miller. *Rethinking Our Classrooms: Teaching for Equity and Justice*, Vol. 2. Milwaukee: Rethinking Schools, 2004.

Bodine, Richard J., Donna K. Crawford, and Fred Schrumpf. *Creating the Peaceable School: A Comprehensive Program for Teaching Conflict Resolution*, Program Guide, 2nd ed. Champaign: Research Press, 2003.

Bolgatz, Jane. *Talking Race in the Classroom.* New York: Teachers College Press, 2005.

Coloroso, Barbara. *The Bully, the Bullied and the Bystander: From Preschool to High School—How Parents and Teacher Can Help Break the Cycle of Violence.* New York: William Morrow Paperbacks, 2009.

Darling-Hammond, Linda, Jennifer French, and Silvia P. Garcia-Lopez, eds. *Learning to Teach for Social Justice.* New York: Teachers College Press, 2002.

Delpit, Lisa. *"Multiplication is for White People": Raising Expectations for Other People's Children.* New York: The New Press, 2012.

Delpit, Lisa. *Other People's Children: Cultural Conflict in the Classroom.* New York: The New Press, 2006.

Elias, Maurice, Joseph Zins, and Roger P. Weissberg. *Promoting Social and Emotional Learning: Guidelines for Educators.* Alexandria: Association for Supervision and Curriculum Development, 1997.

Fergus, Edward, Pedro Noguera, and Margary Martin. *Schooling for Resilience: Improving the Life Trajectory of Black and Latino Boys.* Cambridge: Harvard Education Press, 2014.

Garbarino, James, and Ellen deLara. *And Words Can Hurt Forever: How to Protect Adolescents from Bullying, Harassment, and Emotional Violence.* New York: Free Press, 2003.

Gay, Geneva, ed. *Becoming Multicultural Educators: Personal Journey Toward Professionalism.* San Francisco: Jossey-Bass, 2003.

Harry, Beth, and Janette Klingner. *Why Are So Many Minority Students in Special Education?: Understanding Race and Disability in Schools,* 2nd ed. New York: Teachers College Press, 2014.

Howard, Gary R. *We Can't Teach What We Don't Know: White Teachers, Multiracial Schools,* 2nd ed. New York: Teachers College Press, 2006.

Kozol, Jonathan. *Savage Inequalities: Children in America's Schools.* New York: Broadway Books, 2012.

Lee, Enid, Deborah Menkart, and Margo Okazawa-Rey, eds. *Beyond Heroes and Holidays: A Practical Guide to K-12 Anti-Racist, Mulitcultural Education and Staff Development.* Washington, DC: Teaching for Change, 2007.

Lewis, Amanda E., and Myra Bluebond-Langner, eds. *Race in the Schoolyard: Negotiating the Color Line in Classroom and Communities.* Piscataway: Rutgers University Press, 2003.

Nieto, Sonia, and Patty Bode. *Affirming Diversity: The Sociopolitical Context of Multicultural Education,* 6th ed. Old Tappan: Pearson, 2011.

Schniedewind Nancy, and Ellen Davidson. *Open Minds to Equality: A Sourcebook of Learning Activities to Affirm Diversity and Promote Equity,* 4th ed. Milwaukee: Rethinking Schools, 2014

Stern-LaRosa Caryl, and E.H. Bettmann. *Hate Hurts: How Children Learn and Unlearn Prejudice.* New York: Scholastic, 2000.

Tatum, Beverly. *Can We Talk About Race?: And Other Conversations in an Era of School Resegregation.* Boston: Beacon Press, 2008.

Turner-Vorbeck, Tammy, and Monica M. Marsh, eds. *Other Kinds of Families: Embracing Diversity in Schools.* New York: Teachers College Press, 2007.

Wiseman, Rosalind. *Masterminds and Wingmen: Helping Our Boys Cope with Schoolyard Power, Locker-Room Tests, Girlfriends, and the New Rules of Boy World.* New York: Harmony Books, 2014.

Wiseman, Rosalind. *Queen Bees and Wannabees: Helping Your Daughter Survive Cliques, Gossip, Boyfriends, and the New Realities of Girl World.* New York: Harmony Books, 2009.

Zinn, Howard, and Rebecca Stefoff. *A Young People's History of the United States.* For Young People Series New York: Seven Stories Press, 2009.

CHILDREN'S BOOKS

Books Matter: The Best Kid Lit on Bias, Diversity and Social Justice, www.adl.org/books-matter
   ADL's online bibliography of recommended children's books about bias, bullying, diversity and social justice. This collection of books is representative of the excellent anti-bias and multicultural literature available for educators and parents of children ages 0–12. All the titles in Books Matter have been reviewed by ADL staff and are frequently updated with new and noteworthy books. Integrated into Books Matter is ADL's Book of the Month feature, which highlights a book every month and includes a *Book Discussion Guide* with vocabulary, discussion questions, extension activities and additional resources (see also www.adl.org/book-of-the-month).

ORGANIZATIONS

Collaborative for Academic, Social and Emotional Learning (CASEL), www.casel.org
   CASEL is the nation's leading organization advancing the development of academic, social and emotional competence for all students. Their mission is to help make evidence-based social and emotional learning (SEL) an integral part of education from preschool through high school.

Gender Spectrum, www.genderspectrum.org
   This site provides an array of resources and services that helps to create gender sensitive and inclusive environments for all children and teens.

Facing History and Ourselves, www.facinghistory.org
   Facing History and Ourselves is an international educational and professional development organization whose mission is to engage students of diverse backgrounds in an examination of racism, prejudice, and anti-Semitism in order to promote the development of a more humane and informed citizenry.

The Gay, Lesbian and Straight Education Network (GLSEN), www.glsen.org
   GLSEN is the leading national education organization focused on ensuring safe schools for all students.

Welcoming Schools, www.welcomingschools.org
   A project of the Human Rights Campaign Foundation, Welcoming Schools offers tools, lessons and resources on embracing family diversity, supporting transgender and gender-expansive youth and preventing bias-based bullying.

International Bullying Prevention Association (IPBA), www.ibpaworld.org
   IPBA advances bullying prevention best practices by convening research-based forums, advocating best practices, promoting positive school climate and collaborating across disciplines, sectors and fields.

Morningside Center for Teaching Social Responsibility, www.morningsidecenter.org
   Morningside Center works hand in hand with educators to help young people develop the values, personal qualities, and skills they need to thrive and contribute to their communities—from the classroom to the world.

PACER's National Bullying Prevention Center, www.pacer.org/bullying
   The Center unites, engages, and educates kids, teens, parents and communities nationwide to address bullying.

Rethinking Schools, www.rethinkingschools.org
   Rethinking Schools is a nonprofit publisher and advocacy organization dedicated to sustaining and strengthening public education through social justice teaching and education activism. Their magazine, books and other resources promote equity and racial justice in the classroom.

Share My Lesson, www.sharemylesson.com
   Share My Lesson is a place where educators can come together to create and share their very best teaching resources. This free platform gives access to high-quality teaching resources and provides an online community where teachers can collaborate with, encourage and inspire each other.

StopBullying.Gov, www.stopbullying.gov
   StopBullying.gov provides information from various government agencies on what bullying is, what cyberbullying is, who is at risk, and how you can prevent and respond to bullying.

Teaching Tolerance, www.tolerance.org
   Teaching Tolerance is dedicated to reducing prejudice, improving intergroup relations and supporting equitable school experiences for our nation's children by providing free educational materials to teachers and other school practitioners.

GLOSSARY

This glossary includes terms used throughout the curriculum. Most definitions are appropriate for all children in grades K–5 and there are some definitions only appropriate for grades 3–5 and are specified as such.

Ableism
Prejudice and/or discrimination against people because of their physical or mental disabilities. (Grades 3–5)

Active Listening
Listening clearly to understand the feelings and views of the speaker by being very attentive to what they say.

Ageism
Prejudice and/or discrimination against people based on their age. (Grades 3–5)

Aggressor
Someone who says or does hurtful things.

Ally
Someone who helps or stands up for someone who is being bullied or the target of prejudice.

Anti-Semitism
Prejudice and/or discrimination against people who are Jewish. (Grades 3–5)

Brave
Doing something you would not normally do that may be hard physically or emotionally.

Bullying
When a person or a group behaves in ways—on purpose and over and over—that make someone feel hurt, afraid or embarrassed.

Bystander
Someone who sees bullying or prejudice happening and does not say or do anything.

Classism
Prejudice and/or discrimination against people because of their social class (e.g., how much money people or their families have or do not have). (Grades 3–5)

Collaborate
To work with another person or group in order to achieve or do something.

Communication
Sharing thoughts, feelings or information to another person or group.

Community
A group of people who live in the same area such as a city, town or neighborhood or who share common characteristics or interests.

Cooperation
People working together to do something.

Culture
Parts of daily life that are seen in food, customs, holidays, music and more that a group of people share. (Grades K-2)
Refers to the patterns of daily life that can be seen in language, arts, customs, holiday celebrations, food, religion, beliefs/values, music, clothing and more. (Grades 3–5)

Custom
A way of behaving that is usual and traditional among people in a group or place.

Discrimination
Unfair treatment of one person or group of people because of the person or group's identity (e.g., race, gender, ability, religion, culture. Discrimination is an action that can come from prejudice.

Equality
Having the same or similar rights and opportunities as others.

Homophobia
Prejudice and/or discrimination against people who are believed to be gay, lesbian or bisexual. *(Grades 3-5)*

Inequality
An unjust situation or condition when some people have more rights or better opportunities than other people.

Injustice
Situation in which the rights of a person or a group of people are ignored, disrespected or discriminated against.

Islamophobia
Prejudice and/or discrimination against people who are or are believed to be Muslim. *(Grades 3-5)*

Miscommunication
Failure to communicate clearly.

Multicultural
Including many different cultures.

Name-calling
Using words to hurt or be mean to someone or a group.

Nonverbal communication
Aspects of communication, such as gestures and facial expressions, which do not involve speaking but can also include nonverbal aspects of speech (e.g., tone and volume of voice.

Paraphrase
A statement that says something another person has said or written in a different way.

Prejudice
Judging or having an idea about someone or a group of people before you actually know them. Prejudice is often directed toward people in a certain identity group (e.g., race, religion, gender)

Racism
Prejudice and/or discrimination against people because of their racial group. *(Grades 3-5)*

Sexism
Prejudice and/or discrimination based on a person's gender. *(Grades 3-5)*

Segregation
The practice of keeping people of different races, religions, etc., separate from each other.

Social Change
When elements of a society are altered or changed in some way, including the changes in society's institutions, behaviors, rules or social relationships.

Stereotype
The false idea that all members of a group are the same and think and behave in the same way.

Target
Someone who is bullied or treated in hurtful ways by a person or a group on purpose and over and over.

Teasing
Laugh at and put someone down in a way that is either friendly and playful or mean and unkind.

Weightism
Prejudice and/or discrimination against people because of their weight (e.g., overweight or skinny). *(Grades 3-5)*